COMMON-LAW LIBERTY

COMMON-LAW LIBERTY

Rethinking American Constitutionalism

James R. Stoner, Jr.

University Press of Kansas

Published by the University Press of Kansas (Lawrence, Kansas 66049), which was organized by the Kansas Board of Regents and is operated and funded by Emporia State University, Fort Hays State University, Kansas State University, Pittsburg State University, the University of Kansas, and Wichita State University

Library of Congress Cataloging-in-Publication Data

Stoner, James Reist.
   Common-law liberty : rethinking American constitutionalism / James R. Stoner, Jr.
     p. cm.
Includes bibliographical references and index.
   ISBN 0-7006-1248-3 (cloth : alk. paper)
   1. Constitutional law—United States.   2. Common law—United States.   I. Title.
   KF4552.S76   2003
   342.73—dc21   2003005307

British Library Cataloguing in Publication Data is available.

Printed in the United States of America

10 9 8 7 6 5 4 3 2 1

FOR MY TEACHERS,
Harvey C. Mansfield, Jr.,
and Murray Dry

Customary laws are more sovereign, and deal with more sovereign matters, than written laws; so if a human ruler is less liable to error than written laws, yet he is not less liable to error than the laws based on custom.
—Aristotle, *Politics* III (1287b)

CONTENTS

ACKNOWLEDGMENTS

This book was designed to be an essay, to provoke more questions than it resolves, so in one sense, it was designed to be imperfect. At any rate, I cannot blame its imperfections on the several foundations that generously supported my work, nor on the many friends and scholars who read and commented on earlier drafts. Among the former are the John M. Olin Foundation, which provided a fellowship that enabled the book to be begun years ago; the National Endowment for the Humanities, whose fellowship allowed me to write several chapters and discover the shortcomings of my original plan; the Earhart Foundation, whose summer fellowships allowed the composition of critical chapters; the Lynde and Harry Bradley Foundation, which also provided summer support; and the James Madison Program in American Ideals and Institutions in the Department of Politics at Princeton University, under whose auspices the last tasks were completed. Nor can I neglect to mention the encouragement and the research sabbaticals provided by Louisiana State University, my home institution for a decade and a half. As for my friends and the others who helped by commenting on various parts of the book, I impose on their generosity of spirit by hoping that they will be content with private thanks. Still, I owe special acknowledgment to Robert Clinton, Christopher Wolfe, and Robert Nagel, who gave a critical reading to the entire text, and to my editors at the University Press of Kansas, Michael Briggs, Fred Woodward, and Melinda Wirkus, who patiently brought this text to light.

Several chapters were originally published separately and appear here in revised form, with the publishers' permission. Thanks to Rowman and Littlefield for permission to revise as chapter 1 my essay, "The Idiom of the Common Law in the Formation of Judicial Power," from Bradford P. Wilson and Ken Masugi, eds., *The Supreme Court and American Constitutionalism* (Lanham, Md.: Rowman and Littlefield, 1998): 47–68; to the editors of *Polity* for permission to republish as chapter 3 my "Religious Liberty and Common Law: Free Exercise Exemptions and American Courts," *Polity* 26, no. 1 (fall 1993): 1–24; and to the editors of *The Review of Politics* for permission to republish as chapter 4 "Common Law and Constitutionalism in the Abortion Case," *The Review of Politics* 55, no. 3 (summer 1993): 421–441. A summary version of chapter 5 appeared as part of my essay, "Is Tradition Activist? The Common Law of the Family in the Liberal Constitutionalist World," *University of Colorado Law Review* 73, no. 4 (fall 2002): 1291–1306; thanks to the editors of that review for whatever permission was needed here.

I have accepted the standard practice of hyphenating the term *common law* when it is used as an adjective, as in the title of the book itself. At the risk of being thought pusillanimous, I would note that at issue is whether *common law* is a proper noun (which would suggest no hyphen) or a common noun (which might require a hyphen), and that part of the genius of the common law is to straddle the two: to be specifically ours, as members of a legal community attached to a sovereign government, but also to appeal to every member of that community—and to all who would join them in thought—to accept that law as reflecting their own sense of right and wrong. As the reader will soon discover, I reject the now-common notion that common law is judge-made law, so please do not interpret my use of *common law* to mean *judge-made.* At the same time, I would not make too much of the specific roots of American common law in medieval England; this is an important fact to know, and worth reflecting on in another place, but it is not the whole story. The fruit of common law, which I am not ashamed to call our liberty, is not buried underground.

Finally, I have from time to time revived the archaic practice of matching collective nouns, such as *court* or *community,* with plural verbs and pronouns. There was, I think, real insight in this usage, and that it now sounds odd is some measure of the unconscious corporatism of our age. It is another part of the genius of common law to maintain diversity within unity, to seek not artificial but actual consent. There is a grammar, too, of being free.

Introduction

The American Constitution and American constitutional law cannot be understood without reference to the common-law tradition in which they were formed. That assertion is, in its simplest sense, admitted on all sides. There are terms of art in the federal Constitution, such as the phrases "ex post facto" and "bill of attainder," whose meaning even the delegates at the Philadelphia Convention in 1787 had to confirm in Blackstone's *Commentaries*. But to claim something more—that the common law is a key to understanding the fundamental principles of our Constitution and a guide for deciding contemporary constitutional cases—is to find oneself in the midst of a debate over the meaning of the Constitution and the role of the courts in its interpretation or, rather, in a breach between two parties deeply at odds. I do not ask the reader of an introduction to run with me into that breach, but I do invite you to survey it.

On one side in the debate is the liberal "mainstream" of the law professoriat and the judges they influence and admire.[1] Their articles of faith are the irreversibility of the constitutional revolution of 1937, the soundness of the jurisprudential spirit of the Warren Court, and the sanctity of *Roe v. Wade,* the 1973 decision in which the Supreme Court established a woman's right to an abortion. They see the Constitution through the lenses of the Fourteenth Amendment, which they interpret as establishing judicially enforceable first principles of personal liberty and social equality and as minimizing the independent legal authority of the states. Indeed, when they talk about constitutional Founding, they are apt to posit a Second Founding during Reconstruction or a Third in the New Deal, both of which, to their minds, transcend the Constitution of 1787, with its sordid compromises on the issue of slavery and its staunch provisions securing property rights. As for the First Amendment, they give it a generally libertarian interpretation and see in its Religion Clauses a command for strict separation of church and state, but recent controversies over free speech have tempered their "absolutism" and left them vulnerable to pressure from their more radical members against unregulated free expression. On the whole, their model

1

justice is William Brennan, whose decisions and dissents they still admire and whose place they look for his successors to fill. Though they differ among themselves on whether judges should make progress by bold, theoretically inspired innovation or "one case at a time," they agree in principle and in orientation with the subtitle of former solicitor general Archibald Cox's book on the Warren Court: constitutional decision is an instrument of reform.[2]

On the other, more conservative side are scholars and jurists who decry their opponents as believers in a "living Constitution" that changes from age to age through the policy making of unelected federal judges. They do not deny the need for constitutional change from time to time; in fact, their political friends often have a number of potential amendments to propose. But they would direct the impetus for that change to the amendment process described in Article V. In interpreting the Constitution, they would have judges bound by something unchanging—the text of the document or the intentions of its Framers. They deplore the "activism" of the Warren and Burger Courts, though few, if any, denounce the 1954 decision in *Brown v. Board of Education* in which a unanimous Court, in an opinion by Chief Justice Earl Warren, overturned more than a half century of precedent and ruled public school segregation a violation of the Fourteenth Amendment's Equal Protection Clause. When they speak of the Founding, they mean emphatically the framing of the Constitution of 1787, and they are especially interested in the jurisprudence that entails the elaboration of its leading principles, such as the separation of powers and federalism. Among their leaders on the Supreme Court is Antonin Scalia, who has not been shy in articulating a coherent jurisprudence both off and on the bench. They describe themselves as champions of the democratic process and of judicial restraint. Though increasingly accused by liberal dissenters of activism themselves, judicial conservatives insist that they do not import their personal opinions into their constitutional decisions, only the objectively established law. To them, constitutional adjudication ought to be an instrument not of reform but of the people's will, as formally declared in constitutional text.[3]

On numerous issues of constitutional law, these two constitutional parties have opposite positions, but both would agree to look skeptically on any mention of common law in relation to constitutional interpretation and decision. Justice Scalia, in his book *A Matter of Interpretation,* begins his argument against the modern misconception of the judicial role by ridiculing the way students are trained to think in law school, which he calls the common-law approach. Since Oliver Wendell Holmes, Jr., taught the legal profession to think of common law as judge-made law, professors have taught students to study judicial opinions by putting themselves on the bench, as it were, applying the technique of distinguishing cases to get around the rule of precedent, and "playing judge, which in turn consists of playing king—devising, out of the brilliance of one's mind, those laws that ought to govern mankind."[4] Without impeaching common-law lawmaking in areas such as torts and contracts, Scalia finds the habit of seeking to remake the law judicially to be altogether at odds with democracy; his sympathy for the nineteenth-century codification movement, his dismay at the undeveloped state of statutory interpretation in common-law countries, and his confidence in the cogency of a new textualism in constitutional interpretation all follow from his commitment to written law as an expression of the popular will. He knows, of course, that defining common law as judge-made law was Holmes's innovation, that at the time of the Founding, "the prevailing image of the common law was that of a pre-existing body of rules . . . that judges merely 'discovered' rather than created." On the bench, he has shown himself to be a master of the classic techniques of distinguishing precedents and refining holdings, insightfully comparing the growth of common law to a game of Scrabble, where each word is laid down for its own score but subsequently governs what can come of the board. But Scalia clearly thinks that it is either impossible or undesirable to revive the traditional understanding of common law as something discovered, not invented. Indeed, he is sharply critical of some of the traditional canons of common-law construction, such as the narrow interpretation given statutes derogatory of common law or the rule of lenity in criminal cases. And he titles his essay "Common-Law Courts in a Civil-Law System," suggesting a disproportion between judicial practice and legislative reality and characterizing the constitutional system itself as opposed to the common-law frame of mind. Far from being a solution to the excesses of judicial activism, the common law is, to his mind, its cause.

Liberal authors are, if anything, more hostile to the common law, at least if it is understood traditionally. Also taught by Holmes, they admire the techniques available in common law for judge-initiated legal improvement and have invented whole theories explaining how common-law judging ought to proceed.[5] What they like about common law is its process of rational change, not any particular maxims, rules, or principles; quite the contrary, judicial liberals tend, with varying levels of earnestness, to seek to use the rational techniques of common-law argumentation to reverse the old common law itself, whose substance they see as a repository of traditional economic and moral teachings if not downright prejudice. In areas of the law such as torts, this approach has succeeded in developing concepts that reverse the old common law's presumption in favor of personal responsibility. In constitutional law, it has been used to extend principles of personal liberty and equal protection to abortion and to sexual practices that were not only not protected but actually forbidden at common law. "It is revolting," wrote Holmes in a much-quoted aphorism, "to have no better reason for a rule of law than that so it was laid down in the time of Henry IV," reversing the presumption of the common-law tradition in favor of the spirit of liberal Enlightenment.[6] Judicial liberals today are sophisticated enough to appeal to custom or even the intent of the Framers when it serves their purposes, but their underlying animus is still Holmes's.

In the chapters that follow, we will revisit many of these points, but for now, let me note a few things. First, if neither side is ready to embrace common law, and if both are in some respect apt to distrust it, both nevertheless remain in debt to certain common-law ways of thinking and to specific common-law rights. I already mentioned the liberals' attachment to the common lawyers' manner of argumentation, their skill in distinguishing new cases, their appreciation for the law's adaptability, and their search for logical coherence in the law as a whole. Besides this, the whole postwar jurisprudence of rights represents in some respects a revival of common law against social engineering. Although modern liberals may not share first principles with the old common lawyers nor their stern sense of guilt and innocence, they do share a commitment to due process in criminal proceedings, and it is not in the vocabulary of the common law to criticize "rights talk." On the other side, though conservatives seldom stress the point, the leading ideas of their constitutional hermeneutics descend from common law. Both the first rule of textualism, that one must start with the plain meaning of the words in a written legal instrument, and the principle that if this is not clear, one must look to the framers' intent, are common-law rules of interpretation. The importance of adherence to precedent is at once a basic maxim of the common law and a central tenet of any form of conservatism. Moreover (though again, modern conservatives tend to overlook the point), the common law gave legal force to the traditional moral order of society—defining crime, assigning responsibility, reinforcing the family, and permitting personal liberty—and of course, it specified and jealously guarded property rights.

A second point is that common law in many ways remains a vital part of American constitutionalism today. Not least important is the whole structure of judicial power, which in its outlines would be recognizable to a seventeenth-century Englishman: the mixed regime of judge and jury in the courtroom, adversarial proceedings, a bench drawn from the bar, the legal force accorded precedent, the way first principles of government appear in the context of particular cases, the importance of individual rights and government by law. The influence and continuing authority of common law on legal reasoning and in substantive areas of law are controversial, and much of the burden of the book that follows is to sort out the alternatives in these matters. But the basic matters of structure are, despite occasional calls for reform, so largely settled and widely accepted that they seem invisible. And these are deep structures in the culture: every administrator, even every parent takes precedent into account in making decisions, and rule by law is so central to our thinking that we almost take for granted that the study of law is the preeminent avenue of preparation for a political career.

Third, in the very term *common law* and in the recourse to settled agreement in common-law reasoning, one can see a presumption of or aspiration to social consensus, indicated most perfectly by the common-law requirement that jury verdicts be unanimous. If the paradigm of modern legislation—and of modern law, insofar as it is thought to be an instrument of policy—is the command of a sovereign power, as Thomas Hobbes taught and even William Blackstone echoed,[7] the paradigm of common law is the community's traditional sense of right and wrong. Common law emphasizes assent rather than domination, the community rather than the state, moral authority rather than physical power. Of course, there can be patterns of hidden domination beneath expressed consensus, and authority needs to be reinforced by power; and of course, raw power wants to claim moral authority for itself. Still, it matters what a society says about itself, how it understands itself, and what it looks up to. Any account of American constitutionalism, after all, must explain what it is about the Constitution that raises it above ordinary politics and the partisanship that is inevitable if politics is free. That there should be partisanship in the exposition of the Constitution is to be expected, as the authors of *The Federalist* so perceptively grasped,[8] but it is self-evident that the Constitution must somehow rise above partisan politics, lest it be a mere instrument of party power. At the very least, constitutional discourse, to be genuine, must acquire sufficient autonomy that each party remembers that the arguments used in their favor this time—whether the issue is freedom of speech or the conduct of elections—might be used against them in the future, and thus the parties have a long-term interest in being circumspect in their demands. One of the shortcomings of our present-day constitutional partisans is that they do not seem to acknowledge this, much less seek an account of constitutionalism that can encompass the truths on both sides, as if permanent meaning were incompatible with legal change rather than its presupposition, or as if individual rights were incompatible with rather than essential to the common good.

The chapters that follow represent the common-law dimension of American constitutionalism. The first treats the question of the relation of the Constitution and the common law thematically; the others look at a variety of topics in American constitutional law, considering both how familiarity with common law can illuminate specific constitutional issues and what these issues teach about the constitutional implications of common law. I am not pretending to offer a theory of common-law constitutionalism that will give lawyers fodder for their briefs or judges an algorithm for decision making.[9] As I have argued elsewhere, lawyers and judges in the common-law tradition are skeptical of the claims of any comprehensive theory, at least one that does not pay homage to experience and to the complex multiplicity of human goods.[10] The preference for assent rather than domination appears even in this, for the common law never pretended to be the only kind of law in England or America, though at its moments of greatest strength, it defined where others started and stopped. It should go without saying that, by drawing attention to common law, I do not mean to revive lapsed ethnic privilege. Although I suppose the eclipse of common law in recent years owes something to the rise of a multiethnic America and thus to the decline of Anglo predominance in the culture, common law here was always distinct from its English parent and was a powerful means of assimilating the foreign-born into a shared world.

In this book, I write about constitutional and common law from the perspective of a political scientist trained in the study of political philosophy. I mean to state the law accurately, but not always with the specificity required of legal advice or with the temper of an advocate. I aim to avoid anachronisms or mistakes in historical detail—and I believe that consciousness of common law is essential for a historical understanding of the American Founding and nineteenth-century constitutional law—but my interest is not precisely a historian's, partly because I think that common law is a still-living tradition, not a mentality of the past. But neither do I mean to outline some common-law utopia or best regime and elucidate the principles that underlie it. I start, rather, from the presumption that agreement is more readily achieved on moral questions than on theoretical ones,[11] and I proceed with confidence that casting light on what makes American constitutionalism a vibrant tradition and an important model of the political practice of human liberty is a worthwhile task. If the chapters in this book sketch the paradigm of a constitutionalism that is formed in substantial part by common law, I have achieved my aim. Since I mentioned earlier the problem of partisanship in constitutional scholarship, I should indicate to the reader that I am aware that it will soon enough be apparent to which party I incline in constitutional disputation, but I aspire to write a book that will be useful to both sides. Do not suppose that I always try to find some elusive compromise between the dominant positions; on some matters, I might outflank one of the leading parties, showing its position to be the compromise between true opposites.

Some of the most interesting work on American constitutionalism in recent years involves the study of what is referred to as "the Constitution outside of courts," entailing a renewed appreciation for how the Constitution can structure political development and how that development proceeds by the people's making choices that direct constitutional change and reaffirm what might be called constitutional values.[12] Although I do not think that judges are the exclusive or even the supreme interpreters of the Constitution, I confine myself in this book principally to constitutional law, which is to say, the way the Constitution has been expounded in courts of law, and especially in the Supreme Court of the United States. Common law has influenced Anglo-American civilization as a whole, but it is especially the business of the courts of law; thus, its influence on American constitutionalism is especially notable in the dimension of that constitutionalism that appears in court. The figure of the traditional common-law judge is a formidable one. He was, to paraphrase Justice Scalia, one who discovered and declared the law, not one who self-consciously made legal policy, but he had ample confidence in his judgment and was given to oracular pronouncement, for he had through study and experience so assimilated the common law into his own way of thinking that he could apply it, so to speak, organically, not mechanically. He took pride in his reason—the writing of opinions, especially in appellate work, is another characteristic our judiciary inherited from common law—but it was reason trained as Aristotle thought that practical reason ought to be trained, in the seemingly infinite particularities of moral decision, not in abstract theory alone.[13] The problem of judicial activism today is not a problem of degree, that judges do too much, but a problem of kind, that judges are constantly encouraged to forget their specific business, interfering with others' and neglecting their own. The common law defined and circumscribed the nature of the judicial power as it was understood by the American Founders, who wanted judges to be strong but not supreme. With that original understanding and with an indication of how it changed, I begin.

CHAPTER I

Common Law and Constitution

*Original Understanding, Republican Synthesis, and
Modern Transformation*

In the pitched battles of the "culture wars," whatever our field of engagement, we soldiers of fortune quickly forget our victories and defeats and sometimes even mistake the one for the other. Something like this must explain the disappearance, in the past decade or so, of the question whether we Americans have, in some respects, an unwritten constitution. Scholars were once divided between "interpretivists" and "noninterpretivists," the partisans of the written and the unwritten. Today, however, the conservative insistence on the priority of the written text and the authority of the original understanding of that text by those who wrote and ratified it frames the terms of debate.[1] Perhaps it is only a matter of language; advocates of an evolving Constitution have developed sophisticated theories of interpretation that permit them to reach the same results based on the text that they had sought in unwritten principle.[2] Even the Supreme Court seems more scrupulous in attaching innovations to the written word. In the watershed issue of whether the Constitution licenses an abortion right, the justices have replaced their reference in *Roe v. Wade*[3] to a "right of privacy," supposedly found in the shadows of the text, with reference to the protection of "liberty" in the Due Process Clauses of the Fifth and Fourteenth Amendments, all the while reaffirming that an abortion right is present. Yet the definition they give to "liberty" in the Constitution's text—"the right to define one's own concept of existence, of meaning, of the universe, and of the mystery of human life"—is obviously expansive enough to enact the whole agenda of sexual liberation and much more by judicial decree.[4] This should counsel caution among those who think that the bare text is enough to confine those who would use judicial power as an instrument of partisan change.

In this context, I propose reopening the question of the unwritten constitution or, rather, the question of the implications of the tradition of unwritten law in the midst of which our Constitution was written. Others have, for similar reasons, turned their attention to natural law or natural rights,[5] but I recommend a tandem attention to the common law. Theories of natural law or natural rights are perhaps more satisfying to the mind, but they are, for the same reason, more contentious in the polity; let it be enough for now to point to the radically different conceptions of law and political life in classical natural law on the one hand and modern natural rights on the other.[6] Grounded in custom, and so in consensus, common law gained in practical authority what it yielded in intellectual simplicity. Moreover, at the time of the Founding, natural law and common law were seen as complementary, and more than one effort was made to assimilate the one to the other. My argument for the importance of common law is partly historical. Not only the original intention of the Constitution but also the value of recourse to original intention is oblique if common law is overlooked, for the great document and the Bill of Rights that soon joined it were written in the idiom of common law, and the authority of legislative intent was among the common law's many maxims. Besides, for a century or more, American constitutional development took place in a legal context that took its bearings from common law, and even today our law is replete with precepts and institutions of common-law descent.

I also think that renewed appreciation of common law, not so much in its modern as in its classic meaning, offers for our consideration if not a promise of truce in the "culture wars" at least a way toward restoring what Robert Nagel has called our "constitutional culture," now divided into warring camps.[7] Along with natural law, liberalism, capitalism, Christianity, and much else, the common law has had a formative influence on the American character, and a recognition of what it is and has become is an essential part of understanding our constitutionalism, our possibilities, and ourselves. Let me try in this chapter to sketch what that understanding might entail.

The Original Understanding of Common Law

Like a well-fit ring, ever on hand but never in mind, the common law is rarely noticed by most scholars of the law, and especially of the Constitution. More important, if attended to at all, it is understood in a way that is at odds with its original understanding, that is, with the way it was seen by the Framers of the Constitution and by the English authors they read. Ask lawyers or professors today to define *common law,* and they will answer that it is "judge-made law," devised in cases, extended by precedent, and lim-

ited only by the consensus of the bench and bar or by legislative intervention. This opinion was not entirely unknown to the Founders, but it was the
cynic's perspective, to which no self-respecting lawyer or judge, much less
republican citizen, could admit. The transformation in the meaning of common law was the work of Oliver Wendell Holmes, Jr., in his lectures called
The Common Law and in his influence from the bench, first of the Supreme
Judicial Court of Massachusetts and then for almost thirty years of the
Supreme Court of the United States. I will have more to say about Holmes
later, but it is essential at the outset to suspend allegiance to Holmes's definition if the original understanding of common law is to be grasped.

Common law was, in the first place, the immemorial customary law of
England, enforced in the Court of Common Pleas and the King's Bench and
throughout the realm in local courts called the assizes. These were not the
only courts in England, nor was common law the only law of the realm;
ecclesiastical law and admiralty were separate jurisdictions, both operating
on civil-law principles, and equity was administered by the Chancery in cases
in which strict law did not satisfy the demands of conscience. Common law
governed matters of estate and also crime and punishment (the chief business, respectively, of its two principal courts), and by the seventeenth century, its classic era, its principles gave form to English law as a whole.
Though a written code was lacking, the written evidence of common law was
to be found in the records of cases previously decided. To learn the law meant
to learn these precedents and the rules of law they established, but also to
understand the reasons behind them; it was a maxim at common law that a
precedent that ran against reason was no law. To decide a case at common
law required a determination of what precedents were appropriate to the case
at hand. It was settled in the rhetoric of common law, and held to be fixed in
the character of a common-law judge, that in deciding cases, it was the
judge's duty to discover, not invent, what law governed the case at hand. If
a case seemed genuinely novel, the judge was to proceed by analogy to the
appropriate precedent. As statutes were made, they were assimilated to common law, for the common law had rules by which statutes were to be interpreted. Although it was a maxim of common law that a rule of statute law
supersedes a contrary, unwritten common-law rule, it first had to be determined whether the statute in question modified the common law or simply
declared it in writing. To the most characteristic and perhaps the greatest of
the English common-law judges, Sir Edward Coke, the whole array of customs, maxims, precedents, and statutes appeared as an "artificial perfection

of reason," which referred not to an edifice of science established in a treatise but to the learning and the judgment—that is, the art—that took form in
the mind of a well-read and experienced judge.[8]

The law of what came to be called the English constitution was not,
strictly speaking, common law, since Parliament had its own law and custom and the king his own prerogatives, but the constitution of the courts was
a part of common law, and the larger principles of the English constitution
clearly bore the stamp of common-law thinking. That the English constitution is unwritten astonishes us today, but it was reasonable and indeed
expected in a common-law setting. Because statutes were held to declare
the law as well as make it, the unwritten character of the constitution was
not inconsistent with a tradition of great constitutional documents, from the
Magna Charta (1215) to the Petition of Right (1628) to the Bill of Rights
(1689), that declared the privileges and immunities of subjects of the realm.
Besides, because precedents had the force of law, what Albert Venn Dicey
in the nineteenth century called the conventions of the constitution could
also be considered authoritative, even if their violation would find no remedy in court.[9] The appointment of judges from the bar was among these conventions; lawyers were already considered officers of the court, after all, so
their elevation to the bench had the character of a promotion rather than a
change of profession. That judges declared the law in cases before them,
with the facts determined by a jury of "twelve good men and true," was well
established by the seventeenth century as a matter of common right.[10]
Indeed, trial by jury was the distinctive mark of common law, and not by
accident, for both customary law and jury verdict might be said to register
the understanding of justice in the common mind.

To Coke and his fellows, the common law was the guarantor of English
liberties; its Great Charter was called a charter of liberties, he explained,
because the effect of its many privileges was to make men free, especially
by its assurance in the twenty-ninth chapter of what by Coke's time was
already called "due process of law."[11] The liberty protected by common law
was achieved through the law, not outside it; it was characteristic of common law to protect men's estates or their right to earn a living, so it was no
accident that Parliament anchored its authority not in a general assertion of
sovereignty but in its power over taxation. A liberty that considered due
process its expression and "no taxation without representation" its guarantor was not defined as personal autonomy; it was taken for granted that
crimes were moral wrongs, not just behavior deemed undesirable by the
social power or minimal restrictions on individual license in the name of

others. Due process, and the jury trial at its heart, was a promise that legal proceedings would uncover the truth and that conviction would follow proof of guilt. That it afforded special protection for the accused, forbidding torture and thus involuntary self-incrimination, revealed something of the genius that ran throughout the common law, which was tender toward the innocent and respectful of free will.

When liberal political theory first arrived in the work of Thomas Hobbes, it was as an opponent of the common law, not as its champion, even though on some matters, such as self-incrimination, the traditions converged. By the eighteenth century, however, several great attempts at synthesis were made, first by John Locke, who aimed to reconcile liberal philosophy and the English constitution, and then by William Blackstone, whose *Commentaries on the Laws of England,* appearing in the 1760s, reworked the common law from a liberal perspective and presented its chief rules and maxims in accessible, literary form.[12] Blackstone's contemporary William Murray (Lord Mansfield), meanwhile, had undertaken to reform common law from the King's Bench, most successfully by incorporating into what had been predominantly a law of landed estate the principles of the law merchant, thus developing the common law of contract. Reforming common law from within, Mansfield and Blackstone also taught the sovereignty of Parliament, thus preparing the eclipse of common law even as they infused it with modern ideas.

To assume that the Americans of the Revolutionary era simply accepted the dominant understanding of common law in contemporary Britain would be a serious error. Although Blackstone would, within a generation, replace Coke as the favorite authority on common law among Americans, it was understood that his account of parliamentary sovereignty was inapplicable here—it might even be said that the American Revolution was fought against the assertion of that principle in the colonies—and Mansfield had been an outspoken foe in the struggles leading up to independence. Still, in the course of their struggles, and even on the brink of separation, Americans claimed the common law as their inheritance, most dramatically in the "Declaration and Resolves" of the First Continental Congress, who resolved "That the respective colonies are entitled to the common law of England, and more especially to the great and inestimable privilege of being tried by their peers of the vicinage, according to the course of that law."[13] In the more famous Declaration of Independence not two years later, the choice of independence—or its defense to the world—mandated that appeal be made to the law of nature rather than the law of England, but when abstract terms

such as "absolute Despotism" were given concrete meaning, it was by reference, in the largely unread catalogue of grievances, to numerous rights
and privileges at common law, against which the king and his Parliament
were now found to have transgressed.

Meanwhile, as the colonies re-formed themselves into states, they all
adopted, often by statute or constitutional provision, the common law as the
basis of their jurisprudence—not the common law of England in its entirety,
but, as Joseph Story would write in 1837 for a commission on codification
in his native Massachusetts,

> that portion of the common law of England, (as modified and amelio-
> rated by English statutes,) which was in force at the time of the emigra-
> tion of our ancestors, and was applicable to the situation of the colony,
> and has since been recognized and acted upon, during the successive
> progresses of our Colonial, Provincial, and State Governments, with this
> additional qualification, that it has not been altered, repealed, or modi-
> fied by any of our subsequent legislation now in force.[14]

To the modern reader, this sounds so qualified as to sever all relation, but
Story is merely writing with his customary precision. Although important
parts of the common law such as many of the feudal tenures and all that
related to "the ecclesiastical establishment" had never been known in Massachusetts, he clearly thought that the essence of the common law had been
successfully transplanted and had grown strong and free in its new soil. In
Virginia, where the established church and many feudal tenures had indeed
come across, the project of adjusting the common law upon independence
was more urgent, leading to the appointment of a Committee of Revisors in
1776, with Thomas Jefferson, Edmund Pendleton, and George Wythe among
its members. But even here, the decision was simply to draft model statutes
for reform, not to try to introduce a wholly new order. As Jefferson wrote
of the revisors' deliberations, looking back in 1821,

> to abrogate our whole system would be a bold measure, and probably far
> beyond the views of the legislature; . . . to compose a new Institute . . .
> would be an arduous undertaking, of vast research, of great considera-
> tion & judgment; and when reduced to a text, every word of that text,
> from the imperfection of human language, and it's [*sic*] incompetence to
> express distinctly every shade of idea, would become a subject of ques-
> tion & chicanery until settled by repeated adjudications; . . . [T]his would

involve us for ages in litigation, and render property uncertain until, like the statutes of old, every word had been tried, and settled by numerous decisions, and by new volumes of reports & commentaries.[15]

The decision of the colonies to adhere by and large to their common-law tradition—indeed, to make their case for independence by appeal to the ancient rights they had by common law—makes it plain that, even as they introduced the written constitution to the world, they had no intention of replacing the unwritten law on which their properties were founded and by which their moral and social lives were ordered. This helps explain an over-looked peculiarity in the Declaration of Independence itself—namely, its reference, when condemning acts of parliamentary oppression, to "our constitution," eleven years before the Philadelphia convention was held and before the committee to draft written Articles of Confederation were even appointed, much less successful in their work.[16] Jefferson's draft had the word in the plural (indeed, reprints of the Declaration can be found today with this error), and although the referent then would have been the constitutions of the colonies or states, these too were still, for the most part, unwritten, since Congress had just issued on May 10, 1776, a call to the colonies to suppress crown authority and adopt their own forms of government. But Jefferson's "constitutions" was changed to the singular in committee, leaving no alternative but to suppose an unwritten constitution of British North America, defined in the Declaration itself by the violations alleged to have been made of it by the British Parliament and king. One might say that the constitution there mentioned was dissolved by the very document that names it, but it is not obvious that to "dissolve the Political Bands" between two peoples was the same thing as undoing a constitution, even or especially an unwritten one. Besides, it might be recalled that the Second Continental Congress operated without a written constitution for the course of the fighting, the Articles of Confederation lying unratified for four years because of disputes among the states over the future of the western lands.

Here, then, is a sketch of the understanding of common law on the eve of the Philadelphia convention. It was proudly claimed by Americans as their inheritance, modified to fit the more democratic circumstances of the New World. It was known to have its roots in England, but it was thought to have survived transplanting and to be on the verge of becoming its own tradition. It was, like the legislative power, still principally at home in the colonies-become-states, but such federal action as had begun was not formed on hostile principles and indeed relied at least in part on principles familiar from common law. It formed the law administered in courts, again more democratically than in the mother country, since juries played a greater role and since judges, appointed in colonial times by the crown, were viewed with some suspicion.[17] And it also gave form to the politics of the Revolution itself, which framed the dispute with England in legal terms and thus saw the war that followed as a sort of trial by battle.

My argument is not to deny that, when the break came, it was defended in the natural-rights language of Lockean liberalism or a radical Whiggism that was influenced by this. It is to say that liberalism provided not a theory for the ordering of the whole society but a principle to explain the unusual or extreme case in which the colonists found themselves as the British government moved to crush the assertion of what the colonists saw as their constitutional rights. Liberalism grew in influence as the United States developed, not least as the federal government expanded, and liberalism eventually grew away from its natural-rights foundation, but its role at the outset was to sever "political bands" that had grown destructive and to suggest reforms in the common-law order, something that that order had always allowed. That the change of regime from monarchy to republic occurred with such restraint in America is testimony, in part, to the continuous power of a common law that focused its attention not on the question of regime but on the rights of individuals in particular cases and thus on the whole array of institutions in civil society in the midst of which the people went about their lives. That our lives are so thoroughly politicized today, and thus our politics so bitter, might be testimony to the consequences of dismantling the buffer of common law that stood between the individual and the legislative will.

Common Law in the Constitution

The original understanding of common law, which I laid out at such length because it has largely been forgotten, colors every aspect of the Constitution and thus is essential to a complete account of the original understanding of the Constitution itself. Let me try to put the matter more precisely. The Constitution concentrates on establishing the structure of the federal government; it organizes its institutions according to the principles of the separation of powers and federalism, and it bases the latter especially on a novel scheme; it insists on a form of government that is at once strictly republican, in the sense of drawing all its power directly or indirectly from the people, and entirely representative, in removing the people from the administration of the government; and it puts all this in a positive, written document to be ratified by extraordinary conventions in the states. This owes little to common law and much to the "great improvements" in "the science of politics" praised by Alexander Hamilton in *The Federalist,* as well as to the "manly spirit" of the Founding generation, who had not, in James Madison's words, "suffered a blind veneration for antiquity, for custom, or for names, to overrule the suggestions of their own good sense, the knowledge of their own situation, and the lessons of their own experience."[18] But if the Constitution made an "experiment of an extended republic," its genius was to build with the materials at hand, to temper its innovations with the familiar, to establish a government that was limited not only in its power over individuals but also in its sovereignty over what they considered law. The Constitution was, to be sure, meant to be a written instrument of government, and its engineers were trained in a liberal school, but that does not establish that it undertook to remake man on liberal principles or to narrow all authority to what the new federal government was enabled to achieve. Two states, after all, chose not to write new constitutions, and every state chose to reaffirm its adherence to common law.

To fully establish the argument I have just sketched would require an investigation—beyond the bounds of this essay—into law and politics in the states in 1787, which the Constitution was meant to constrain but not to replace. What is worth examining here is the presence of common law in the Constitution itself. It is universally acknowledged that this appears, in the first place, in the language of the document. Whether at issue is "the Privilege of the Writ of Habeas Corpus" or "ex post facto Law" or "natural born" or "good behavior," the common law must be consulted for definition. Moreover, in contrast to the Virginia Plan at the convention, which spoke of the "National Legislature" and the "National Executive," the Constitution proceeds, common law–like, even when fashioning new institutions, to give them established names, most obviously in the case of Congress, but even in the use of "President" for the chief executive. The influence of common law appears not only in the words but also in the style of the document, especially in the way the Constitution articulates by enumeration rather than by definition, most famously in the list of the powers of Congress in Article I, section 8. Here again, the contrast to the Virginia Plan is instructive. That plan would have defined rather than enumerated the power of the National Legislature: "to legislate in all cases to which the separate States are incompetent, or in which the harmony of the United States may be interrupted by the exercise of individual Legislation."[19] Although the convention at first approved such an approach, the Committee of Detail returned to an enumeration of powers, as in the Articles of Confederation, and the delegates readily acquiesced.

My point in drawing attention to the common-law language in the Constitution is not to deny that old words can assume new meanings, but rather to suggest that the presumption was meant to run the other way: to presume stability in language and continuity in law, except where there was explicit, written text to the contrary or a clear, logical implication derived from the text. That, at least, was the practice in interpreting statutes at common law, and there is no reason to suppose that the Framers meant for their Constitution to be read any differently, at least in court. The Constitution was a new kind of statute, of course, a fundamental law stamped with popular approval. How that Constitution was to be read—whether strictly, as were penal statutes, or liberally, as were statutes against fraud,[20] or whether powers were to be read one way and rights another—needed fresh determination, so it was no accident that constitutional law in its early years was concerned with precisely this. But allowing for a liberal interpretation of congressional powers need not deny stability in meaning and may even be thought to demand it. The fact that the Framers anticipated the need for flexibility in government to meet changing exigencies is an argument against their having left their words infinitely supple. As for the persistence of enumerating powers and rights rather than defining them abstractly, it betrays a common-law willingness to respect the multiplicity of human concerns rather than to insist on theoretical perfection.

In the second place, common law appears in the Constitution specifically in Article III, where the judicial power is established, and again it appears not in terms but as presupposition. Ironically, this is clearest in the text at the very moment the Framers depart from common-law practice by assigning "all Cases, in Law and Equity," to a single set of courts, for the understanding of "law and equity" here is obviously specific to the English tradition, where a settled practice of equity adjudication developed alongside the common-law courts. Likewise, trial by jury, the trademark of common law, is guaranteed, although again, a few modifications of common-law practice are indicated—the subject of much dispute in the ratification debates, by the way. That the judicial power was understood in a common-law manner is nowhere more evident than in *The Federalist,* where Hamilton, in Number 78, takes it for granted that judges will be "bound down by strict rules and precedents"; that they must devote themselves to "long and laborious study" of "the records of precedents[, which] must unavoidably swell to a very considerable bulk"; and that they will have to "quit a lucrative line of practice to accept a seat on the bench"—that is, he takes for granted that they will, in common-law fashion, be appointed from the bar and that they will study and judge in the common-law mode. Nor, in this light, is it accidental that their power to set aside unconstitutional statutes remains unwritten, to be deduced on analogy to the rule for interpreting conflicting statutes, a "mere rule of construction, not derived from any positive law, but from the nature and reason of the thing," in Hamilton's words. That he expects federal judges to protect individual rights even when no written constitutional command is crossed, by "mitigating the severity, and confining the operation of such laws" as are "unjust and partial," further suggests that he expects them to possess, by virtue of the judicial power itself, the common-law judge's tools of art.[21]

A third place where the common-law way of thinking appears in the Constitution is in the Supremacy Clause of Article VI: "This Constitution, and the Laws of the United States which shall be made in Pursuance thereof; and all Treaties made, or which shall be made, under the Authority of the United States, shall be the supreme Law of the Land; and the Judges in every State shall be bound thereby, any Thing in the Constitution or Laws of any State to the Contrary notwithstanding." What is remarkable here is not the fact of federal supremacy but the manner in which it was to be secured, namely, through the courts of law. Once again, the Virginia Plan had something very different in mind—a power in the National Legislature "to negative all laws passed by the several States, contravening in the opinion of the National Legislature the articles of Union." The Supremacy Clause, instead, comes from the alternative New Jersey Plan, where it appeared in a version very similar to its final form. (Interestingly, this plan refers several times, in a different context, to the "Common law Judiciary" in the several states.)[22] What made the unique arrangement of American federalism possible, at least in the early years of the Republic, was its mediation by a judiciary trained to focus not on abstract questions of sovereignty but on questions of right and power as they arise in a particular case. This allowed the logic of the novel system to be worked out over time, as issues developed, rather than forcing a settlement before the advantages and disadvantages of any scheme had become clear. It allowed the judiciaries of each part of the system to reach unobtrusively into the other as needed to settle the case at hand: the state courts enforcing claims under federal law when these arose in cases within their jurisdiction; the federal courts deferring to the law of the states in settling diversity suits and even, under the original Judiciary Act, in ordering their own legal process. Moreover, it allowed state law to develop in parallel fashion in the several states, as common-law precedents came to be cited across state boundaries and as legal treatises of national scope, such as those of Supreme Court Justice Joseph Story or the *Commentaries on American Law* of New York Chancellor James Kent, made American common law readily available to lawyers and judges in a land growing and changing at a rapid pace. How much of this can be attributed to the intention of the Framers is uncertain, but it is clear, at least from Hamilton's essays in *The Federalist,* that they understood that no written constitution by itself would anticipate every difficulty:

> The erection of a new government, whatever care or wisdom may distinguish the work, cannot fail to originate questions of intricacy and nicety; and these may in a particular manner be expected to flow from the establishment of a constitution founded upon the total or partial incorporation of a number of distinct sovereignties.'Tis time only that can mature and perfect so compound a system, can liquidate the meaning of all the parts, and can adjust them to each other in a harmonious and consistent WHOLE.[23]

Although the passage occurs in the context of a discussion of the relation of state and federal courts, Hamilton does not suggest that only the judiciary is involved in the work of maturity and adjustment. Indeed, no one should expect such a suggestion from a mind trained, like Hamilton's, in the common law, where courts settle novel issues when they arise in the context of a legal dispute, and legislatures can alter not past verdicts but the future course of the law.

To these three aspects of common law in the Constitution was added a fourth, the Bill of Rights. Enumerated in traditional fashion, drawn from the English experience, and largely concerned with the legal process (especially the Fourth through Eighth Amendments), these rights that were protected against federal infringement make explicit the common-law demeanor of the new federal government, reinforced by the story of their enactment. Over the protests of leading Federalists, who thought such a catalogue of rights unnecessary or positively dangerous, many of the state ratifying conventions insisted on a promise of amendments to ensure traditional rights that were thought insecure in, if not positively threatened by, the new federal regime. The case of trial by jury, that emblem of common law, is most indicative. Though established in general terms for criminal trials in Article III of the original document, it was not above criticism in *The Federalist,* where its virtue in civil cases is somewhat impeached and the difference between Federalists and Anti-Federalists on the issue is aptly captured: "the former regard it as a valuable safeguard to liberty, the latter represent it as the very palladium of free government."[24] The Bill of Rights edges the government toward the second view, specifying in some detail the rights of the criminal jury trial and adding, in the Seventh Amendment, protection for juries in "Suits at common law." That James Madison and other Federalists in Congress were readily able to introduce a series of amendments that would meet the promise of the ratification compromise without undermining the original document suggests that enough of them saw the amendments as merely declaring unwritten law—if at the price of reducing Congress's future room for maneuver—rather than as retrenchment on the Constitution's own reforms.[25] Moreover, the Ninth Amendment, a written tribute to unwritten rights, loses much of its uncertainty if understood from the common-law perspective. Then, it appears not as a license for inventive judges but as testimony to the unwritten store of rights discovered in common-law privileges and immunities, perhaps the very sort of thing Hamilton had in mind when he attributed to judges a duty to mitigate and confine the statute law.

Common Law and Constitutional Law in the Early Republic

How was the written Constitution assimilated into the common-law world? This is a more complex story than can be told here, but the simplest way to grasp the synthesis is to consult the jurisprudential writings of Justice Joseph Story, appointed to the Supreme Court by James Madison, colleague and companion to John Marshall, and simultaneously Dane professor of law at Harvard, in which capacity he authored a number of leading texts. As mentioned earlier, it is characteristic of the common-law jurist not to set out the principles of his or her legal thinking in theoretical form; like the principles of the common law itself, they are better gathered from the bulk of a judge's writing, in case and in commentary. Still, for our purposes, a useful introduction to Story's thought is the *Discourse* he delivered upon accepting his professorship at Harvard.[26] The founder of the chair, a prominent lawyer, legal scholar, and Revolutionary statesman, had apparently designated its duties as encompassing five areas of study—"the Law of Nature, the Law of Nations, Maritime and Commercial Law, Equity Law, and, lastly, the

Constitutional Law of the United States"—and toward the end of the address, Story speaks briefly of these in turn. He begins, however, with a general discussion of the science of jurisprudence, which "in its widest extent . . . may be said almost to compass every human action," including, as it does, "the elements of morals and ethics, and the eternal law of nature, illustrated and supported by the eternal law of revelation." On this extended meaning of law he quotes Cicero and a modern poet, but he quickly turns to "contemplate [jurisprudence] in a narrower view, as a mere system of regulations for the safety and harmony of civil society; as the instrument of administering public and private justice; as the code, by which rights are ascertained, and wrongs redressed; by which contracts are interpreted, and property is secured, and the institutions, which add strength to government, and solid happiness to domestic life are firmly guarded." Of this narrower jurisprudence—whose "design will yet appear sufficiently grand, and its execution sufficiently difficult, to have strong claims upon the gratitude and admiration of mankind"—Story explains: "The common law purports to be such a system."[27]

Story pretends to no originality in his account of common law—seeing John Taylor of Caroline's book titled *New Views of the Constitution,* he exclaimed, "What right has a man to start new views upon it?"[28]—but neither is his treatment characterized by the sort of antiquarianism one finds in the writings of, say, Sir Edward Coke. He begins with the traditional distinctions between common law and civil or Roman law, and between common and statute law:

> [Common law] is composed of customs, and usages, and maxims, deriving their authority from immemorial practice, and the recognition of the courts of justice. . . . Much, indeed, of this unwritten law may now be found in books, in elementary treatises, and in judicial decisions. But it does not derive its force from these circumstances. On the contrary, even judicial decisions are deemed but the formal promulgation of rules antecedently existing, and obtain all their value from their supposed conformity to those rules.

Brought with the English colonists "as their birthright," common law remains the basis of American jurisprudence, and thus common law, "in its largest extent," will "furnish the means of a better juridical education, to those who are destined for the profession, as well as . . . scholars and gentlemen." Though he speaks highly of Edmund Burke throughout this address and his writings more generally, Story does not share Burke's view that legal study sharpens the mind by narrowing it: "I do not exaggerate its value, when I express the deliberate opinion, that there is not, within the compass of human attainment, any science, which has so direct a tendency as this, to strengthen the understanding, to enlarge its powers, to sharpen its sagacity, and to form habits of nice and accurate discrimination." The common law, for Story, remains above all a practical science in an old-fashioned, perhaps one should say Aristotelian sense, embodied not in its books but in the man who can master it, allowing his mind to be formed according to its mold, making its many rules and principles his own, bringing it to life in the exercise of judgment. While the common law "employs a most severe and scrutinizing logic," threatening "enslave[ment] by scholastic refinements," "common sense has at all times powerfully counteracted the tendency to undue speculation in the common law, and silently brought back its votaries to that, which is the end of all true logic, the just application of principles to the actual concerns of human life."[29]

If the attitude toward common law I have just described could be equally found in the writings of Coke, in the scorn of "scholastic refinements" and "metaphysical subtilties and abstractions," one hears as well the modernizing cadence of William Blackstone. Coke, who wrote that the common law "hath been fined and refined by an infinite number of grave and learned men,"[30] would have allowed Story's statement that "law is a science, which must be gradually formed by the successive efforts of many minds in many ages," but he would never have said so frankly that the common law "must for ever be in a state of progress, or change, to adapt itself to the exigencies and changes of society; that even when the old foundations remain firm, the shifting channels of business must often leave their wonted beds deserted, and require new and broader substructions to accommodate and support new interests," though Story cites Coke's successor Sir Matthew Hale in support of his claim. Story does not hesitate to recount with some amusement certain reasons attributed to legal rules in Coke, and at the end of the *Discourse,* in speaking of commercial law, he notes that "much of its excellence, it must be admitted, is the growth of modern times," the work most especially of Blackstone's contemporary Lord Mansfield, who, in marked contrast to Coke and "the old common lawyers," "borrowed much from foreign jurisprudence."[31] What enabled the smooth transition, indeed the continuous mixing, of Coke's medievalism and modern political economy in common law was its openness to reason and thus improvement, for it is an ancient maxim at common law that a precedent that goes against reason does not bind. What was little noticed, at least apparently by Story, was that from medieval times to modern, what counts as reason had fundamentally changed.

If the modern moment in Story's jurisprudence comes through in his discussion of commerce, his traditionalism appears in passages like the following: "One of the beautiful boasts of our municipal jurisprudence is, that Christianity is a part of the common law, from which it seeks the sanction of its rights, and by which it endeavours to regulate its doctrines. . . . There never has been a period, in which the common law did not recognize Christianity as lying at its foundations." Story of course recognizes that the distance from the early common law of Catholic England to the America of the (albeit early) First Amendment is great, and so he quickly mentions "the error of the common law" in not tolerating dissent and thus debasing justice. The Christianity he has in mind seems to be chiefly a moral and ethical doctrine, coincident with natural law but more certain in its convictions, resting as it does on revelation, not reason alone. (Though brought to Harvard by his Congregationalist minister uncle, he migrated during his students days to Unitarianism.) In this way, Story's Christianity might be said to mirror his view of common law: to be learned for its tradition and for the sake of continuity with the past, but most interesting in its more modern and rationalized forms. The self-consciously Burkean character of the result— adapted, of course, for the republican setting—appears in his description of "the perfect lawyer": by "search[ing] the human heart, . . . walk[ing] abroad through nature, . . . examin[ing] well the precepts of religion, . . . [and] unlock[ing] all the treasures of history for illustration, and instruction, and admonition," the perfect lawyer "will thus be taught to distrust theory, and cling to practical good; to rely more upon experience, than reasoning; more upon institutions, than laws; more upon checks to vice, than upon motives to virtue."[32]

When Story turns to the American Constitution and to constitutional law, he brings along his views of common law as general jurisprudence, but he accords special recognition to the singularity of his subject. Here alone does he make reference to "the delicacy and reserve becoming my official station," suggesting the already special status of constitutional law in the work of the Supreme Court. Whereas the drift of his account of commercial law— and of the common law as a whole, insofar as he saw in commercial law its growing end—was toward the cautious and learned fostering of improvement, his emphasis now is on adherence to the "great experiment of self-government" formed by the Framers, and he promises that his principal source of doctrine will be "the admirable production of Hamilton, Madison, and Jay":

> If by such means I shall contribute to fix in the minds of American youth a more devout enthusiasm for the constitution of their country, a more sincere love of its principles, and a more firm determination to adhere to its actual provisions against the clamours of faction, and the restlessness of innovation, my humble labours will not be without some reward in the consciousness of having contributed something to the common weal.[33]

Four years after his inaugural *Discourse,* Professor Story produced the *Commentaries on the Constitution of the United States,* which was meant to secure this last end. Here too, the common law appears as background, but the author's principal devotion is to the Constitution itself, with each provision expounded in accordance with the special end it meant to foster, but also with an eye to the aim of the whole. Common law appears most readily in the two short books that introduce the long book on the Constitution, the first describing the state of the law in the American colonies, the second the nature of the legal changes brought about by the Revolution. That any statute ought to be interpreted in light of the common law it declared or modified and the mischief it was meant to relieve was a settled principle at common law, so it is no surprise to find that Story's interpretation of the Constitution includes an account of the orders it replaced and the evils it sought to cure; it is perfectly appropriate for him to examine these in great breadth when at issue is the interpretation not of an ordinary statute but of a new sort of fundamental law, a written constitution. Still, Story gives the Constitution its own authority and standing as a fundamental but positive law. The common law provides the background out of which the Constitution emerged and establishes the general principles of jurisprudence it invokes and that aid in its interpretation, but a written constitution makes a new beginning. It is not to be submerged, like the British constitution, in the immemorial tides of common law.

The Great Transformation

Until well into the twentieth century, common law not only helped shape American law and legal culture generally and American constitutional law in particular but also had a specific role in federal law. As announced by Justice Story in the 1842 case *Swift v. Tyson,*[34] the federal courts thought themselves bound, when deciding common-law matters under their diversity jurisdiction (that is, in cases between citizens of different states), to rest their decisions on "the general principles and doctrines of commercial jurisprudence." At issue in the case was the interpretation of section 34 of the Judiciary Act of 1789, "that the laws of the several States . . . shall be regarded as rules of decision in trials at common law in the courts of the United States, in cases where they apply," and in particular whether the "laws of the several States" include precedents of their courts, even when these run against general legal practice, as did some of the New York precedents arguably applicable here. Determining that "the decisions of courts . . . are, at most, only evidence of what the laws are, and are not of themselves laws," because such decisions "are often re-examined, reversed, and qualified by the courts themselves, whenever they are found to be either defective or ill-founded, or otherwise incorrect," Story concluded that "the laws of a State are more usually understood to mean the rules and enactments promulgated by the legislative authority thereof, or long established local customs having the force of laws."[35] Thus, while common law could acquire a local character concerning local matters, such as real estate, the federal courts would settle common-law cases that came within their jurisdiction by what would come to be known as federal common law.[36]

The demise of *Swift v. Tyson* came in 1938 in an opinion by Justice Louis Brandeis in the case of *Erie R. Co. v. Tompkins,*[37] and it was part and parcel of the "constitutional revolution" that had begun the year before. Like *Swift, Erie* turned on interpretation of section 34 of the Judiciary Act of 1789, but Brandeis chose not to reverse the long-standing statutory reading solely on the basis of better information about its framers' original intent—perhaps because it is generally held that precedent ought to be especially strong in the interpretation of statutes, since legislative acquiescence even in a historical error is presumed to indicate current legislative will.[38] Although the bulk of Brandeis's discussion illustrated what he held to be "the mischievous results" of the *Swift* doctrine, he relied on what he called "the unconstitutionality of the course" of decisions under *Swift,* which had the effect of discriminating in favor of noncitizens over citizens of a state. The former could choose the forum of the federal courts when these decided cases under a more favorable rule than did the courts of the state where the complaint arose, and this "rendered impossible equal protection of the law." Instead, Brandeis would read the Judiciary Act's command to include among the "laws of the several States" not only their statutes but also the entire common law as it now stood established by precedent in the state whose laws would apply. The federal judiciary would subsequently have no recourse of its own to common law but must defer to whatever had been announced as common law by state judges.

Erie has been considered the death of federal common law, in its technical sense, but in fact, it was only its death knell, for underlying the opinion was the radical reorientation in the meaning of common law that had been introduced in the generation leading up to *Erie* by Justice Holmes: if judges are lawmakers, then it is surely perverse to exclude their decisions from the law of the states to which the federal courts must defer. Holmes's project, introduced as early as his 1881 lectures, was first of all "to insist on a more conscious recognition of the legislative function of courts."[39] If this statement contains the germ of a critique of the Constitution, structured as it is on the notion of separate and analytically distinct powers of government, Holmes's strategy is not to assault the Constitution or, for that matter, American constitutional law head-on, but rather to act by indirection, through the underbelly of that constitutionalism in common law. In a speech about John Marshall delivered from the Massachusetts bench, he confessed, "My keenest interest is excited, not by what are called great questions and great cases, but by little decisions which the common run of selectors would pass by because they did not deal with the Constitution or a telephone company, yet which have in them the germ of some wider theory, and therefore of some profound interstitial change in the very tissue of the law."[40]

His book *The Common Law* is a study of just such change, usually unintentional, initiated by judges whose views of policy inevitably colored their decisions at law. The book is historical, but as he explains in his celebrated essay "The Path of the Law," he is interested in history because "it is the first step toward an enlightened skepticism, that is, toward a deliberate reconsideration of the worth of those rules" that govern common-law adjudication, now on self-conscious policy grounds. "For the rational study of the law, the black-letter man may be the man of the present, but the man of the future is the man of statistics and the master of economics."[41] Still, Holmes's economist does not work as a classical legislator; he is no architect of comprehensive political and social change. Rather, as a judge, he legislates little by little, adjusting the rules of decision case by case on the basis of a larger theory. He is a craftsman of judicious or surreptitious change, and thus he shies away from constitutional law, with its bright spotlight in the midst of party politics. Or he makes his contribution to constitutional law as he would to common law, quietly adjusting doctrine in the direction, but not the name, of new principles—as Holmes succeeded in doing with the constitutional law of free speech. He is guided toward rather than confined by "interstices," for like the modern atom discovered by his contemporaries, Holmes's law is wide open between charged particles, though its surfaces seem solid to superficial minds.

The school of legal analysis Holmes fostered has come to be called *legal realism,* and Holmes's claim was first of all to describe what judges actually do, and only then to teach them better ways to do it. As I noted before, his basic account of common law as a process of judicially managed legal change is now orthodox in the legal academy, even if only occasionally employing economists as its priests.[42] Was it a fair description of the American common-law judge in Holmes's time? Perhaps, but Holmes did not do justice to the serious reflection on the relation between permanence and change in the great publicists of common law in the early Republic. Already by the time of the Revolution, the notion was alive, through the practice of Lord Mansfield and the writings of Blackstone, that the common law carried within it a reforming principle, at least in commercial matters, and that the current practice of merchants was entitled to respect in the courts. Moreover, in the early years of the American Republic, the maxim that nothing against reason could be lawful itself became an engine of common-law reform in two related but distinguishable ways. In the first place, the power of the common-law judge to confine a precedent and even control a statute that went against reason seems to have referred especially to his duty to keep the law consistent with itself.[43] The demand here was not that he deduce a fully articulated theory or model of the law from a few axioms; again, the common law welcomed a multiplicity of rules, even of kinds and sources of law, that any rigorous demand for consistency would have squelched. At the same time, contrary rules brought to bear on the same case could not be tolerated, and one must be obliged to yield. In the early years after the Founding, with the change of regime from monarchy to republic and with a vast expansion in the sources of law—the addition of a federal government with its own Constitution, legislature, and judiciary; the political independence and growing economic interdependence of the states, not to mention the steady growth in their number—numerous questions of law for which there were no adequate precedents were to be expected, and the courts at every level had to reason their way through the new order of things. In the second place, however, under the influence of the same Enlightenment that helped set in motion these changes, the meaning of reason in the public sphere began to alter, so that courts might be called on to consider not so much the consistency of law within its own immemorial order as its compatibility with the discoveries of modern social science, and especially the new science of political economy. Here the common law became an important part of the story of the economic development of the continent; the old genius of individual initiative embedded in the common law was now allied with modern reforms concerning the rights of property to give the edge to commercial improvement and acquisition over landed and inherited wealth.[44]

By the time Holmes wrote, the malleability of common law that he supposed already had some precedent in American common law, partly in the adjustment of English practices to fit the circumstances of the American federal republic, partly in a more open-ended engagement with the scientific and economic developments characteristic of the modern world. Nor was change in common law innocent of hope of moral improvement; although common law in England was more or less independent of ecclesiastical law, it still accommodated an established church, which American law would soon enough do without. Still, for all his Unitarian optimism, Story had proclaimed, "There never has been a period, in which the common law did not recognize Christianity as lying at its foundations."[45] With Holmes, that period arrived. He reserved his religious awe for the dispensations of unfathomable fate, even as he reserved for himself the role of oracle. The detachment of common law from its ancient ground, whether in natural law or in Christian faith, made inevitable its becoming an empty form of flux and so prepared the course by which, in a constitutional jurisprudence that unfolded like Holmes's common law, the right to procreate and educate one's children became the right to abort.[46] But of this, more later, as I turn from this general sketch of the relation of common law and Constitution to more specific questions and doctrines of constitutional law.

CHAPTER 2

Fighting Words

Common Law and Liberalism in the American Doctrine of Free Speech

In 1990, when the U.S. Supreme Court handed down one of their flag-burning decisions and members of Congress scurried to propose a constitutional amendment against desecration of the American flag, two Louisiana state representatives had a different idea: they proposed that the state legislature abolish the threat of imprisonment and reduce to twenty-five dollars the fine for assault and battery against someone defiling the flag.[1] With rustic frankness, this brings to light what the Supreme Court's doctrine concerning "fighting words" both is and is not: a right of reply to offensive speech with the fists. Announced in Justice Murphy's unanimous opinion in the 1942 case *Chaplinsky v. New Hampshire,* and honored since then more in the breach than in the observance, the "fighting words" doctrine holds that "insulting or 'fighting' words—those which by their very utterance inflict injury or tend to incite an immediate breach of the peace"—are, together with "the lewd and obscene, the profane, [and] the libelous," "well-defined and limited classes of speech, the prevention and punishment of which have never been thought to raise any Constitutional problem."[2] Since 1942, suppression of the lewd and obscene, the profane, and the libelous has certainly been challenged as problematic, but "fighting words" remained in principle a category of unprotected speech for fifty years until, in the case of *R.A.V. v. St. Paul,* the Supreme Court struck down a Minnesota "hate speech" statute on the grounds that, in prohibiting some but not all fighting words, it violated the principle of "content-neutrality."[3] The right to fight in defense when insulted has become the right to insult with impunity.

In this chapter, I use the notion of "fighting words" as a point of entry to discuss the nature of freedom of speech and its relation to the common law on the one hand and to liberalism on the other. From the earliest controversy under the First Amendment to recent disputes about libertarian and republican justifications for the system of free expression, a contest between the common law and liberalism has persisted, although it seems to have been taken for granted by scholars that in the matter of free speech, the common law represents the benighted past and liberalism the enlightened future. My point is not to deny that contemporary free-speech doctrine, if not always its practice, is chiefly informed by some version of liberal ideas, but I mean to examine the extent to which the common law has shaped the American understanding of free speech and to raise the question of whether something useful might be learned from it for our present quandaries. I begin with a sketch of the context of free speech in the history of political philosophy, then look in some detail at the early history of the First Amendment, concluding with a few remarks on the modern judicial doctrine of free expression.

Free Speech and the Political Animal

When Holmes wrote in his famous dissent in *Abrams v. United States* that "persecution for the expression of opinions seems to me perfectly logical,"[4] he chose his words precisely or said more than he knew, for *logos*—the ancient Greek word for speech or reason—was at the center of the Aristotelian understanding of politics that liberalism undertook to replace. As Paul Rahe has written:

> For Aristotle, *logos* is something more refined than the capacity to make private feelings public: it enables the human being to perform as no other animal can; it makes it possible for him to perceive and make clear to others through reasoned discourse the difference between what is advantageous and what is harmful, between what is just and what is unjust, and between what is good and what is evil. It is the sharing of these things, Aristotle insists, which constitutes the household and the *polis* each as a community (*koinonia*).[5]

The word "sharing" is carefully chosen by Rahe as a translation for *koinonia* in the passage of *Politics* he is paraphrasing. Just as Aristotle thinks that man is by nature a political animal because he is both irrational and rational—his irrationality making political rule necessary, his rationality making it possible[6]—so the sharing in *logos* has a sort of ambiguity, or in-between character. On the one hand, political speech involves deliberation about what the city ought to do and thus necessarily demands a certain freedom to present alternatives. On the other hand, Aristotle makes it clear that deliberation is about means, not ends[7]; the city depends on a certain agreement (the

Greek word is *homonoia*) or authoritative opinion about first principles, that is, about the advantageous, the just, and the good, and the opinion that rules each city determines, or is determined by, its regime (*politeia*). The "persecution for the expression of opinion" that Holmes derides as "perfectly logical" is, from an Aristotelian point of view, only partly so. The author of the *Rhetoric* was no enemy of public speaking, but he did hold that there was a limit to public debate implicit in the premises of a regime.

The relation of classical political philosophy to free speech appears from another perspective as well. In the *Republic,* Plato divides the soul (and the city) into three parts: the calculating, the spirited, and the appetitive. The scheme of the dialogue is to forge an alliance of the first two against the third or, more precisely, to attach spiritedness to reason in the control of the appetites. While Aristotle does not adopt this psychology in his political works, emphasizing simply the division between the rational and the irrational, his account of politics seems likewise to involve an alliance between the love of honor and reason, with the appetitive relegated to the prepolitical sphere of the household. Though it might be foolish or at least unhistorical to push the analogy too far, one can see in the Platonic or Aristotelian scheme a sort of model for American free-speech doctrine as late as the mid-twentieth century: speech that merely fed the appetites (commercial speech and, even more, obscenity) could be regulated even to the point of prohibition, whereas speech imbued with spiritedness (fighting words and, more generally, incitement and sedition) engaged a spirited response. From a classical perspective, it is no accident that most controversy over free speech involves spirited speech, or that the freedom of speech presents itself as a noble cause, or that men fight for what they think is the truth.

Now, if classical political philosophy forms a sort of background to the common-law understanding of free speech, more immediately in the foreground is the influence of Christianity and monarchy. Christianity added to classical philosophy at least the following ingredients: the priority of law to the regime (a reversal of the classical order), based on a greater certainty about good and evil in revelation than in reason, and on a confidence in the public declaration of good; the infinite value of the human individual as a being with an eternal soul and as the object of God's particular providence and, sometimes, His grace; the doctrine of free will; and the distinction between church and state, implicit in the three previous principles but unknown to the ancient world. With its origin in medieval European civilization, English common law counted heresy, witchcraft, and other Christian sins among its crimes, and among its maxims was that "Christianity is a part of the common law." Moreover, common law undoubtedly drew prestige or at least self-assurance from the enhancement of law effected by Christianity, and in the central importance of the particular case at common law one sees an image of the infinite individual with free will. At the same time, the common-law courts were largely independent of the ecclesiastical courts, so that one finds in the old common law not only elements that present-day Americans consider an impermissible mixture of religion and secular law but also the seeds of an independent judiciary.[8] As for monarchy, the common-law courts recognized the king's claim to ligeance, generally respected his prerogatives, and administered justice in his name, but they insisted that it was not part of a king's prerogative to displace the judges in their business of doing his justice, thus insisting that the king rule by law and providing in the courts of law (including the "High Court of Parliament") a forum for contention and dispute. The phrase "freedom of speech," incidentally, first appears in this context. In Coke's *Institutes* and in the English Bill of Rights of 1689, it is a privilege of free debate belonging to members of Parliament. Its more popular parallels were the right to petition the Parliament and the right to vindicate one's rights in court.

Liberalism arose especially as a challenge to the influence of Christianity in politics, in response to the Inquisition and its civil penalties on the one hand and to the religious warfare and sedition that accompanied the Reformation on the other.[9] This appears both in its institutional program for revising the relationship of church and state—firm state control of the church, a scheme of separation and toleration, or a mixture of the two[10]—and, even more dramatically, in its philosophical principles of the state of nature and the social contract, which implicitly deny the Christian doctrine of the Fall (not to mention the Redemption) and the maxim of Scripture that all power comes from the Lord. About monarchy, liberalism was at first more circumspect, although the earliest liberals did not hesitate to reconstitute its basis in consent or to adjust its institutions better to secure individual rights; the liberal principle that forms of government have value not in themselves but as means to independent ends at once deprives monarchy of its sacred claims and deprives republicanism of its sacred honor. That liberalism challenged to the core the classical philosophy of politics was perhaps less apparent—since some of the practical champions of liberal ideas also imbued classical models—but was no less decisive. Liberal philosophy rejected the ancient notion that man was naturally political because naturally rational, and it consequently sought a basis for public order not in practical wisdom and political rhetoric, supported by a popular religion and a retiring philosophy, but in a scientifically based public philosophy supported by enlightened self-interest. Although by the nineteenth century a maturing liberalism discarded its natural rights foundation—this was suspect anyway, as it borrowed language from the thought it attacked—the liberal commitment to public enlightenment and individual self-development persisted, even as, with the twentieth century, a liberalism influenced by the same radical critiques that hoped to surpass it shifted its concerns from the rights of property to the rights of self-expression.[11]

The implications of the appearance of liberalism and its subsequent development for the American doctrine of freedom of speech are several. First, that liberalism arose in response to the religious question meant that the liberty of speech and of the press was associated with religious liberty and was often treated as ancillary to it. This appears not only in the words of the First Amendment but also in the development of modern legal doctrine in the Supreme Court, where many of the first successful free-speech claims were made in cases involving a religious sect, the Jehovah's Witnesses.[12] Second, just as the question of the form of government was secondary to the early liberal, free speech in political matters was not always as forthcoming as it was in religious matters; even if politics could be placed on a scientific foundation, there was thought to be some residual need for public doctrine, at least among those liberals who doubted that ours would be entirely a nation of philosophers.[13] The development of liberalism away from defense of the natural rights of property and toward encouragement of historically emergent rights of self-expression has been widely noted, as have the consequences for judicial doctrine in the United States, perhaps most succinctly in the most famous sentence from Holmes's *Abrams* dissent: "When men have realized that time has upset many fighting faiths, they may come to believe even more than they believe the very foundations of their own conduct that the ultimate good desired is better reached by free trade in ideas—that the best test of truth is the power of thought to get itself accepted in the competition of the market, and that truth is the only ground upon which their wishes safely can be carried out."[14] And because liberalism grounded its opposition to public Christianity on a critique of classical political philosophy, this meant that its effort to define the course of free expression in America would come up against the freedoms of speech and press as they came down in common law.

The Alien and Sedition Controversy

Here is Holmes again in *Abrams:* "I wholly disagree with the argument of the Government that the First Amendment left the common law as to seditious libel in force. History seems to me against the notion. I had conceived that the United States through many years had shown its repentance for the Sedition Act of 1798, by repaying the fines that it imposed."[15]

That the controversy over the Alien and Sedition Acts settled the meaning of free speech and press in America for a century is today generally accepted, but less clear is the prior status of common law and the extent to which the settlement reached at the turn of the nineteenth century differs from the libertarian doctrine that developed in the middle of the twentieth. Leonard Levy's study of freedom of the press in the colonial and Revolutionary periods, written from the libertarian perspective, finds in the common law and American practice a "legacy of suppression" renounced not in the original intention of the First Amendment but only by the most advanced Jeffersonians—significantly, not by Jefferson himself—who in the course of dispute over the Alien and Sedition Acts were first driven to articulate the libertarian position that there can be no such crime as seditious libel in republican government.[16] Walter Berns, by contrast, finds the dispute between the Federalists and the Republicans principally concerned not with conflicting interpretations of freedom of the press but with conflicting positions on federalism; both parties agreed, in Berns's telling, that republican government presupposes a power to limit the right of free speech to those who do not try to subvert that form of government either by preaching sedition or by corrupting republican virtue.[17] What both Levy and Berns underestimate, in my opinion, is the extent to which the solution reached (not just one side of the argument) was influenced by the Founders' way of thinking and arguing within the framework of common law.

The controversy over the Alien and Sedition Acts had several stages and several dimensions. Not the least significant of the latter was that this controversy was the forge in which Americans developed their understanding of the character of legitimate party competition. And the temporary character of the parties formed, as well as the fundamental character of the issues over which they contended, suggests that this development was, from the later perspective of American politics, incomplete.[18] Jefferson's magnanimous Inaugural Address—"We are all federalists, we are all republicans"—was as much a denial as an affirmation of party competition. In fact, the bitter dispute between the parties, which always had in its background conflicting positions over the French Revolution, was alleviated in part by the eighteenth Brumaire. By suppressing the French Republic, Napoleon helped spare the American Republic, for this freed us from making a precipitous choice between liberal republicanism and British liberties, allowing us to persist, as we have done, in having it both ways.[19] The Founders' healthy ambivalence toward political parties—evinced, for example, in Madison's *Federalist* Number 10, where factions are defined as enemies of private rights or public good but then are described as involved in "the necessary and ordinary operations of Government"[20]—survived the first bitter partisan competition under the Constitution not only because one side won decisively but also because the other eventually had its day in court.

The stages of the dispute over what we call seditious libel were, first, the Federalist attempt at common-law prosecutions of Republican editors, which eventuated in the Sedition Act; second, the Republican remonstrance against the act, most notably the Virginia and Kentucky Resolutions, which culminated in what Jefferson called the "Revolution of 1800"; third, the prosecution of Federalist editors at the state level, which issued in a new and authoritative definition of the American common law of libel under the influence of Alexander Hamilton; and finally, the 1812 decision of the Supreme Court that there is no federal common law of crimes. The last stage is perhaps the most easily disposed of, for the decision in *United States v. Hudson and Goodwin,* issued from an apparently unanimous Supreme Court by the pen of Jefferson's appointee William Johnson, announced that the matter had been "long since settled in public opinion" and had received "the general acquiescence of legal men."[21] In the 1790s, however, the issue was far from settled, as Federalists argued that despite the Constitution's enumeration of specific objects of federal power, the very composition of a government with a judicial branch entailed incorporation of as much of the common law as befitted that government's form and function. Holding that the government's authority to protect itself from libelous assault was so incorporated, federal prosecutors successfully brought suit against several editors after 1797. The Sedition Act, in the minds of its Federalist authors, then, appeared not as an innovation but as a declaration of what they considered unwritten law. Indeed, they claimed that whatever innovations it contained— making the intent of the publisher an element of the crime, allowing the truth of the statement to vindicate the defendant, and making the jury the arbiter of intent and truth—were reforms or interpretations of the common law in the direction of greater liberty.[22]

Today, the standard source for the common law at the time of the Founding is William Blackstone's *Commentaries on the Laws of England,* published between 1765 and 1769 and quickly a favorite in the colonies and the new states. What is less well understood by modern scholars is that Blackstone's authority was not accepted without argument by lawyers in the

Founding period, not least because of his association with Lord Chief Justice Mansfield and the opponents of the colonial cause in the constitutional dispute that led to the American Revolution. Jefferson preferred the authority of Sir Edward Coke to Blackstone, and when original Supreme Court Justice James Wilson modeled his law lectures on the *Commentaries,* he emphasized the importance of adapting Blackstone to the American Republic.[23] On libel, Blackstone's position is complex. He treats the matter twice: in book 3, chapter 8, "Of Wrongs, and Their Remedies, Respecting the Rights of Persons," and in book 4, chapter 11, "Of Offenses against the Public Peace." The first concerns slander and libel insofar as it injures an individual and is redressed by a civil suit for damages. The second concerns "malicious defamations of any person, and especially a magistrate, made public by either printing, writing, signs, or pictures, in order to provoke him to wrath, or expose him to public hatred, contempt, and ridicule"; since "the direct tendency of these libels is the breach of the public peace, by stirring up the objects of them to revenge, and perhaps bloodshed," they can give rise to an indictment and punishment by fine and corporal penalty.[24] In civil suits, the truth of the statement at issue can be pleaded in defense against a judgment, but in a criminal case, it is no defense, for "the tendency which all libels have to create animosities, and to disturb the public peace, is the sole consideration of the law." Coke's report of the 1605 Star Chamber Case *De Libellis famosis* is cited here, and Coke wrote in that case, "It is not material whether the Libel be true," but Blackstone omits the reason that followed: that "in a settled State of Government the Party grieved ought to complain for every Injury done him in an ordinary Course of Law, and not by any Means to revenge himself, either by the odious Course of Libelling, or otherwise."[25] As to whether the jury can rule on anything beyond the defendant's responsibility for publication, Blackstone does not say, although Lord Mansfield would decide cases limiting the jury to just that, as discussed later. It is worth noting that, despite the implication in Levy, Blackstone draws no formal distinction in criminal libel between members of the government and other individuals beyond that quoted above, although one can suppose that public prosecutors most vigilantly protect their own. The prohibition of seditious libel alone—against the government and its officers—was apparently another innovation of the Sedition Act.

The discussion of criminal libel concludes Blackstone's chapter on wrongs against the public peace, and he takes the occasion for a general paragraph about the freedom of the press. "This consists," he writes, "in laying no *previous* restraints upon publications, and not in freedom from censure for criminal matter when published. Every freeman has an undoubted right to lay what sentiments he pleases before the public. . . . But if he publishes what is improper, mischievous, or illegal, he must take the consequences of his own temerity." If Blackstone's acquiescence in discounting truth as a defense in criminal libel reflects a Hobbesian concern with public peace above all else, his account of the freedom of the press has the authentic ring of the traditional common law. The absence of a public licenser means "the will of individuals is still left free; the abuse only of that free will is the object of legal punishment." "To censure the licentiousness, is to maintain the liberty, of the press."[26]

Although Levy finds several pamphlets more worthy from a libertarian perspective, the most authoritative public statements in opposition to the Sedition Act belong to the pen of James Madison: the Virginia Resolutions of December 1798, the "Address of the General Assembly to the People of the Commonwealth of Virginia" of January 1799, and especially the "Report on the Resolutions" of 1800.[27] As Berns points out,[28] the resolutions are chiefly concerned with questions of federalism: how far the powers of the federal government extend in light of their enumeration; the unconstitutionality of acts that go beyond the implicit limits; the right of the states, as constituent bodies of the Union, to "interpose" and declare such acts unconstitutional, at least for the purpose of urging on the other states concerted action to amend the Constitution and stop the evil. But Madison's "Report," though it works through the resolutions one by one and reinforces them with careful argumentation, devotes nearly half its length to a matter treated in only half a paragraph in the resolutions, namely, the unconstitutionality of the Sedition Act. This Madison establishes by three arguments. First, to show that the absence of a power over the press delegated to Congress is decisive, Madison meets head-on the argument for a federal common law. While admitting that "particular parts of the common law may have a sanction from the Constitution, so far as they are necessarily comprehended in the technical phrases which the powers delegated to the Government; and so far also as such parts may be adopted by Congress as necessary and proper for carrying into execution the powers expressly delegated," he denies any general incorporation of common law into the federal charter. Referring to the colonists' constitutional dispute with England, and in particular their denial of any power in Parliament to legislate for any of the colonies and their assertion of the right severally to legislate for themselves, Madison shows that what common law was brought along or adopted by each colony "was the separate law of each colony within its respective limits" and in fact "not the same in any two of the Colonies"; "the common law never was, nor by any fair construction ever can be, deemed a law for the American people as one community." And good riddance, too, he suggests. To find the common law implicit in the Constitution would mean that "the whole code, with all its incongruities, barbarisms, and bloody maxims, would be inviolably saddled on the good people of the United States."[29]

Madison's impeaching the authority of common law in the course of his constitutional argument concerning the independent legislative powers of the states seems to prepare his second argument, that the words "freedom of speech, or of the press" in the First Amendment do not form the sort of technical phrase that can be interpreted simply by reference to common law. Taking "no previous restraint" as the common-law definition, Madison shows that the different forms of government in England and America require different forms of press freedom. In England, where danger is expected from the monarch, the absence of a royal licensor is sufficient to put the people's mind at rest; indeed, so thoroughly do they expect danger only from the king that they allow their Parliament to claim omnipotence. In America, by contrast, where the tendency of Parliament to overreach was learned in colonial times, and where the tendency of legislatures in the new states was seen to be the same, danger is anticipated from all branches of government; the absence of a licensor is no protection against a legislature that would make publications criminal at its will. More generally, "the nature of governments elective, limited, and responsible in all their branches, may well be supposed to require a greater freedom of animadversion than might be tolerated by the genius of such a government as that of Great Britain," with its hereditary parts. Add to this the practice of the press "in every state," which has decided "that it is better to leave a few of its noxious branches to their luxuriant growth, than, by pruning them away, to injure the vigour of those yielding proper fruits," and the argument that the American understanding of freedom of the press is wider than that in English common law is almost complete. To clinch the case, consider the analogous status of religious liberty—mentioned also in the First Amendment—in common law: "It will never be admitted that the meaning of [freedom of conscience and religion], in the common law of England, is to limit their meaning in the United States."[30]

Madison's third major argument develops the phrase in the resolutions pronouncing the freedom of the press "the guardian of every other right."[31] Here he stresses the constitutional power of impeachment and especially the people's right to elect their representatives. Election is the chief means of guarding rights in a republic, but free election is possible only with free discussion; fair elections, too, need free speech, but the Sedition Act shields incumbents while leaving challengers exposed. To the claim that the reforms of Blackstone's common law in the act protect free discussion, Madison replies, first, that the defense of truth is inadequate, both because even true facts cannot always meet judicial standards of proof and because "opinions, inferences, and conjectural observations" are not subject to judicial proof, and second, that the need to show criminal intent is no protection when the exposing of corruption is made a crime.[32]

What is remarkable about Madison's "Report" is the extent to which its arguments, at least those concerning freedom of the press, however derogatory of common law, rely on forms of reasoning characteristic of common law itself. This is especially true of the second argument just reviewed, for it was a maxim of common law that inconveniences or inconsistencies in the law demanded resolution, since the law could contain nothing "against reason"; if the rule defining freedom of the press as simply "no previous restraint" could be shown to conflict with the form of constitutional government legitimately established (as I think Madison ably shows), that rule must be adjusted. This was a point generally admitted by those who would incorporate the common law in America, even if they differed over its application in the matter of a free press. Moreover, Madison's argument from practice or custom had a certain force at common law, if not against a law of undoubted authority, at least as evidence of what the law was understood to mean. To be sure, there are arguments in the "Report" that draw on principles foreign to the common law, even in its American formulation: that the people of the United States possess "absolute sovereignty" or that the laws of the United States are a "legislative expression of the general will."[33] But these are the echoes of Rousseau and of the French Revolution, not the American language of 1787 and 1788.

As Berns has noted, the burden of the Virginia and Kentucky Resolutions was not to deny the common law of libel as such, but only to insist that it belonged to the states and could be modified only in their legislatures. Even Madison, some of whose arguments are readily adopted by the libertarian cause, admitted that individuals' reputations could still be vindicated against libels "under the same laws, and in the same tribunals, which protect their lives, their liberties, and their properties," namely, the state courts.[34] In this sense, the Jeffersonians were true to their word once they were in power, for Jeffersonian governments in several states instituted libel prosecutions against those who derided their chief. In New York, the critical case came in 1803, *People v. Croswell,* in which a Federalist editor was indicted and convicted for libel of President Jefferson—the assertion in question being that Jefferson had paid a certain James Callender to libel George Washington. The judge in the case, also chief justice of the New York Supreme Court, had charged the jury under the rule enunciated by Chief Justice Mansfield in the *Case of the Dean of St. Asaph,* namely, that the jury could determine only the fact of publication and whether the innuendoes drawn out by the prosecution were correct.[35] Moving before the entire state supreme court for a new trial the following year, Croswell had the benefit of the services of Alexander Hamilton, who argued that the question of criminal intent should have been left to the jury, and that evidence of the truth of the publication ought to have been admitted as a material factor in establishing intent. "The Liberty of the Press consists, in my idea, in publishing the truth, from good motives and for justifiable ends, though it reflect on government, on magistrates, or individuals," Hamilton asserted, and he aimed to show not only that this understanding comports with American institutions but also that it is warranted by the common law properly understood.

Hamilton's argument about institutions is much terser than Madison's had been, and not only because he spoke at the bar, not to the House. Like Madison, he begins with the need for free discussion in a "free and elective government," though he adds that he would preserve the distinction between liberty and license, a distinction Madison thought impossible in legal practice to enforce.[36] His chief concern, however, is with the independence of the judiciary and its trustworthiness as an impartial administrator of the law of libel, which he finds even more unreliable in America than in England: "But with us, it is the vibration of party. As one side or the other prevails, so of that class and temperament will be the judges of their nomination."[37] Presuming, apparently, the people to be less partisan than the elite, this distrust of judges recommends leaving the question of intent to the jury, which in criminal cases under the common law has the final say concerning the application of law to fact. To argue the appropriateness and the possibility of a jury determination of intent in libel cases, Hamilton canvasses the criminal law as a whole. As for the authority of the *Dean of St. Asaph* and other modern cases cited, Hamilton indicates contrary precedents, albeit mostly from earlier eras, to show that "the law was never thus settled[; i]t was a mere floating of litigated questions," enabling the courts of New York to make a fresh decision. And he urges the judges explicitly to "pursue the precedents . . . more emphatically our own," namely, the Sedition Act, which, "on common law principles," admitted the point contended for. Regarding "the applicability of the common law, to the Constitution of the

United States," though it would be "a long detail to investigate," Hamilton confidently asserts, "It is evident . . . that parts of [the Constitution] use a language which refers to former principles. . . . Such is the general tenor of the constitution of the United States, that it evidently looks to antecedent law. What is, on this point, the great body of the common law? Natural law and natural reason applied to the purposes of Society. What are the English courts doing now but adopting natural law."[38] Hamilton then, like Madison, makes an appeal to reason, but while the latter treats the common law as the positive enactment or custom of a sovereign state, the former finds it in the application of reason to the forms and precedents that constitute the society at hand.

Hamilton thus promotes the following definition of libel: "a slanderous or ridiculous writing, picture, or sign, with a malicious or mischievous design or intent, towards government, magistrates, or individuals." Truth is no absolute bar to conviction but "is a reason to infer that there was no design to injure another," overridden if it can be shown that the author "uses the weapon of truth wantonly, . . . [or] for the purpose of destroying the peace of families, . . . [or] for relating that which does not appertain to official conduct."[39] The New York Supreme Court was evenly divided on the question, and Hamilton lost his case, but he won the war, so to speak, for the New York legislature, many of whose members had attended the pleadings, soon passed an act incorporating into New York law the position for which he had contended—a provision later included in the 1821 constitution of that state.[40] Moreover, James Kent, who had sat on the court before which Hamilton argued and who defended the clause at the 1821 constitutional convention, included Hamilton's principle in the discussion of libel in his influential *Commentaries on American Law,* as a signal attempt "to preserve equally, and in just harmony and proportion, the protection which is due to character, and the protection which ought to be afforded to liberty of speech and of the press."[41]

On the matter of libel, then, both the Republicans and the Federalists made a contribution. The Republicans returned the matter to the states, and the Federalists there had the opportunity to anchor the American understanding of freedom of speech and the press in the context provided by the common law, rationally adjusted to republican circumstances. The principle of responsibility was saved, but so was a practical freedom of the press, at least for the publication of sentiments that could win credibility in that register of public opinion and palladium of the common law, the jury. Tocqueville, visiting America in the aftermath of this settlement, could take for granted that Americans enjoy an unlimited freedom of the press in practice.[42] But words that hurt could be fought back against, at least to the extent that truth and good motive were allowed to vindicate themselves.

Modern Libertarianism and Postmodern Regulation

It is one of the peculiarities of the modern Supreme Court that it has often succeeded in nearly erasing the common-law dimension of American constitutionalism while making decisions ostensibly in its name. Arguably, this explains the course of property rights at the end of the nineteenth and the beginning of the twentieth centuries, during which the rich texture of the common law of property and contract was reduced to a few hardened principles thought vindicated by the modern science of political economy, only to have the whole thing discarded in the name of the regulatory state once scientific developments and unanticipated events discredited the principles evolved. When, coincident with the constitutional revolution of 1937, the Supreme Court began turning its attention to the vindication of civil liberties against the burgeoning power of the modern state, a resurgence of interest in a neglected side of common law might have been expected, since so many of the protections in the Bill of Rights had their source in common law. Even the business of incorporation of the Bill of Rights through the Fourteenth Amendment to become applicable to the states might appear to be in the spirit of common law, countering the divergence among the states Madison had already seen in his day. And there are indications of this in a number of opinions from the age of Stone and Vinson, Black and Frankfurter, perhaps especially in those of Robert Jackson.[43]

But the common law had come to be perceived differently in the interim, under the immense influence of the poet Justice Holmes and his army of admirers. No longer an inheritance of reason, entrusted to judge and jury in their proper parts, it became in Holmes's light mysterious custom, fascinating in its development to the detached observer, but lacking the generative power now attributed to modern science. Holmes's free-speech opinions display this attitude, nowhere more obviously than in the contemplation of proletarian dictatorship in the *Gitlow* dissent,[44] but even in the "clear and present danger" standard, which bases the test for speech not on its intrinsic character but on its accidental circumstances. The "fighting words" doctrine of *Chaplinsky* becomes, from this perspective, just an especially vivid and individualized instance of the danger apprehended. Quoting the New Hampshire Supreme Court, itself capturing the spirit of Holmes's "reasonable man" test,

Justice Murphy agrees that "'the test is what men of common intelligence would understand would be words likely to cause an average addressee to fight.'"[45] But why place the burden on the speaker, when it is the other man who starts to push? This doubt, which begins to surface in cases such as *Feiner v. New York,* eventually leads to the modern routine of massive police protection being accorded a handful of, for example, Nazi pretenders. The absolutization of speech accompanies the relativization of meaning.

More important than the development of "fighting words" jurisprudence for contemporary discourse was the Court's reopening of the question of the relation of libel to free speech in *New York Times v. Sullivan* (1964) and its licensing of profanity, even in the pages of its reports, in *Cohen v. California* (1971). In the first case, on one level, the Court opinion appears to be simply an attempt to extend a common-law rule developed in several jurisdictions to a national standard: the actual malice test comes not out of thin air but from the pages of the *Kansas Reports.*[46] But the most quoted lines are not these, as Justice Black in concurrence feared, but Justice Brennan's mention of "a profound national commitment to the principle that debate on public issues should be uninhibited, robust, and wide-open," moving from Hamilton's notion that truth be admitted in defense to prove no malice to the position—not quite contradictory to the first, but surely of a different tenor—that falsity is not evidence of bad intent.[47] In *Cohen,* by contrast, no mention is made of common law, as another of the categories of excluded speech in *Chaplinsky* is buried by the Court's most able common lawyer. Tempted by the claim of a right in the states "to maintain what they regard as a suitable level of discourse with in the body politic," Justice Harlan nevertheless concludes that no principle can justify excluding only some words from the public vocabulary, since the fluidity of language is apparently such that "one man's vulgarity is another's lyric."[48]

Cohen marks the apogee of libertarianism in free-speech doctrine,[49] but such retrenchment as has occurred involves not a return to a common-law perspective but adoption of a distinctively modern interest in regulation, illustrated in the denouement of the "fighting words" doctrine, the 1992 case of *R.A.V. v. St. Paul.* Here, the Minnesota State Supreme Court had tried to save a local ordinance that banned as disorderly conduct the placement of symbolic objects or graffiti aimed at arousing "anger, alarm or resentment in others on the basis of race, color, creed, religion or gender" by interpreting the ordinance as limited in its reach to constitutionally unprotected "fighting words." The Supreme Court reversed, however, finding the ordinance impermissibly "content-based," since it excludes only insults of one ideological class. Thus, even "fighting words" come under the Supreme Court's protection, as the principle that regulation of speech in relation to its time, place, and manner should not ordinarily be based on the content of what is said, and even less on the viewpoint represented, is expanded to a principle of fair speech in a regulated environment that overrules the common-law approach of restricting speech by kind and category, confidently judging what matters and what does not. Implicit in Justice Scalia's opinion is a sense, foreign to common law, that social consensus has disappeared to such an extent that efforts at preserving public discourse are bound to be partisan in character, and perhaps there is even some resignation to the eclipse of reason in public life: "St. Paul [he means the city, of course] has no such authority to license one side of the debate to fight freestyle, while requiring the other to follow Marquis of Queensberry Rules."[50] "Fighting words," no longer a category of unprotected speech, become the paradigm of discourse itself in the age of "culture wars."

In his book *Democracy and the Problem of Free Speech,* Cass Sunstein makes the observation (from a perspective opposite my own) with which I conclude this chapter.[51] Calling for "A New Deal for Speech," he promotes an expansion of regulations designed on the model of the now discarded "Fairness Doctrine" to foster equal political debate unbiased by the power of money in the marketplace of ideas. He explicitly presents this program as a counterweight to what he describes as the common-law regime of speech under which we now operate. This project, the serious thought behind what appears in the media as "political correctness," seems to me to overlook two related, though apparently contradictory, dangers. The first is whether an unforced consensus can be found to support a regime of deliberation not limited to means, as Aristotle thought deliberation must be, but even or especially about values or ends. In other words, how can relativism be made an absolute? The second is whether it will foster in practice the sturdy individuals willing to defend what they say and able to say things worth defending. Alexander Hamilton, champion of the American common law of free speech, died, a few months after his argument in *Croswell,* in a duel.

CHAPTER 3

Religious Liberty and Common Law

Free-Exercise Exemptions and American Courts

Contrasting the dispositions associated in his day with the civil and the common law, Alexis de Tocqueville wrote in *Democracy in America* of lawyers in his native France and in the English-speaking world: "A French lawyer will deal with no matter, however trivial, without bringing in his own whole system of ideas, and he will carry the argument right back to the constituent principles of the laws in order to persuade the court to move the boundary of the contested inheritance back a couple of yards." In contrast, "The English or American lawyer denies his own reasoning powers in order to return to those of his fathers, maintaining his thought in a kind of servitude."[1]

Since Tocqueville's time, American lawyers, or at least their professors, have certainly learned how to be enamored of their "own whole system of ideas," but the rule of precedent has not been extinguished, nor has American legal discussion abandoned its focus on the particular case. In approaching the question of the relation of religious liberty to common law, then, to begin abstractly is already to risk distortion. Rather, to recapture an understanding of the common-law perspective that informed our original constitutionalism and that persists by force of form and process in our law today, it is better to begin not with first principles but with a particular case at law. Actually, I discuss two cases, separated in time by almost two centuries, but both involving a matter of some moment in the law of religious liberty: whether or when judges must grant an exemption from generally applicable law to those who claim that compliance with the law would interfere with their religious obligations—in other words, with their free exercise of religion. In the more recent case, the Supreme Court refused a claim based on sacramental use of a proscribed drug; in the older case, a common-law court excused a priest from testifying about matters learned in the confessional. After an analysis of the recent case, I turn to a discussion of the liberal theory of religious liberty on which it seems to be based, then to some general reflections on common law, before returning to the older case as an

46

illustration of a common-law approach. My aim here is not to design an alternative judicial doctrine of free exercise but to suggest that attention to the common-law perspective may serve at once the spirit of religious liberty and the spirit of American law.

Modern Judicial Doctrine: The Peyote Case and Its Context

The case of *Employment Division, Department of Human Resources of Oregon v. Smith* involved two drug rehabilitation counselors, Alfred Smith and Galen Black, who were dismissed from their jobs with a private organization "because they ingested peyote for sacramental purposes at a ceremony of the Native American Church, of which both are members."[2] Their applications for unemployment compensation were denied on the grounds that they had been discharged for work-related misconduct, but their appeal from the Employment Division to the Oregon courts was initially successful. The state supreme court determined that, under a line of federal precedent dating back to the 1963 Supreme Court case *Sherbert v. Verner,* benefits could not be denied to workers whose employment was terminated as a consequence of religiously motivated conduct.[3] On first hearing, however, the Supreme Court found in the case a potentially new circumstance. The religious conduct at issue in the earlier cases had been perfectly legal (the refusal to work on Saturday, for example, or the refusal to build weapons), even though it resulted in the loss of a job.[4] Here, in contrast, as the Employment Division stressed, the misconduct in question involved a violation of Oregon law. Finding it unclear from the record whether ingesting peyote was a crime in Oregon, the Court remanded the case.[5] On remand, the state supreme court held that under the Oregon criminal statutes, ingesting peyote is indeed against the law, but they then held that the use of peyote in religious ritual is protected by the Free Exercise Clause of the U.S. Constitution. The Supreme Court cannot gainsay a state's interpretation of its own statutes, but on the free-exercise question, it reversed: the counselors had no free-exercise right to exemption from generally applicable criminal law, the Court ruled; therefore, the Employment Division was not constitutionally barred from denying them benefits after their dismissal for misconduct.

Reaction to the Supreme Court's decision in *Smith* was sharp, and it came from many quarters, including a bill in Congress aimed at defeating its effect. That bill, titled, portentously, "The Religious Freedom Restoration Act," was eventually passed, but it was struck down by the Court, albeit on grounds of Section 5, not Section 1, of the Fourteenth Amendment.[6] In dissents from the bench in *Smith* and in Congress, what provoked the most controversy was the Court's apparent abandonment of the reigning standard in free-exercise adjudication: that state-imposed burdens on the free exercise of religion can survive only if the state can show a compelling interest in the regulation under dispute.[7] Justice Scalia, though admitting that this formula had often been alleged, denied that it had ever really been applied, at least to sustain a free-exercise claim. He explained the unemployment compensation cases under a particular rule: "where the State has in place a system of individual exemptions, it may not refuse to extend that system to cases of 'religious hardship' without compelling reason."[8] As for several other cases in which exemptions from general law had been granted to religious groups, Scalia insisted that in each instance the free-exercise claim had been asserted "in conjunction with other constitutional protections, such as freedom of speech and of the press [here he cited *Cantwell v. Connecticut* and *Murdock v. Pennsylvania*] or the rights of parents . . . to direct the education of their children [here, *Pierce v. Society of Sisters* and *Wisconsin v. Yoder*]."[9] The illegality of peyote use apparently destroyed the claim of "religious hardship" under the unemployment compensation rule, and since "the present case does not present . . . a hybrid situation, but a free exercise claim unconnected with any communicative activity or parental right," the Court found itself unbound by any adverse precedent. Thus, the issue was simply the constitutional claim to an exemption from a generally applicable criminal law on the basis of conflicting religious practice. Scalia's response was categorical: "Any society adopting such a system [that would exempt conflicting religious practices from general criminal law, absent a government showing of a compelling interest in the particular law] would be courting anarchy, but that danger increases in direct proportion to the society's diversity of religious beliefs, and its determination to coerce or suppress none of them." Exemptions must be sought in the legislature, not in court. And although he acknowledged the political difficulty this imposes on minority religions, he concluded, "that unavoidable consequence of democratic government must be preferred to a system in which each conscience is a law unto itself or in which judges weigh the social importance of all laws against the centrality of all religious beliefs."[10]

Students of American constitutional jurisprudence will recognize in that last remark, and perhaps in the whole case as described, an echo of the thought of Justice Felix Frankfurter. Scalia openly pays his debt by quoting Frankfurter in support of the basic principle announced in the case, "that an individual's religious beliefs [do not] excuse him from compliance with an otherwise valid law prohibiting conduct that the State is free to regulate."[11] But several things about the reference to Frankfurter merit pause, besides the fact that the quotation employed to vindicate "the record of more than a century of our free exercise jurisprudence" is taken from *Minersville School District v. Gobitis,* a case overturned three years after it was first announced.[12] First, as my summary of Justice Scalia's objections to the compelling-interest test suggests, and as his other opinions make plain, Scalia is an implacable foe of the various balancing tests deployed by the Court in a variety of constitutional settings; he prefers a jurisprudence that distills rules from a strict reading of past decisions to a jurisprudence of doctrinal formulas that structure the reasoning in judicial opinions more than they guide the results.[13] Frankfurter, by contrast, was one of the architects of judicial balancing, even if his literary sensibility and his deferential set of scales kept him from penning many of the modern multipronged judicially administered "tests." Second, Frankfurter's staunch opposition to exemptions was not limited to free-exercise adjudication but informed his reluctance in Establishment Clause cases to sanction legislative accommodations of religion. He dissented from the Court's opinion in the first modern establishment case, *Everson v. Board of Education,* and he joined the majority when they struck down a released-time program in the public schools and dissented when they upheld one. When he voted with the Court in upholding Sunday-closing laws, it was by a separate opinion of a hundred agonizing pages.[14]

Scalia not only welcomed legislated exemptions in his concluding remarks in *Smith* but also joined in opinions sustaining laws against establishment challenges or dissenting from judicial prohibition of practices on establishment grounds. Indeed, what makes the *Smith* opinion so striking is that it seems to mark one flank of an emerging jurisprudence of the Religion Clause as a whole, the other flank of which is an approach to establishment cases that is less insistent on strict separation of church and state and more respectful of governmental attempts to accommodate religion than the test devised in *Lemon v. Kurtzman* (1971), which requires that government action "(1) reflect a clearly secular purpose; (2) have a primary effect that neither advances nor inhibits religion; and (3) avoid excessive government entanglement with religion."[15] The Court's recent fragmentation in establishment cases has left the *Lemon* test in force, despite calls over the last decades from an apparent majority of the current justices for its abandonment. Nevertheless, the alternative has been articulated with some consistency since Chief Justice Warren Burger's 1983 majority opinion in *Marsh v. Chambers* (the legislative chaplain case): by Justice Kennedy's partial concurrence in *County of Allegheny v. ACLU* (1989), by Justice Scalia's dissent in *Lee v. Weisman* (1992), and, most recently, by Justice Thomas's concurrence in *Mitchell v. Helms* (2000).[16]

In *Allegheny,* the Court, through a mixture of opinions, condemned a Christmas crèche display in a county courthouse in Pittsburgh while allowing a Christmas tree and a menorah to stand together in front of the city-county building a block away. Justice Kennedy's opinion—joined by Chief Justice Rehnquist and Justices White and Scalia—would have permitted both displays. Finding no need to challenge the *Lemon* framework in the instant case, but expressing his doubt as to its value, Kennedy recommended instead an approach to establishment cases that would look benignly on government attempts to accommodate religion unless there was evidence of coercion, for instance, in compelling participation, conditioning benefits, delegating power, or proselytizing on behalf of a faith. Rejecting what he dubbed the majority's "jurisprudence of minutiae" and the "no endorsement" test proposed in several of Justice O'Connor's opinions, he explained: "The First Amendment is a rule, not a digest or compendium. A test for implementing the protections of the Establishment Clause that, if applied with consistency, would invalidate longstanding traditions cannot be a proper reading of the Clause."[17]

In the *Weisman* case, Kennedy found coercion at work in an invocation and benediction delivered as part of a public school graduation ceremony, parting company in this judgment of fact with those who had joined him in *Allegheny.* Besides disputing the fact of coercion here, Scalia's dissent—joined by Rehnquist, White, and the newcomer Thomas—stressed the "longstanding American tradition of nonsectarian prayer to God at public celebrations," traceable to the era of the Founding, which to his mind "displays with unmistakable clarity that the Establishment Clause does not forbid the government to accommodate it." Coercion by force of law would be proscribed in his reading of the Establishment Clause, as would government's endorsement of a single religious sect "in the sense of specifying details upon which men and women who believe in a benevolent, omnipotent Creator and Ruler of the world are known to differ (for example, the divinity of Christ)," but "characteristically American" public expressions of belief would stand untouched.[18] Indeed, as he remarked in dicta, whatever their value as prayer, such exercises directly serve the public purpose of fostering the cause of religious liberty: "maintaining respect for the religious observances of others is a fundamental civic virtue that government (including the public schools) can and should cultivate."[19]

Scalia's dissent in *Weisman* was as welcomed in the religious community as his *Smith* opinion was decried, although the combined effect of the two decisions by almost opposite majorities induced no little despair. Although the Court has lurched from side to side on these matters in recent years, it seems worthwhile to consider more fully the implications of the jurisprudence of the whole Religion Clause suggested by Scalia's several opinions and apparently supported by a consistent bloc of justices that occasionally grows to form a majority. To explain this approach solely in terms of an attitude of judicial restraint and of an aspiration for legal rules to replace judicial balancing is insufficient, if only because such an attitude and aspiration, however independent from certain "substantive" areas of law, cannot be presumed to stand apart from the inquiry into first principles that a consideration of religious matters necessarily entails. My approach is to examine the theory of the First Amendment with which Scalia's Religion Clause opinions seem most congruent, that of Professor Walter Berns.

Liberalism, the Constitution, and Religion

For over forty years now, Berns has written as a critic of the modern Supreme Court and a staunch defender of the liberal republicanism of the American Founders against all sorts of modern, or late modern, heresies. He interprets the Founding itself squarely in the light of the political theory of early liberalism; directly or indirectly, those who wrote the Constitution and the Bill of Rights went to school with Hobbes, Locke, Spinoza, Montesquieu, and the like. Nowhere does this reading of the Constitution have greater consequence than in the interpretation of the Religion Clause of the First Amendment, for, as Berns has written, "In the beginning of free and liberal government, no question was more important than the question of religion, and none played so prominent a role in the thought of the pertinent theorists—Hobbes, Locke, Spinoza, Bayle, and to a lesser but still significant extent, even Montesquieu."[20] According to Berns, the solution to the problem of religion defined by the early liberal philosophers was seized upon by the Founders, and their handiwork bears the unmistakable mark of its parentage. In his formulation, that solution was a compound one:

> Americans had, as Tocqueville observed, succeeded in combining the spirit of religion and the spirit of liberty, but they did so by subordinating the former to the latter. Not only were they wise to do so, he suggested, but the two could not be combined in any other fashion. Still, if

he was right, "the whole nation" held religion "to be indispensable to the maintenance of republican institutions," and it was his opinion that only so long as this combination was maintained would the crisis of liberalism be avoided.[21]

In Berns's America, it was understood that priestly authority would not compete with legal authority: as he put it with characteristic frankness, "Congress does not have to grant an exemption to someone who follows the command of God rather than the command of the law because the Congress established by the Constitution of the United States denies—to state the matter harshly, as the Supreme Court has forced us to do—*that God issues any such commands*."[22] Not Creation, Covenant, and Incarnation but the state of nature was for the Founders the beginning of political reflection and the common discourse of political debate, and the state of nature, for Berns, is a concept deeply at odds with Christian faith. At the same time, the Founders understood the political advantages of religion—or, rather, of religious differences—and "doubt[ed] that a civil society founded on the rights of man could sustain itself in the absence of the extraneous support provided by religious belief." No one was more expert at finding the perfect mix than George Washington: always cordial to or even solicitous of religious belief, never orthodox or even particularly Christian in reciting the names of God.[23]

For Berns, the two parts of the Religion Clause nicely reflect this compound attitude: the prohibition on establishment expresses the secular foundation, and the guarantee of free exercise allows the proliferation of religious sects. But Berns is roundly critical of modern cases in which the Supreme Court has sought to apply the two commands independently. Because the basis of the government is squarely secular, free-exercise exemptions from generally applicable law are entirely out of order, according to Berns, at least when granted judicially as a matter of right, as in *Wisconsin v. Yoder.* On the other side, since republican government depends on a moral people, and since religion, at least in a competitive setting, can help cultivate virtue, the establishment prohibition should not be read to thwart government encouragement of religion generally—more precisely, government encouragement of religion for secular ends[24]—but only preference for one sect over another. Starting, then, from the first principles of early modern liberalism, Berns sketches an approach to the Religion Clause similar to that which now beckons Justice Scalia and those who join him on the Court.

Berns's interpretation of the clauses has come under criticism, not from the strict separationists he had opposed from the start but from Professor—

now Judge—Michael McConnell, who had previously written in support of an accommodationist reading of the Establishment Clause and had participated in several religion cases before the Court in the early 1980s as an official in the Department of Justice.[25] Writing in the *Harvard Law Review* in 1990—and reiterating his argument in a lengthy critique of *Smith*—McConnell favors an interpretation of the Free Exercise Clause that permits or even requires courts to grant exemptions from generally applicable law to religious objectors, and he attempts to show that this was, or is at least consistent with, the original understanding of those who framed and ratified the First Amendment.[26] Interested in the political theory underlying the Religion Clause, accepting an interpretation of Locke not unlike Berns's, and acknowledging Locke's influence on Jefferson, McConnell's strategy is to limit the reach of Jefferson's influence on the American doctrine of religious liberty by carefully distinguishing Jefferson's notorious anticlericalism from Madison's "Memorial and Remonstrance" and the deeds it informed. Whereas Jefferson is intent to remove religious opinions to the private sphere, Madison premises his argument for disestablishment on the priority of man's "duty towards the Creator" and the recognition that a man enters civil society "with a saving of his allegiance to the Universal Sovereign."[27] This saving brings Madison's case for disestablishment into accord with the teaching of dissenting or evangelical sects, especially the Baptists, whose political support of the Virginia Bill was critical to its passage and whose electoral support of James Madison in his campaign for a seat in the first Congress under the Constitution was won by a promise to introduce in that body a bill of rights. In short, not liberalism alone but an alliance of liberal rationalism and dissenting Christianity made possible the First Amendment, at least to the extent that matters in Virginia were, if not typical, then paradigmatic.

Unlike the *Everson* Court and some of its defenders, however, McConnell does not leave the matter in Virginia.[28] Rather, he surveys the religion clauses in the constitutions of the original states and reads these in the light of each state's colonial arrangements regarding the relation of religion and government. Following the work of Thomas Curry,[29] he catalogues the variety of colonial schemes: the decentralized Congregational establishments of New England; the Anglican establishment under government control in Virginia and, later, throughout the South; the benign neglect of New York and New Jersey; and the various, mostly unstable, experiments providing havens for religious dissenters (Maryland, Rhode Island, Pennsylvania, Delaware, and Carolina). In these last, McConnell writes, "the free exercise of religion emerged as an articulated legal principle,"[30] though not in most cases without subsequent development, not to mention emulation on the part of other emergent states. Reviewing meticulously the fragmented record of the debate over the wording of the Religion Clause in the first Congress, taking into account the treatment of religion in the original Constitution of 1787 and the typical issues involving religious exemption in the states at the time (disputes over oaths, military service, assessments for the support of ministers, and the like), and asserting the Founders' widespread anticipation of judicial review, McConnell concludes that the original understanding of the First Amendment leaves room for judges to develop free-exercise exemptions from general laws in cases in which conscientious obedience to a "Universal Sovereign"—McConnell adopts Madison's term—conflicts with secular commands. Outside of an occasional footnote, McConnell does not comment in this article on contemporary free-exercise adjudication, but he does examine several state cases in the young Republic in which exemptions were at issue and concludes that, when faced with a free-exercise claim, the Court should ask, in the spirit of Madison's *The Federalist* Number 51, not "'Will this advance religion?,' but rather, 'Will this advance religious pluralism?'" He concludes, "The happy result of the Madisonian solution is to achieve *both* the unrestrained practice of religion in accordance with conscience (the desire of the religious 'sects') *and* the control of religious warfare and oppression (the goal of the Enlightenment)."[31]

McConnell's account of the origin of the Free Exercise Clause raises two challenges to Berns's reading of the American doctrine on religion and the state—the first, an implicit difference on the discernment of original intention, and the second, more directly, a matter of principle or prudence. First, McConnell's evidence of the mixed intentions at work in the framing of the First Amendment—not just the usual confusion of a mixed body, but a deep difference of first principles—calls into question any approach that would find a legally binding intention of the Framers exclusively in the thought of the admittedly secular liberal minds whose energy and insight brought the Constitution before the people. To be sure, Berns often writes as though the authority of the Founders derives as much from their wisdom as from their law, but to the extent that the doctrine of original intention to which he subscribes refers to the latter rather than the former, the understanding in the minds of the people who ratified the Constitution and its amendments is a constitutive part of the original intention; indeed, this was the view of the Founders themselves.[32] If evidence of compromise or merely practical understanding in such settings sometimes vitiates recourse to theoretical principle in constitutional interpretation, it also spares us from the tyranny of a Locke or a Hobbes. As Berns has explained as eloquently as anyone, the modern era of constitutional crisis results in part from the intellectual development of the train of thought that Hobbes and Locke helped initiate, whereas the people, whose opinions draw on resources perhaps less sharp but at least less brittle, often remain a reservoir of good sense and loyalty to the Constitution.[33]

The second challenge implicit in McConnell's attention to the religious roots of the First Amendment turns on what he called, in another context, "the special status of religion."[34] Berns had argued that, according to the Framers, liberal society is not founded on religious faith but is dependent on the persistence of some kind of religious practice to supply the moral character essential to republican government. The question is how that practice can be maintained in the face of the public denial of, or at least indifference to, its premise. Government accommodation of religion in a general and nondiscriminatory way, as Berns suggests ought to be allowed under a correct interpretation of the Establishment Clause, may do the trick in part. But if Madison and Jefferson are correct about the risk of discredit incurred by any religion that associates with the state, such accommodation alone may not be sufficient, especially if, when a genuine conflict appears between the law of the state and the law of God, the state proves unaccommodating by brusquely refusing to recognize any free-exercise claim against its own statutes. Tocqueville's admonition to democratic leaders that they should act as if they believe even when they doubt may ease the dilemma,[35] but there are matters at law when the difference cannot be suppressed, at least so long as justices feel obliged to render reasoned opinions, and these opinions receive the scrutiny of the pious.

In fact, though he is reluctant to admit it, this objection applies as well to McConnell's own remarks celebrating our current condition of religious pluralism. His "happy" solution of promoting pluralism is, as he recognizes, classic liberal fare, drawn not from Madison's "Memorial and Remonstrance" but from his asides in *Federalist* Numbers 10 and 51.[36] It supposes that widened pluralism is unobjectionable to all religions and an unmixed blessing to the state, neither of which is necessarily so. Madison himself, in *Federalist* Number 51, may draw a strict parallel between the multiplicity of interests and the multiplicity of sects, but the drift of the argument in *Federalist* Number 10 is to suggest that factions based on interest are preferable to those based on religious or political zeal, because they are more stable and more accommodating.[37] Moreover, while Madison advocates an extended sphere that would accept the diverse interests that arise spontaneously in society, he never recommends, as McConnell's solution seems to allow, that government actively promote social division, much less religious zealotry. As for the attractiveness of pluralism per se to churches, it is surely only a lesser evil to persecution rather than a positive good, at least to faiths that worship one God, a fact at which McConnell hints when he contrasts the imperative of pluralism to the prayer of ecumenism. Alternatively, if the American solution is found entirely congruent with the theology of certain Christian sects, for others, it is at most a moral necessity, so that the result is not perfectly unbiased among the creeds it mediates.[38] In short, McConnell's attempt to bridge, at the level of theory, the inevitable gap between religious and political authority does not escape Berns's dilemma: liberalism might tolerate religion, but it remains jealous of its supreme authority over social rules, and its jealousy shows believers the bounds of its benevolence.

Religion, Liberty, and Common Law

To deny that the gap between religious and political authority can be bridged in liberal theory is not, of course, to deny that adequate accommodation can from time to time be achieved in law.[39] To be fair to McConnell, it is probably this he has in mind.[40] His own examples of cases from the early Republic raising the question of free-exercise exemptions do not, however, establish his claim unproblematically, as he recognizes, since they are not entirely in his favor. To understand the leading case he cites, and even to understand the course of free-exercise adjudication today, requires appreciation of the importance of common law in the American judicial process. Since, as I argued at the outset, common law is best approached through attention to cases, let me turn to its consideration not by theoretical summary but by reviewing how features of common law figured in the matters I have already discussed.

First, Justice Scalia's attempt in the *Smith* case not to rely on a formula for balancing interests but to cull from the relevant precedents a rule for the case at hand—taking the force of precedent to lie in the holding in the circumstances of particular cases, rather than in dicta concerned with doctrinal formulas—pays homage to the classic process of reasoning at common law.[41] His actual treatment of precedents in *Smith* has been widely criticized. McConnell, for instance, argues that the attempt to distinguish apparent precedents by separating simple free-exercise claims from claims "made in conjunction with other constitutional protections" is unpersuasive, since almost any religiously based conduct (such as the Native American cere-mony at issue here) is expressive and thus could also raise a free-speech claim.[42] Still, from the point of view of common law, even if these criticisms are valid, the fault would lie rather in the execution of the task than in the aspiration for a legal rule to replace the previous balancing framework. As McConnell himself acknowledges, the "compelling interest test" in religious freedom cases had been honored more in the breach than in performance, since, with the exception of *Yoder* and the unemployment compensation cases, almost every government interest asserted was found adequate to override the religious claim.[43]

Second, a common-law element can be seen in the crucial importance attributable to the factual situation of the particular case at hand and to the Court's judgment of how to subsume the facts under an appropriate rule or precedent. In *Lee v. Weisman,* both Justices Kennedy and Scalia accepted the precedential authority of *Engel v. Vitale* on the one hand, which forbids teacher-led classroom prayer in public schools, and *Marsh v. Chambers* on the other, which allows invocations at legislative sessions; their opposite opinions turn on the judgment of whether graduation prayers resemble more the first or the second. The unavoidable exercise of judgment in subsuming particular cases under established rules is the peculiar and typically over-looked essence of the judicial task in a common-law or any other judicial system, and the ability to make sound judgments on this score is no small part of the virtue of a great judge. It was the boast of the common law that, by granting the force of law to precedent cases and thus requiring its judges to study not only established rules but also the factual settings in which they were declared, it effectively trained their faculty of judgment. One might add, in this context, that McConnell's most cogent criticism of *Smith* is that, in their eagerness to declare a general rule, the Court seized on a case whose legal facts did not demand constitutional decision: the Oregon Supreme Court had ruled both times that, as a matter of state law, the criminality of the action leading to an employee's dismissal for work-related misconduct is irrelevant to the consideration of whether unemployment benefits should be granted.[44]

A third way in which common law figured in the foregoing was the at-tention paid to the circumstances surrounding the establishment of the Con-stitution and the First Amendment as an aid to understanding their meaning. It was one of the maxims of common-law interpretation, recounted, for example, in Blackstone, that a statute was to be understood not only in reference to its plain words and its authors' intentions—though these were important—but also in light of the prior state of the law (since some statutes were understood to be declaratory of existing law rather than introductory of new law) and in light of the mischief the new act was intended to remedy.[45] Obviously, when the statute in question is not a legislative act but a constitutional provision, the common law will take account of the difference, but there is no reason to suppose that the courts' whole structure of reasoning will be altered, even if, as Chief Justice Marshall famously supposed, a constitution by its nature deserves a more liberal construction. In reference to the Religion Clause, these observations counsel attention to the law of the states, not just the vision of the Founding Federalists. Establishments of some sort or other continued to exist in a number of the states at the time, and debate in Congress makes it clear that the First Amendment was not intended to disturb these. Moreover, many state constitutions included free-exercise or liberty-of-conscience clauses of their own—sometimes, as in Massachusetts, alongside an established religion—and these provisions and the practices that developed under them might provide guidance to courts in search of the meaning of the Free Exercise Clause at the federal level.[46] The effort of the common-law mind always to understand change in the context of continuity reflects the customary status of the old common law in England. But even in America, where common law was often declared adopted by constitutional or statutory provision, the appeal to common law as ancient custom has not been absent. Indeed, the tendency to allow custom a certain authority in law is evident in the remark by Justice Kennedy quoted earlier (and seconded emphatically by Justice Scalia), which demands that any rule for applying the Establishment Clause not "invalidate longstanding traditions."

To attend to the common-law moment in exploring the law of free exercise is, in other words, to examine as a source of law the American experience of religious liberty, as it can be collected from constitutions and statutes, from customs and practices, from particular cases brought before the courts, and even from the laws and traditions of particular churches. Obviously, these various sources of law will not weigh equally in a court's determination of a particular dispute before it, but it is characteristic of common law to determine the applicability of rules in the context of the facts of the instant case, not to seek a single rule or theory to encompass all imaginable cases. It is, for example, not irrelevant to such a consideration that common law itself arose in a particular religious context. This may offer a clue not only about the meaning of religious liberty but also about civil liberty generally, for instance, that it cannot, John Stuart Mill to the contrary notwithstanding, be understood apart from the question of free will.[47] Nor is it irrelevant to such a consideration that American circumstances with regard to religion, at the time of the Founding and perhaps still today, are unique, and that those circumstances vary markedly from state to state.[48] To recommend a common-law perspective, then, is to suggest avenues of inquiry rather than to propose a ready theory. Yet it does suppose a certain openness to experience, both in its deference to the wisdom collected in tradition and in its willingness to entertain the possibility of a genuinely new and unanticipated case.

I can anticipate the following objection regarding the use of historical common law to help explain religious liberty, and it is an objection I can imagine Berns raising: Though certain elements of common-law thinking may have influenced the particular form in which Americans settled the religious question, surely the source of that solution is modern liberal political theory. The old common law, as it was understood in England at the time of the Founding and by members of the Founding generation in America in light of their study of English texts and experience with colonial forms, was anything but friendly to religious liberty on the American model. When Blackstone speaks of the religious liberty of the English, he refers to the liberty of the Church of England from the pope in Rome; according to Coke and his more immediate successors, as Blackstone notes with some embarrassment, heresy, blasphemy, and witchcraft remained crimes at common law.[49] What toleration there was in England in the eighteenth century was the result of an act of Parliament—the Toleration Act—and by American standards even before the Constitution, its reach was limited: Protestant dissenters in England could worship freely, but Catholic priests were banished from the realm (including Ireland, of course), officeholding was limited to members of the Church of England, and that church was (and still is today) supported by public funds and under parliamentary government. In any event, what religious liberty there was owed nothing to common law.

This is not an objection to be dismissed, nor one that can be easily answered, but neither can it be flatly admitted. In the first place, as McConnell is quick to point out, although the logic of Locke's plea for toleration works against establishment—if religion is a private matter, why does it merit public support?— his explicit program itself does not challenge an establishment of religion in England, only an establishment that would preclude dissent.[50] Besides, Lockean toleration was to be denied atheists and Catholics if the latter held to their allegiance to Rome.[51] These implications were lost neither on the Massachusetts preachers, who regularly invoked Locke's political authority while benefiting from their own establishment, nor on Blackstone, who explains the English establishment entirely on the grounds of the contribution it makes to civil society. To the extent, then, that our objection to English practice results from its persisting establishment, it applies to liberal theory as much as to common law—a point, of course, not overlooked by Berns, who would have us learn from liberal theorists to calm our horror of establishment.

This leads to a second observation in defense of common law. It is important to remember that the theological-political crisis of early modernity had two stages. The first, which the Reformation sought to answer, had its roots in the reach of the pope's authority. The second, which the Reformation fueled if not caused, was brought on by the wars of religion of the sixteenth and seventeenth centuries. The common law, of course, antedates both in its earliest sources, and though its classic formulation by Coke and others came between the crises, in another respect, it made its progress independent of religious developments—a fact brought home most strikingly by the continuity of process in the courts during the English civil war. Before and after the Reformation, the courts of common law sat alongside separate courts of ecclesiastical jurisdiction, which handled matters relating to marriage, wills, bankruptcy, and wards.[52] Although there was, of necessity, some borrowing back and forth, and in Coke's age quite a bit of dispute over respective jurisdictions, it is important to remember the limited reach assigned the king's common-law courts. Obviously, things would be different in the American setting, and different in each state, but the fact that traditional common-law courts had little cognizance of religious concerns might be seen to have planted a seed of religious liberty at the start.[53] This, at least, can be said: insofar as the American Founders—I speak now of those who made the states as well as those who made the federal government—drew their idea of judicial power from the common-law courts, they drew on a tradition of limited involvement of secular law in matters of religious concern.

Finally, the process of reasoning embedded in the common law—moving to general principles from particular cases, following precedent but holding to the maxim that precedents against reason are not good law—had within it the ability to assimilate particular insights of liberal theory without, at least initially, having to accept the whole. Eventually, this was perhaps its undoing—again, in Holmes and Cardozo, the mooring to preliberal thought was severed—but at the time of the Founding, American courts could accept the principle of religious freedom without being disabled by it in their business of determining the manifold cases that came before them. Let me illustrate by example what this might mean in a particular case.

Common Law and Constitution: A Privilege against Testimony by Priests

In the spring of 1813, a court in New York City was faced with the question of whether a Catholic priest can be forced to testify in a court of law concerning matters he learned in the confessional. The issue arose in the case of Mr. and Mrs. Daniel Philips, who were indicted for the misdemeanor of receiving stolen goods, which goods had been restored to their owner by a priest, the Reverend Anthony Kohlmann, rector of St. Peter's Church in New York. It was surmised that the priest had arranged the restitution in the course of hearing the confession of a parishioner, and so he was called to testify, first at the police station, then before the grand jury, then at the trial proper. Every time he was called, he refused to answer, despite the general duty of a witness in a legal proceeding to tell the whole truth. He explained that he knew nothing of the matter in his private capacity and that he was forbidden by his religious principles from violating the secrecy of the confessional: "it would be my duty to prefer instantaneous death or any temporal misfortune, rather than disclose the name of the penitent in question. For, were I to act otherwise, I should become a traitor to my church, to my sacred ministry and to my God. In fine, I should render myself guilty of eternal damnation."[54]

When Father Kohlmann first made his claim in court, it was argued by counsel for the defendants that the case "was novel and without precedent," and as a result, the proceedings were deferred. In the interval, the original district attorney became so convinced that the priest had a privilege of silence that he switched sides, arguing the matter for the defendants. It seems that his successor agreed to continue the prosecution only at the urging of the board of trustees of St. Peter's, who were apparently confident of victory and anxious to gain a precedent. The gamble paid off, at least in the case at hand. Resting on arguments at common law and on the Free Exercise Clause of the New York Constitution, the court found that the priest could not be compelled to testify about secrets he had learned while administering the sacrament of penance. For want of other testimony, the indictment was dismissed.

Although the New York court drew on both the common law and the New York Constitution in granting the privilege of silence to Father

Kohlmann, it devoted most of its argument to the case at common law.[55]
Looking back over English reports, the lawyers for the defendants could
discover only a couple precedents in which the testimony of priests had been
required in court, and they devoted much of their effort to impeaching their
validity. One case, it seems, had been decided in a minor court and was
reported only by an attorney in a subsequent case, where it was commented
on with disapproval by Lord Kenyon, a widely respected English judge. The
other case came from a court with authority, but in Ireland, and the court
determined—after a passionate argument from an Irish exile turned New
York attorney—that the Irish case ought to be disregarded, given the religious oppression under which that country then bent.[56] Having dismissed
the contrary precedents, the court decided that the privilege against testifying that was granted to an individual in his or her own case, to one spouse
in the case of the other, and to an attorney in the case of a client ought to be
extended to a priest in the case of a parishoner he had confessed, given the
infamy the priest would incur should he violate his vow of secrecy:

> It cannot, therefore, for a moment be believed, that the mild and just
> principles of the common Law would place the witness in such a dread-
> ful predicament; in such a horrible dilemma, between perjury and false
> swearing: If he tells the truth he violates his ecclesiastical oath—If he
> prevaricates he violates his judicial oath—Whether he lies, or whether
> he testifies the truth he is wicked, and it is impossible for him to act
> without acting against the laws of rectitude and the light of conscience.
> The only course is, for the court to declare that he shall not testify or act
> at all.[57]

Having settled the case at common law, the court nevertheless proceeded to
the constitutional question (*Ashwander*[58] parsimony is actually a more recent
development than is often recognized), a step it referred to as a move "to
more elevated ground; upon the ground of the constitution, of the social
compact, and of civil and religious liberty." It began thus: "Religion is an
affair between God and man, and not between man and man. The laws
which regulate it must emanate from the Supreme Being, not from human
institutions." This set the context of the court's quotation of Article 38 of
the New York Constitution then in force:

> And whereas we are required by the benevolent principles of rational
> liberty, not only to expel civil tyranny, but also to guard against that spir-

itual oppression and intolerance, wherewith the bigotry and ambition of weak and wicked princes have scourged mankind, This convention doth further in the name, and by the authority of the good people of this state, ordain, determine, and declare, that the free exercise and enjoyment of religious profession and worship, without discrimination or preference, shall hereafter be allowed within this state to all mankind. Provided, that the liberty of conscience, hereby granted, shall not be so construed as to excuse acts of licentiousness, or justify practices inconsistent with the peace or safety of this state.[59]

The court found the secrecy of penance worthy of its respect: "It is essential to the free exercise of religion, that its ordinances should be administered—that its ceremonies as well as its essentials should be protected." It dismissed the prosecutor's claim that the practice was "inconsistent with the peace or safety of the state" by insisting that the general rule be established on the basis of the practice's usual effects, not a speculative extreme case, and then by determining that, on the whole, confession does much more good than harm. To the objection that this established a discrimination or preference in favor of the Catholic faith, the court suggested that it would equally respect the sacraments of all faiths, but that different faiths had different sacraments.

A few points of contrast between the decision of the early-nineteenth-century New York court in *Philips* and the contemporary Supreme Court in *Smith* make up my conclusion. First, the earlier court saw the argument at common law and the argument in constitutional law as congruent. In fact, the reluctance to privilege constitutional argument in such a way as to elevate it apart from the law as a whole is typical of early constitutional jurisprudence, but this is often overlooked in analysis today. In the *Smith* case, by contrast, the issue was forced to the constitutional level, even though the widespread exception for ceremonial peyote use in other jurisdictions and in federal law, the administrative context of the case, and the Oregon Supreme Court rulings suggest avenues for decision short of invoking the U.S. Supreme Court's full constitutional power. This is hardly the place to embark on a discussion of the character of modern judicial review and its departure from earlier practice,[60] but the different results in the two cases suggest that liberty is not necessarily best assured by raising all disputes over rights to the modern constitutional plane.

Second, the court in New York did not hesitate to inquire into the canons of the church—or even into its reputation as law-abiding. In this way, its inquiry foreshadowed the free-exercise exemption from compulsory education laws granted several decades ago to the Amish in Wisconsin, although the customary, communitarian character of the Amish religion apparently precluded reference to formal church law.[61] In contrast, Justice Scalia decided in *Smith* that any sort of inquiry into the law, custom, or character of a religion was beyond judicial competence, and he cited in support of this position both the *Thomas* case involving unemployment benefits and various cases involving church property disputes. Although the issue raised in *Thomas*—whether an individual's religious claim can be asserted at law absent any showing of religious duty beyond personal testimony[62]—is a matter of genuine difficulty, it does not follow that all claims of superior religious duty are similarly difficult to judge. The property cases, in particular, while urging civil courts to defer to religious tribunals in cases of schism, necessarily involve the courts in examining religious canons, if only to determine where religious authority lies. Besides, the difficulty they are meant to avoid—civil interference in doctrinal disputes—is not present in a case like *Smith,* where the character of peyote worship in the Native American church is not at issue.[63]

Finally, it seems to me that in the older case, but not in the more recent one, the court found a way to both respect the claim of superior religious duty and awaken a sense that the justice of civil and political law depends on something more than the force of a sovereign. Again, this is hardly the place to develop an account, much less a critique, of the liberal theory of sovereignty or the theory of consent. But I suggest that an account of American constitutionalism that is dismissive of religious obligation that goes beyond civil statutes and constitutions cannot do justice to our common sense of all that is at stake when we invoke the name of law. If obedience to law is for some citizens always (and perhaps for all citizens sometimes) the result of a Hobbesian calculation of utility, short term or long, it defies experience to deny that for others it is a virtue or a duty whose roots lie in religious faith. Religious liberty, all would agree, is not secure if government claims divine sanction for all its demands. But neither is it imaginable in a setting where law itself is stripped of all affinity to a higher source than political power or unabashed popular will.

CHAPTER 4

Common Law and Constitutionalism in the Abortion Case

To the observer of public affairs and perhaps to any citizen of the Republic, the temptation to read in political terms the Supreme Court's June 1992 decision in *Planned Parenthood v. Casey* is almost overwhelming. There was the dramatic development of a split among the justices appointed by Presidents Reagan and Bush, signaled the previous week in the graduation prayer case; a centrist bloc emerged, highlighted by the unusual jointly signed opinion; and the result was ambiguous, expressly reaffirming *Roe v. Wade*[1] while upholding most of the provisions of the Pennsylvania statute. And all this occurred on the eve of the presidential nominating conventions in a volatile political year that eventually saw the White House pass from a pro-life to a pro-choice tenant. Together, these factors impede detached analysis of the case as a matter of constitutional law rather than constitutional politics. Indeed, the Joint Opinion seems at times to place itself on the latter footing, as in its opening sentence—"Liberty finds no refuge in a jurisprudence of doubt"— or in its discussion of the Court's legitimacy and the importance of the instant decision to the maintenance of the rule of law. Still, it would be a mistake to give the case only a political reading—as if the justices had found, or at least proposed, the much-sought-after but elusive great compromise on the abortion question. Precisely if the reflections on constitutionalism in the Joint Opinion are a clue to its authors' meaning, they urge us to pay attention not to the political debate about abortion but to the argument at law.

In the pages that follow, I attempt to do two things: to bring to bear on the interpretation of the decision the perspective offered by the common-law dimension of American constitutionalism, and to use *Casey* to illustrate something about the condition of our constitutionalism today. My thesis is that, whatever the personal views of the justices on abortion and related moral or "lifestyle" issues, the fracture on the present Court in the jurisprudence of the Due Process Clause results from a severing of two elements that were once united in the classic form of common-law adjudication: (1) the rule of precedent, or *stare decisis*, and (2) the customary or traditional character of common law. I do not mean to suggest that the abortion crisis itself is rooted in the severing of these two elements, nor that it would be solved by their repair, although it is no accident which legal element is allied with which moral position. I do think that an understanding of this fracture can impart a sense of the consequences of the abortion issue for our constitutionalism as a whole.

Planned Parenthood v. Casey: An Overview

The case of *Planned Parenthood of Southeastern Pennsylvania v. Casey* was decided June 29, 1992, by the sort of split decision that has become familiar to students of the modern Supreme Court. Originating in federal district court as a (barbarously called) "facial challenge" seeking declaratory judgment and injunctive relief, the case required the Court to review five provisions of the Pennsylvania Abortion Control Act of 1982, as amended in 1988 and 1989: an "informed consent" requirement that a physician provide certain information to women twenty-four hours in advance of an abortion; a requirement that minors seeking an abortion receive the "informed consent" (as previously described) of one parent or the approval of a judge; a command that married women certify that they have notified their husbands of their plans before obtaining an abortion, but excusing wives in a few situations; a series of reporting requirements placed on abortion clinics; and a definition of medical emergency under which the various consent and notification rules could be waived.[2] Four justices (Rehnquist, White, Scalia, and Thomas) signed two opinions (by the chief justice and Justice Scalia) that would have upheld all provisions of the law and overruled *Roe v. Wade*. The other five subscribed in whole or in part to an opinion jointly authored by Justices O'Connor, Kennedy, and Souter. The part of the opinion that explicitly reaffirmed *Roe*, upheld the medical emergency definition as interpreted by the lower court, and struck down the spousal notification requirement qualified for Opinion of the Court status; the remainder of the Joint Opinion—upholding the provisions regarding informed consent, qualified parental consent, and medical reporting[3]—did not, since Justice Blackmun refused to approve reporting, and both Justices Stevens and Blackmun would have struck the requirements for informed consent. In short, the Court unanimously upheld the challenged definition of medical emergency, upheld the reporting scheme by eight to one, and upheld the informed and parental consent requirements by seven to two, but by a vote of five to four it struck down required spousal notification, and it reaffirmed by the same vote what it called the "central holding" of *Roe v. Wade.*

Key to the Joint Opinion is the distinction between *Roe*'s "central holding" and its "specific rule,"[4] that is, the trimester scheme whereby abortion must remain virtually unregulated in the first trimester of pregnancy, can be regulated only in the interest of the mother's health in the second, and can be regulated in the third at discretion, even to the point of disallowance, since the fetus is presumed to be viable. Never mentioning the right of privacy, except in a single quotation from *Eisenstadt v. Baird,*[5] the central holding of *Roe* is now characterized as affirming "the woman's right to terminate her pregnancy before viability," a right discovered in the sphere of liberty guaranteed by the Due Process Clause of the Fourteenth Amendment. That protected liberty is described as having at its center matters "involving the most intimate and personal choices a person may make in a lifetime, choices central to personal dignity and autonomy. . . . At the heart of liberty is the right to define one's own concept of existence, of meaning, of the universe, and of the mystery of human life."[6] Although the characterization of due process liberty and the accompanying support for reaffirming *Roe*'s central holding earn the approval of Justices Blackmun and Stevens, the authors of the Joint Opinion are on their own when they actually specify *Roe*'s holding in such a way as to allow them to discard the trimester scheme as inadequate. Finding that scheme to fail because it refuses to allow any state regulation before fetal viability in the interest of the potential life, the Joint Opinion develops an "undue burden" test, according to which abortions cannot be denied women before fetal viability (now acknowledged, thanks to medical advances, to come somewhat before the third trimester). State regulations in the interests of maternal health or potential life will now pass constitutional muster if they do not impose a substantial obstacle to, or an undue burden on, a woman's exercise of her right to abort. As noted by the partial dissenters on both sides, this new standard is apparently a balancing test that discards the language of "fundamental" rights, "strict scrutiny," and "compelling interests." "Abortion is a unique act," the joint authors write early in the opinion, and thus they apparently conclude that abortion regulation can be subjected to a unique constitutional test.[7]

The mixed verdict of the justices on the various provisions of the Pennsylvania statute accords with the different forms of due process analysis employed: Justices Blackmun and Stevens would adhere to "strict scrutiny" of regulations interfering with a "fundamental" abortion right; Chief Justice

Rehnquist and Justices White, Scalia, and Thomas would treat the right to terminate a pregnancy as a nonfundamental liberty interest and thus ask only that regulations be "rationally related" to a legitimate state aim; and Justices O'Connor, Kennedy, and Souter would apparently find the abortion right an ultimate liberty of women before fetal viability but would allow regulations that create no "undue burden" on the exercise of the right. It seems clear that the authors of the Joint Opinion mean by their test to give recognition to both sides in the abortion debate: to those who insist on a woman's right to choose and to those who "deem [abortion] nothing short of an act of violence against innocent human life."[8] The pro-choicers get their right to abort, and the pro-lifers get their right to try to persuade women against its exercise; the former are denied constitutional protection for abortion on demand, and the latter are forbidden to use the state's coercive power to protect the fetus. Though not expressed as such, this line between regulations that aim to persuade and regulations that effectively coerce corresponds to the distinction between the provisions of the law that were upheld and the rejected spousal notification provision—at least as the likely effect of the latter is described in three full pages repeating expert testimony and summarizing published studies on battered women. Needless to add, such a reading is consistent with the Joint Opinion's firm announcement that a law that would deny an abortion to any woman carrying a fetus not yet viable outside the womb has no chance of being allowed.

The Common Law, Take One: Precedent

How does an appreciation of the common-law elements of American constitutionalism contribute to an analysis of *Planned Parenthood v. Casey* in particular and of the constitutional law of the due process privacy or liberty right in general? In this section and the following one, I suggest two ways: by illuminating the meaning of precedent, and by clarifying the legal status of custom and tradition. Behind each discussion is the complex tale of the transformed meaning of common law, and I should clarify at the outset that I do not think the question of the place of common law in American constitutionalism has been adequately or decisively settled, even by such authorities as Cardozo and Holmes. Rather, this question remains an open one, both for scholars and for judges. The following remarks are meant to be one part of an attempt to address it.

Precedent emerges in the Joint Opinion in *Casey* not just in the usual way, providing authority for legal rules or principles employed in the reasoning, but as an independent ground for the decision: "While we [here, a full majority of the Court] appreciate the weight of the arguments made on behalf of the State in the case before us, arguments which in their ultimate formulation conclude that *Roe* should be overruled, the reservations any of us may have in reaffirming the central holding of *Roe* are outweighed by the explication of individual liberty we have given *combined with the force of stare decisis*."[9] The Court's discussion of *stare decisis,* the common-law rule that precedents ought to be followed, is neatly divided into three parts: the first announcing, on the authority of precedents, four exceptions to the rule of *stare decisis* and then examining whether the present case conforms to any such exception; the second contrasting the legal authority of *Roe* in the *Casey* Court to the discredited authority of *Lochner v. New York* (1905) in 1937 and to the likewise discredited authority of *Plessy v. Ferguson* (1896) in the Court weighing *Brown v. Board of Education* (1954); and the third meditating on the Court's legitimacy when overruling a precedent it had itself established.

Each of the four exceptions that the Joint Opinion considers proves inadequate, in its view, to justify overruling *Roe*. First, *Roe* as a whole has not proved unworkable. Second, there is no absence of a class of people "who have relied reasonably on the rule's continued application." Although, as the opinion acknowledges, this argument against overruling a precedent classically applies in a commercial context when property has been risked on the assumption that the precedent is good law, the Court treats as the relevant class not the providers of abortion services but all women, indeed all people, in a position to find abortion convenient or necessary: "for two decades of economic and social developments, people have organized intimate relationships and made choices that define their views of themselves and their places in society, in reliance on the availability of abortion in the event that contraception should fail. The ability of women to participate equally in the economic and social life of the Nation has been facilitated by their ability to control their reproductive lives."[10] Third, "no evolution of legal principle has left *Roe*'s doctrinal footings weaker than they were in 1973." In fact, the opinion suggests, *Roe* has been woven deep into the fabric of the law in two related lines of precedent, one concerning "the liberty relating to intimate relationships, the family, and decisions about whether or not to beget or bear a child," and the other concerning "personal autonomy and bodily integrity" in relation to state power over medical treatment. Even treated *sui generis,* as involving the unique abortion right, *Roe* has been consistently, if not always explicitly, reaffirmed. Fourth, the factual assumptions on which *Roe* was based have not been significantly altered: abortions are a little safer than in 1973, and fetal viability comes a little earlier, but neither change has been significant enough to disturb *Roe*'s assumptions of a limited state interest in the medical regulation of abortion and of noncompelling state interest in fetal life before viability.

In turning from legal rules that specify exceptions in the rule of *stare decisis* to considerations of constitutional history and present legitimacy, the Joint Opinion moves, quite consciously, I think, from a strictly legal to a more political plane. The Court, it is argued, could safely overrule *Plessy* in *Brown* and *Lochner* in *West Coast Hotel Co. v. Parrish* because the "fundamentally false factual assumptions" underlying the earlier precedent in each case had come to be recognized as such by society at large; in relation to *Brown* and *Plessy,* "Society's understanding of the facts upon which a constitutional ruling was sought in 1954 was thus fundamentally different from the basis claimed for the decision in 1896."[11] Chief Justice Rehnquist, in his dissent to this portion of the Joint Opinion, notes that the falseness of the facts presumed in the earlier cases had been recognized by dissenters at the time the cases were decided. But true as this is, it does not undermine the argument the Court is making, since the point is not that the facts themselves must necessarily change but that, over the course of a generation or two, the basic opinions of society on such fundamental matters as the nature of the economy and the equality of the races had altered or, as political scientists might say, had realigned. In relation to abortion rights, the opinion observes, no decisive shift in the social mind has been registered—despite the presumably unanticipated fact of more than a million abortions each year in the United States since *Roe*.[12] Abortion was controversial in 1973, and it remained so in 1992. Although this in itself gives the justices no further reason to reaffirm their holding, it apparently supplies to their mind no reason to abandon it.

The political reason not to abandon *Roe* comes to light in the Joint Opinion's consideration of what it calls the Court's legitimacy. Without citing Alexander Bickel's early classic,[13] the authors of the opinion seem to accept his argument that the Court's legitimacy depends on its adherence to principle and its ability over the long run to persuade the people to follow its lead on matters of principle. Justice Scalia, in his dissent, correctly notes that this understanding of the judicial program betrays an ambition to set the direction of social change, but his arguments do not sway the Court majority here, who are confident of the long-range prospects for the sort of personal liberty they would foster. The color of that ambition appears most clearly in the following passage from the Joint Opinion:

> Where, in the performance of its judicial duties, the Court decides a case in such a way as to resolve the sort of intensely divisive controversy reflected in *Roe* and those rare comparable cases, its decision has a dimension that the resolution of the normal case does not carry. It is the dimension present whenever the Court's interpretation of the Constitution calls the contending sides of a national controversy to end their national division by accepting a common mandate rooted in the Constitution.[14]

To say of this passage—which asserts the need not to "surrender to political pressure, and [make] an unjustified repudiation of the principle on which the Court staked its authority in the first instance"—that it voices "a truly novel principle"[15] is not entirely accurate. To the joint authors, *Casey* stands to *Roe* not as *Brown* stands to *Plessy* but as *Cooper v. Aaron,* the Little Rock desegregation case, stands to *Brown.* Compare these passages:

> *Cooper:* [*Marbury v. Madison*] declared the basic principle that the federal judiciary is supreme in the exposition of the law of the Constitution, and that principle has ever since been respected by this Court and the Country as a permanent and indispensable feature of our constitutional system. It follows that the interpretation of the Fourteenth Amendment enunciated by this Court in the *Brown* case is the supreme law of the land, and Article VI of the Constitution makes it binding on the States "any Thing in the Constitution or Laws of any State to the Contrary notwithstanding."

> *Casey:* [Americans'] belief in themselves as . . . a people [who aspire to live according to the rule of law] is not readily separable from their understanding of the Court invested with the authority to decide their constitutional cases and speak before all others for their constitutional ideals. If the Court's legitimacy should be undermined, then, so would the country be in its very ability to see itself through its constitutional ideals.[16]

Making allowance for differences of tone and context, the message is identical. Though the Joint Opinion in *Casey* is silent on *Cooper,* it openly suggests the analogy: the "call . . . to end [a] national division" is something "the Court is not asked to do . . . very often, having thus addressed the Nation only twice in our lifetime, in the decisions of *Brown* and *Roe*."[17] The Court's reference on the next page to its implicit "promise of constancy" to the constituency that "approves or implements a constitutional decision where it is unpopular," and especially to "those who themselves disapprove of the decision's results when viewed outside of constitutional terms, but who nevertheless struggle to accept it, because they respect the rule of law," parallels what the *Cooper* Court must have thought (but in a less politicized era dared not say) in regard, respectively, to the civil rights movement and to southern whites who did not join the campaign of "massive resistance." That the *Cooper* order was issued in a rare joint opinion—signed, however, by all nine justices—makes the analogy complete.

The treatment of precedent in the *Casey* Joint Opinion is criticized by the dissenters as incoherent, in that it argues that *Roe* must be retained, not overturned, and then proceeds to retain only *Roe*'s "central holding" and to discard the trimester framework that governed most of the subsequent abortion cases brought to the Court. In the process, say the dissenters, the Joint Opinion explicitly overturns parts of the Court's rulings in intervening cases such as *Akron v. Akron Center for Reproductive Health* and *Thornburgh v. American College of Obstetricians and Gynecologists*.[18] Actually, several of the particular legal exceptions that militate against overturning *Roe* as a whole cut the other way when only the trimester rule is at issue, according to the Joint Opinion: that framework is precisely the part of *Roe* that has proved "unworkable" or that has been extenuated by new facts. Moreover, if in abandoning the trimester rule the Joint Opinion seems to retreat from the holding in *Roe* and its "progeny" by allowing more scope to state regulation in the interest of protecting potential life, its reformulation of the right at issue in *Roe* arguably advances its central holding. Gone is not only the term "right of privacy" in favor of direct reference to due process "liberty" but also any vestige of medical paternalism: *Roe* had spoken of "the woman's decision whether or not to terminate her pregnancy," but in its summary the Court wrote, "the abortion decision and its effectuation must be left to the medical judgment of the pregnant woman's attending physician."[19] Indeed, nowhere is the distance from *Roe* to *Casey* more striking than in those passages in the latter that clearly echo contemporary feminist legal and historical theory: the much-quoted mention of the sacrifice and suffering of pregnancy, the discussion (quoted earlier) of reliance on abortion rights in the modern regime of sexual equality, and the ample reference to research on battered women in disposing of spousal notification.

By formulating the right of personal decision as broadly as they do, the authors of the Joint Opinion in *Casey* intend to do to *Roe* what the Court in *Roe* did to *Griswold v. Connecticut:* to carry its logic a step further by refor-mulating the theory that underlies its rule. Though the practical short-run meaning of *Casey* is to allow expansion of abortion regulation, its long-run purpose seems to be to better ground the abortion right and to formulate principles to advance other rights of sexual autonomy. In entering the flux of precedent that unfolds according to the progress of the social mind—in their own metaphor, by affirming the "covenant running from the first gen-eration of Americans to us and then to future generations . . . a coherent suc-cession"[20]—and then attempting to guide such progress by theoretical innovation, the authors of the Joint Opinion exhibit the familiar pattern of common-law craftsmanship modeled by Holmes and Cardozo, here applied in a constitutional setting. That theirs is not the only meaning inspired by common law will become clear as we turn to consider tradition and custom.

The Common Law, Take Two: Tradition

The legal force of precedent distinguishes what is still dubbed a common-law legal system from a civil-law system built on adherence to a code. In another sense, however, it is odd to use the term *common law* to describe the approach taken by the authors of the Joint Opinion, for in their sole employment of the term, in the context of rejecting the provision for spousal notification, the justices note the demise in recent years of the traditional attitude of common law toward the family, whereby the legal identity of a wife was subsumed for most purposes into that of her husband.[21] Although the authors of the Joint Opinion note that "these views, of course, are no longer consistent with our understanding of the family, the individual, or the Constitution," they do not stop to consider how that understanding changed—whether by judicial innovation or through constitutional amend-ment (i.e., the Nineteenth) and legislative changes in the marital regime—nor do they mention the role played by lingering notions of coverture in establishing the zone of marital privacy from which the right they assert in *Casey* descends. Indeed, it is striking that the Joint Opinion makes no other mention of common law except to dismiss it, since the opinion of the Court in *Roe* made much of the purported "lenity of the common law" toward abortion,[22] and since the Court in *Casey* was briefed on historical research since *Roe* that calls this conclusion into doubt.[23]

Common law in the sense of the previous paragraph refers to the ancient customary law of England and America. Its place in the story of the modern right to privacy is twofold—as the point of departure for evolving notions among the advocates of a progressive Constitution, and as a point of reference for those who see the Constitution's meaning as, absent amendment, essentially fixed. The use of common law by the latter has most prominently appeared in the case of *Bowers v. Hardwick,* where the Court made reference to the criminal status of sodomy at common law in its finding that the Due Process Clause of the Fourteenth Amendment could not have been intended to forbid modern statutory prohibitions of the same.[24] The common law in this context carries authority not in itself but as a key to discern the meaning of the Constitution. In a rule of interpretation typical of the classical common law, it is presumed that a constitutional provision that at the time of its adoption apparently left undisturbed an existing common-law or statutory regime cannot later be invoked to destroy it. Justice Blackmun's quotation from Holmes in his *Bowers* dissent—"it is revolting to have no better reason for a rule of law than that so it was laid down in the time of Henry IV"—underscores the competition this rule offers to the progressive transformation in law that his own opinion in *Roe* exemplifies and that the Joint Opinion in *Casey* seeks to steer and propel.[25] While Blackmun would have struck down the Georgia sodomy statute as violating "the fundamental interest all individuals have in controlling the nature of their intimate associations with others," a right he finds implicit in the line of privacy cases since *Griswold,* Justice White's majority opinion in *Bowers* treats the various precedents as establishing a series of rights—for example, to rear one's child, to marry, and to procreate. Though roundly criticized, White's opinion exhibits the typical preference of traditional common law for enumeration rather than theoretical synthesis, a preference evident, of course, in the Constitution itself (e.g., Article I, section 8) and the Bill of Rights.[26]

The approach to substantive due process claims proferred by White in *Bowers* was refined by Justice Scalia's plurality opinion in *Michael H. v. Gerald D.* In that case, a man who had apparently fathered a child during an adulterous liaison with a married woman sued to overturn the statutory presumption in California law that the woman's husband was the child's father, a presumption open to rebuttal only at the motion of the husband or wife. Noting that "the presumption of legitimacy [of a child born within a marriage] was a fundamental principle of the common law," and citing Cardozo's adage that due process liberty includes only those rights "so rooted in the traditions and conscience of our people as to be ranked fundamental,"

Justice Scalia dismissed the due process claim and allowed the California presumption, now statutory, to stand undisturbed.[27] In referring to "tradition"—including, of course, the common law, but also statutes widely adopted and consistently in force, as well as practices whose legality has gone unchallenged—Scalia makes it clear that he means to take traditions or customs one by one, not subsumed in an abstract theoretical concept; he refers in a footnote "to the most specific level at which a relevant tradition protecting, or denying protection to, the asserted right can be identified."[28] Again, the preference here expressed for specificity in the enumeration of rights and the distrust of abstract formulation call to mind the classical attitude of the judge at common law. In *Casey,* then, Scalia and the dissenters should have no objection in principle to treating the abortion right as *sui generis.* But their favored mode of analysis would indicate that *Roe v. Wade* was decided incorrectly: statutory tradition since the mid-nineteenth century and the common law even before then, carefully read, indicate that a right at least to nontherapeutic abortion is not so anchored in our traditions as to deserve due process protection against most legislative claims.

It is ironic, perhaps, that the development of an approach to due process litigation that stresses the importance of specific traditions in contrast to abstract conceptualization should be recent, but it is apparent that it arose in reaction to the progressivist judicial craftsmanship that reaches its apogee in the abortion cases. Indeed, as Scalia's quotation of Cardozo in *Michael H.* indicates, and as his willingness in *Casey* to treat the liberty interest in abortion under "rational relation" analysis makes plain, the critical break with tradition—perhaps, we can say, with common law—is of more recent vintage than, say, the "constitutional revolution" of 1937. Instructive here is the quotation in the early pages of the *Casey* Joint Opinion from Justice Harlan's dissent in *Poe v. Ullman,* a case involving a challenge, dismissed by the plurality as nonjusticiable, to the same Connecticut anticontraceptive law overturned four years later in *Griswold.* The principal extract is worth quoting in full:

> Due Process has not been reduced to any formula; its content cannot be determined by reference to any code. The best that can be said is that through the course of this Court's decisions it has represented the balance which our Nation, built upon postulates of respect for the liberty of the individual, has struck between that liberty and the demands of organized society. If the supplying of content to this Constitutional concept has of necessity been a rational process, it certainly has not been

one where judges have felt free to roam where unguided speculation might take them. The balance of which I speak is the balance struck by this country, having regard to what history teaches are the traditions from which it developed as well as the traditions from which it broke. That tradition is a living thing. A decision of this Court which radically departs from it could not long survive, while a decision which builds on what has survived is likely to be sound. No formula could serve as a substitute, in this area, for judgment and restraint.[29]

Except perhaps for the mention of "rational process" (if that term is taken to refer to theoretical synthesizing rather than to the reason of the common-law judge that assembles and assimilates, rejecting only what utterly contradicts) and the certainty expressed on the eve of the activist decade that "unguided speculation" has never trumped attention to tradition (a certainty perhaps naive even when voiced, and almost surely obtuse or disingenuous when repeated today), there is nothing in the approach to judging here described that Scalia and those who join him would not acknowledge. Everything turns, it seems, on what is meant by reason, on what can be counted a tradition, and on whether a living tradition grows like a single human being, to a natural fulfillment that reason can discern, or like an ecological population, to an equilibrium impossible to foresee.

The foregoing analysis of the *Casey* decision and its relation on the one hand to *Roe* and on the other to *Bowers* and *Michael H.* leads to the conclusion that the fracture evident in contemporary due process adjudication can be traced to the severing of two moments or principles of common-law judging: the development of law from precedent to precedent in the name of reason, on the one hand, and the anchoring of law in custom and tradition freely attested and consented to, on the other. To determine where that fissure first occurred is beyond the scope of this chapter, but it is worth listing several possibilities: after *Roe,* when what had been a medical decision effectively became a consumer right; between *Eisenstadt v. Baird* and *Roe,* when the Court moved from permitting contraceptives to permitting abortion; between *Griswold* and *Eisenstadt,* when what had been introduced as a right to use contraceptives strictly in terms of a right to privacy in the traditional sanctity of the marriage bed was extended to a right to distribute contraceptives to the unmarried in a public setting; or even with *Griswold* itself, where the right to procreate and raise a family was transformed into a right to "contracept." Although the theory of personal autonomy can account for every step, its logic is not so inexorable as to force anyone who admits parents' due process liberty to govern the religious and cultural education of their children—at issue in *Meyer* and *Pierce* in the 1920s[30]—to accept a constitutional right to abortion on demand.

Nor should a choice between these two moments at common law be made too hastily by observing their apparent implications for the *Casey* decision alone. On the one hand, abortion advocates should recall that, as late as *Roe,* reference to a specific common-law tradition on the matter of abortion was taken as evidence of a traditional liberty to abort before "quickening." Although subsequent research has shown that such liberty as there was hardly deserves the status of a moral right, it seems that some liberty did in fact exist, whether because, in an era of limited medical knowledge, the difficulty of discerning early pregnancy and of distinguishing induced abortion from natural miscarriage made it impossible to meet common-law standards of proof, or because common law was reluctant to step fully into areas once belonging to ecclesiastical jurisdiction. Abortion opponents, on the other hand, before dismissing all attempts to adjust ancient traditions to modern discoveries, might consider not only the limited protection under traditional common law for fetal life but also the argument that the nineteenth-century antiabortion statutes sought not to overturn the common law but to bring its general protection of human life up-to-date with advances in medical science, in particular with the discarding of the ancient theory of quickening and the discovery of the processes of conception and fetal growth.[31] In any event, it seems to me imperative that the meaning of common law be considered if the fracture in our constitutional law and in our polity brought on by abortion is to stand any chance of being healed. I confess that I find the Joint Opinion in *Casey* no more a compromise than was *Roe,* which was not lacking in moderate sentiments, nor do I think *Casey* more likely to solve the abortion dispute than *Cooper v. Aaron* settled the segregation controversy or *Dred Scott v. Sandford* resolved the clash over slavery. Besides, the current neglect of common law seems to be part and parcel of our nagging postmodern predicament: we distrust any sort of authority, we reject on principle that anything can be truly common, and we obstinately refuse to look for present wisdom in our past.

CHAPTER 5

The Common Law of the Family and the Constitutional Law of the Self

For all the concern now expressed by both political parties about the family in America, it must be admitted at the outset that the Constitution of the United States makes no mention of the family or its relations by name. There is in the Preamble the promise that the blessings of liberty will be secured for posterity, so the Framers cannot be accused of entirely forgetting family matters, but to find any more of an allusion to familial things, one has to strain. The minimum age requirements for holding office might be cited as evidence of the Framers' recognition that maturity is attained, not immediate. The president must be a "natural born" citizen, suggesting that, at least at the top, parentage matters. The Bill of Rights twice makes reference to "houses," which one might suppose are family homes, though the text of the Third and Fourth Amendments includes only "the Owner," "the people," and "persons." Indeed, the closest the Constitution comes to mentioning the family is to deny its relevance to the matter in question: "no Attainder of Treason shall work Corruption of the Blood" (Article III, section 3). And I suppose the prohibition, on both the federal government and the states, against granting titles of nobility restricts a form of recognition that was, in the mother country and her kindred in Europe, regularly bestowed on a couple and usually inherited by their brood.

All this is obvious and would go without saying, were it not for the fact that so much has been found in the Constitution that was not obviously—or was obviously not—written there that it behooves us to pay some attention to the Constitution's silences, however enigmatic they might be. This is especially so for those who look for the Constitution's "original understanding" and then confine themselves to the Constitution's text and contemporary commentaries on it. But even those who concentrate on the text alone must heed its legal context if the language is to be understood. The absence of explicit protection for the family in the Constitution has occasioned a deep bias against the family in modern constitutional law, where the Due Process and Equal

78

Protection Clauses have been expansively interpreted so as to undermine the family's legal status. In this chapter, I suggest that the modern bias results from a misunderstanding of what constitutional law was supposed to entail, caused in part by the eclipse of common law or by its redefinition. I begin with a few remarks on the Constitution and common law, then turn to the common law of the family and its development in the nineteenth century, before considering the constitutional developments of our own time.

The Constitution and the Common Law

Today, as at the time of the Founding, we describe the Constitution as fundamental law, but what we mean by "fundamental" has changed. Supposing that law is the decree of the sovereign power, or a social rule made according to a rule of recognition, or public policy written and formalized, we think of the Constitution as fundamental because it establishes the rules by which laws are made, as well as rules that limit lawmaking. At the time of the Founding, by contrast, common or unwritten law was the basis of the law in all the colonies, with legislation understood as its supplement or its corrective. Legal cases were decided in accordance with precedents as well as statutes, and statutes were interpreted in the light of common law, which they might be understood to declare, to modify, or to reinforce. As the nascent states began writing constitutions upon Congress's call, once independence was imminent, they fashioned instruments of government, partly ratifying and partly modifying existing arrangements, with declarations of rights securing customary privileges against infringement by these same governments. These constitutions were so far from radically remaking social order that, one by one, the states chose to adopt the common law, to the extent that it was not inconsistent with their constitutions and statutes, rejecting proposals for new-modeled comprehensive legal codes. Despite the use of state-of-nature language to justify political revolution, the colonists did not think that their properties or their families—indeed, even their states— would be dissolved by independence. Political discontinuity overlay a basic continuity of legal order, though the latter was sometimes amended—for instance, in the matter of entail and primogeniture—to take account of the choice of a republican rather than a monarchical political form.

The federal Constitution of 1787 was in one sense an even less fundamental document than the state constitutions that preceded it. Besides being largely limited to matters of governmental structure, the government it established was limited in its objects to certain enumerated concerns, mostly involving defense, commerce, and the ability to provide for itself. To be sure, in another sense it was innovative: unlike the Articles of Confederation it replaced, the Constitution did not just ratify existing arrangements but designed wholly new political institutions, and the very idea of a completely formed government at the federal level was novel. If, as Alexander Hamilton argued in *The Federalist Papers,* the "radical vice" of the Articles was "the principle of LEGISLATION for STATES or GOVERNMENTS, in their CORPORATE or COLLECTIVE CAPACITIES," the radical innovation of the Constitution was its establishment of an unmediated relation between the federal government and the individuals it would govern.[1] The creation of a federal judiciary was naturally one essential part of this new relation, for it involved the federal government in the disposition of individuals' property and in the protection of their liberties and lives. Though it seems to have been taken for granted that that judiciary would proceed for the most part by familiar common-law forms, whether an independent body of federal common law existed was a hotly contended issue. It was eventually determined that there was no federal common law of crimes but that there was a general commercial law, even in the absence of congressional regulation. Landed property and domestic relations were governed, of course, by the common and statute law of the states.

The American state constitutions and in particular the federal Constitution, then, not only established limited government but were themselves limited as forms of law. Federal law is supreme over state law, constitutions are supreme over statutes, and statutes are supreme over common law, but these hierarchies are not simple or absolute. Federal laws are supreme only if pursuant to the Constitution, and traditional common-law privileges and immunities are often embodied in constitutional bills of rights. More generally, although the federal Constitution might be said to have been formed largely on liberal republican principles—limited, as it was, to providing security for peace, prosperity, and individual rights—and although the state constitutions became increasingly democratic in the early republican period, the persistent force of common law allowed for the continuation of traditional practices, not only in society but also in the law itself. To a mind that demands uniformity, a change of principles in one sphere of life demands a change in all, but to a mind that accepts differentiation among life's spheres, the logic works the other way. Just as the kingdom of God might as readily be held to forbid as to demand monarchical politics, so republican or democratic politics need not entail the demise of the traditional family. That the democratic mind tends to uniformity is undeniable, but the common law itself tended to reinforce differentiation. Besides, in promising every man his day in court and involving that most democratic of institutions, the jury, in the most serious legal business, common law was not without a claim to democratic respect.

The Common Law of the Family

For the sake of convenience, the state of the common law of the family at the time of the Founding is probably best established with reference to the *Commentaries on the Laws of England* of Sir William Blackstone, who covers what he calls "private oeconomical relations" in four chapters toward the end of his first volume on the rights of persons.[2] The basic elements of his account are these: Marriage is a civil contract in which the common law closely tracks ecclesiastical law (that it is a contract between one man and one woman is implicit in the chapter title, "Of Husband and Wife"). There are limits concerning who is eligible to consent to marriage, and divorce *a vinculo matrimonii,* that is, a divorce that dissolves the marriage, is allowed only if eligibility was not genuine. Otherwise, marriage is for life, although divorce *a mensa et thoro,* or divorce by separation of bed and board, is permitted. A recent statute (Lord Hardwicke's Marriage Act of 1753) had greatly formalized the requirements for a valid marriage in England, mandating that it be performed in a church after the couple had obtained a license or had published banns,[3] but this act had no authority in America, where "common-law" or informal marriage by open consent of the parties was generally valid and dissolvable only on the terms just mentioned.

The central doctrine of the common law on married life was coverture, described by Blackstone as follows: "By marriage, the husband and wife are one person in law: that is, the very being or legal existence of the woman is suspended during the marriage, or at least is incorporated and consolidated into that of the husband: under whose wing, protection, and *cover,* she performs every thing."[4] Though the wife retained title to the property she brought to the marriage, its management and use were at her husband's discretion unless there was a prenuptial agreement to the contrary, and she was generally disabled from making any contracts in her own name and from suing in a court of law. At the same time, the husband became responsible for her debts and for her maintenance, unless she "elopes, and lives with another man." Since the union was civil, husband and wife could be indicted and punished for their own crimes, but neither was allowed to testify against the other, except where the husband's "offence is directly against the person of the wife." However, the common law gave the husband the right of "moderate correction" of his wife, "as he is to answer for her misbehaviour," although "in the politer reign of Charles the second, this power of correction began to be doubted: and a wife may now have security of the peace against her husband; or, in return, a husband against his wife."[5]

When Blackstone turns from the marital relation to the parental—no distinction is made at first between the father and the mother—he finds that the parents have the duty of maintenance, protection, and education, and their power to correct and to consent to their child's marriage when he or she is underage derives, he says, from their duties. Only when speaking of the power to manage the child's estate does Blackstone restrict his discussion to the father alone. Parents in need are entitled not only to their children's "honour and reverence" but also to their support. To bastards the only parental obligation is maintenance. "Of Guardian and Ward" and "Of Master and Servant" complete Blackstone's account of domestic relations, the latter notable for his assertion that slavery "does not, nay cannot, subsist in England."[6]

James Kent's *Commentaries on American Law,* which first appeared in the 1820s and quickly established its author as the American Blackstone, treats family law more expansively than the original, and not only because Kent must account for variations among the states and the special complications that arise from these.[7] He accords special chapters to marriage and divorce, the latter now apparently expanded, especially in his home state of New York, to cover cases of alleged adultery. Coverture remains and is discussed at great length, with the adjustments typically granted in equity duly noted. Kent contrasts the common-law doctrine of coverture with the community-property system of the civil law in Europe and Louisiana, then concludes, somewhat ambiguously, "it cannot be denied, that the pre-eminence of the Christian nations of Europe, and of their descendants and colonists in every other quarter of the globe, is most strikingly displayed in the equality and dignity which their institutions confer upon the female character."[8] Kent's discussion of parenthood differs from Blackstone's chiefly in its catalogue of the provisions made by the various states for public schools and its endorsement of their mission. And of course the lecture on master and servant must treat slavery at some length, which Kent, who denies its justice, does in part by discussing the law of emancipation of New York.

Even from this brief overview, it is evident that the common law of the family had achieved a certain stability and a measure of coherence. The regime of coverture presupposed the husband's role as provider. The relatively free choice of occupation or trade provided by common law must in turn have reinforced the doctrine of coverture, for it opened opportunities for enterprising men even as coverture gave them additional resources and responsibilities. There is little or nothing in either Blackstone's or Kent's account of the law to suggest how the regime might have functioned to promote the exceptional fecundity of the women who lived in common-law countries during this era. Perhaps, as Tocqueville suggests, because the wife's resignation of her rights as a *feme sole* (single woman) was, in effect, her choice, she embraced the roles of wife and mother with the energy people devote to their own voluntary arrangements.[9] It is clear that marriage was expected to be stable, except for untimely deaths, and the family was seen as the original locus of education. Religion not being legally established in America, marriage was a civil institution according to the law, but the common-law heritage ensured a pattern for the family that was not at odds with the predominant Christian teaching—though the common law of marriage was not entirely formed on the traditional Christian pattern, since, for example, it refused to legitimate children who had been born to a couple before their wedding.[10] In other words, no human law could make a family Christian, but the law was designed to protect the Christian family or, at the very least, was not intended to unsettle or undermine it.

Discussion of family matters is a delicate thing, even among seasoned scholars, so let me be completely clear. My point is not that the common law of marriage is fixed in the Constitution. Again, the Constitution says next to nothing about the family; although it was always said to be a fundamental law, it was never understood to be comprehensive regarding the fundamental things. The Constitution is an instrument of government, and only of the federal government at that, and government in America was thought to be limited to specified purposes, not constitutive of every relation in life. The Founding Fathers could suppose that the law of marriage was based on its own reasons and did not think that their Constitution, based on reasons of *its* own and dealing with its own concerns, undermined them. Indeed, they saw it as a vice that monarchy transgressed against the integrity of life's separate realms and sought to make the king the father of the state.

Developments in the Law, 1839–1964

Between the beginning of the middle third of the nineteenth century and the end of the middle third of the twentieth, the American law of the family followed a course of liberalization that nevertheless preserved a substratum of the old common-law understanding and thus gave legal recognition to the traditional family despite enormous political, economic, and social change. This story is usually told from the perspective of equal rights for women, to which this whole period forms a sort of prehistory, but I think that perspective, though illuminating in some respects, cannot do justice either to the real character of women's lives in America before the modern regime or to the real community of interests among men, women, and children that the family, at least in its ideal, is meant to serve. Alongside the liberalization of the family ran the transformation of American common law, and the modern regime rushed into place in the late 1960s and early 1970s only after these two streams merged. I can offer here no more than the barest sketch of both developments.[11]

In 1839, in the wake of bankruptcies caused by the panic of two years earlier and as a means of protecting wives from their husbands' economic misfortune, Mississippi passed the nation's first married women's property act, altering the common-law regime of coverture and allowing married women certain rights to property independent of their husbands.[12] By 1860, about half the states had modified the common law, with the others following suit in subsequent decades. Higher education for women in America can be dated from the 1840s, with professional schools first admitting women in the 1870s; the industrial revolution had, of course, brought many women out of the home and into the mills throughout the century. Naturally enough, these changes were variously caused by and the causes of legislative activity, even though, except in a few western states, women lacked the right to vote. Political organization on behalf of women's rights initially proceeded hand in hand with the antislavery movement in the North. Its founding is usually dated from the Seneca Falls Convention of 1848, and its triumph arrived in 1920 with the ratification of the Nineteenth Amendment, according the right to vote to women throughout the nation.

Before this constitutional change, however, the question of women's economic equality had been raised in federal court, first in relation to the professions, and later in relation to the mills. Both times, at issue was the first section of the recently ratified Fourteenth Amendment. In *Bradwell v. State,* decided as a companion case with the *Slaughter-House Cases* in 1873, the Supreme Court upheld the Illinois Supreme Court's rejection of Myra Bradwell's application for a license to practice law. Justice Miller's majority simply reaffirmed the narrow interpretation of the Privileges and Immunities Clause announced in *Slaughter-House* and thus denied her petition, but the four justices who had dissented in *Slaughter-House* on the grounds that the Privileges and Immunities Clause meant to protect certain common-law rights against state infringement could not follow suit, and one, Chief Justice Chase, would have decided for Mrs. Bradwell, although he wrote no dissenting opinion. Justice Bradley's opinion, for himself and Justices Field and Swayne, is notorious among modern feminists, but in fact, with some allowance for Victorian idealization, it is eloquent testimony to the mind of the common law on the matter. Explaining that the right to practice law is not a fundamental privilege or immunity of women, Justice Bradley wrote:

> the civil law, as well as nature herself, has always recognized a wide dif-ference in the respective spheres and destinies of man and woman. Man is, or should be, woman's protector and defender. The natural and proper timidity and delicacy which belongs to the female sex evidently unfits it for many of the occupations of civil life. The constitution of the fam-ily organization, which is founded in the divine ordinance, as well as in the nature of things, indicates the domestic sphere as that which prop-erly belongs to the domain and functions of womanhood. The harmony, not to say identity, of interests and views which belong, or should belong, to the family institution is repugnant to the idea of a woman adopting a distinct and independent career from that of her husband. So firmly fixed was this sentiment in the founders of the common law that it became a maxim of that system of jurisprudence that a woman had no legal existence separate from her husband, who was regarded as her head and representative in the social state; and, notwithstanding some recent modifications of this civil status, many of the special rules of law flow-ing from and dependent upon this cardinal principle still exist in full force in most States.[13]

Similarly, when the laissez-faire position of Justices Field and Bradley gained a majority on the Court at the turn of the century, maximum-hour legislation was upheld for women when it was struck down for men as a violation of the liberty of contract implicit in the Due Process Clause, again with reference to woman's role as mother and with acknowledgment of the law's design that she be dependent on men.[14] Only after the passage of the Nineteenth Amendment, and with specific reference to that amendment, did the liberty of contract become sex-blind.[15]

Despite his language of "divine ordinance" and his reference to "the nature of things," Justice Bradley did not insist that divine or natural law gave Myra Bradwell a constitutional duty, enforceable in court, to abandon her business ventures and depend on her husband. In the traditional way of American jurisprudence, and in some contrast to his colleague Field's opinion in *Slaughter-House,* Bradley invoked natural law not as a barrier to legal change but as a background justification for the established legal order. Neither his argument in *Bradwell* nor Justice Brewer's in *Muller* attempted to write the common law of different roles for husband and wife into the Constitution as a limit on legislative action. Rather, both insisted on the power of the legislature, exercising the police power of the state, to make adjustments to the existing order. In the parts of two centuries under discussion, this is precisely what was done, not only in relation to the relative privileges of men and women but on a whole host of matters, leading eventually to the establishment of big governments with extensive economic and social responsibilities on both the federal and state levels. As the American welfare state was established, the familial roles of the father as provider and the mother as nurturer were supplanted in part by the new responsibilities assumed by the more powerful, if not more devoted, state. Still, the American welfare state was designed around families of the traditional cast and was often defended in their name, as a means of protecting them against the disintegrative forces of modern economic life. Whether the issue was Social Security, Aid to Families with Dependent Children, or veterans' benefits, the legislation presumed a family structure similar to that sustained by the common law. At the same time, the welfare or administrative state was, in its mode of operation and in its conception of law, entirely at odds with the common-law economic regime.[16] Moreover, as a result of the theoretical work of such leading jurists as Oliver Wendell Holmes, Jr., and Benjamin Cardozo, both of whom came to the Supreme Court after important careers on state common-law courts, the common law itself was reconceived as judge-made law, created interstitially in novel cases, rather than as customary law that found expression in particular cases but was adjusted only to preserve a settled maxim or principle in novel circumstances or to restore reasoned order to an altered whole. By the time, in what was almost a legislative accident, discrimination on the basis of sex was outlawed by the Civil Rights Act of 1964, the common law had suffered not only its relative marginalization by the administrative state but also its redefinition from within.

Hostile Silence: The Constitution and the Family Today

The vast changes in American society over the past forty years, brought about by the parallel but by no means identical sexual and feminist revolutions, cannot be explained solely by developments in constitutional law. The Court, after all, has generally proclaimed itself only to be following public opinion, not leading it, although its members sometimes drop their modest garb. Still, even if the Court lags behind elite opinion, it often remains at odds with common opinion away from the coasts or the universities, and more to the point, once it constitutionalizes a modern notion, it blocks the way to sober retreat. In the paragraphs that follow, I consider two realms of modern constitutional law where the Court has introduced new standards hostile to the traditional pattern of family life: its creation of a right to an abortion alleged in the Due Process Clause, and its use of the Equal Protection Clause to strike down state programs that distinguish between the sexes. With the common law and its traditional reason out of sight and opaque to the modern judicial mind—or, more precisely, with the reference point of common law now over the horizon—surviving statutes appear to be arbitrary, and legislatures seem irrational when they meant only to accommodate the unwritten but established law on which society was based. In this sense, the whole debate about "level of scrutiny" misses the point: even moderate compromises concerning individual rights or social equality will appear arbitrary and thus will not clear the lowest hurdle if a judge accords tradition no authority at all.

The abortion right has its proximate origin in the 1965 case of *Griswold v. Connecticut,* a follow-up to a similar case, *Poe v. Ullman,* which had been decided just a few years before. In *Poe,* the Court per Justice Frankfurter rejected as nonjusticiable a complaint seeking a declaratory judgment of unconstitutionality against a Connecticut law that forbade the distribution and use of contraceptives; since the law had long been unenforced, Frankfurter chose judicial restraint in the absence of real controversy. Justice Harlan dissented, not only accepting the justiciability of the controversy but also arguing the unconstitutionality of the statute. Insisting precisely on the deeply embedded tradition of marriage in the law, he argued for a right of marital privacy that was violated by the statute against the use of contraceptives, a right he explicitly said would not extend to "adultery, homosexuality, fornication and incest."[17] Harlan cannot be accused of ignoring common law—he was probably its most adept admirer on the Court at the time—but his Holmesian willingness to treat legal tradition as a "rational process"[18] always in flux disposed him to accept the then-modern notion of marriage as a den of sexual intimacy and to discard that side of the tradition in which marriage involves public recognition of a sexual liaison for the sake of replenishing human life. Harlan concurred in *Griswold,* where the prosecution was actual and Frankfurter was retired, but he did not join Justice Douglas's opinion finding a right of privacy in the "penumbras, formed by emanations from those guarantees" in the Bill of Rights.[19] Though his specific objection was to Douglas's implicit endorsement of the doctrine of incorporation of the Bill of Rights, something Harlan resisted to the last, perhaps he also foresaw that if texts have penumbras, so might precedents; thus, the right of privacy, still tied by Douglas in a concluding paragraph to the marital relation, might spread a longer shadow.

This, of course, is what happened seven years later, with Harlan retired and Justice Brennan writing for a bare majority of a seven-man Court in *Eisenstadt v. Baird.* In that case, by the sort of reasoning that would become common in subsequent Equal Protection cases, the Court first forbade the obvious purpose of an anticontraceptive statute, then devised plausible purposes that proved too attenuated to justify the legislation, and finally concluded that the Massachusetts ban on the distribution of contraceptives "violates the rights of single persons under the Equal Protection Clause of the Fourteenth Amendment":

> the marital couple is not an independent entity with a mind and heart of its own, but an association of two individuals each with a separate intellectual and emotional makeup. If the right of privacy means anything, it is the right of the *individual,* married or single, to be free from unwanted government intrusion into matters so fundamentally affecting a person as the decision whether to bear or beget a child.[20]

It is hard to imagine a script that could more precisely reject the community implicit in the common law of marriage. In this passage, marriage is treated as contingent rather than constitutive, even in relation to an individual's sexual life, and the begetting of children is seen not as a natural consequence of marital relations but as a personal choice. To this principle, *Roe v. Wade* is merely an afterthought, an unavoidable consequence. And the notorious definition of liberty in *Planned Parenthood v. Casey*—"At the heart of liberty is the right to define one's own concept of existence, of meaning, of the universe, and of the mystery of human life"—seems only a more enthusiastic, and more naive, expression of the solipsistic life. Nor is it surprising that in *Casey* the justices struck down a provision that would have required a husband's consent to his wife's abortion, and that they took the occasion once again to dismiss the common law as "of course . . . no longer consistent with our understanding of the family, the individual, or the Constitution."[21]

It was probably no accident that the critical privacy case *Eisenstadt* took an equal protection form and occurred just after the term in which the Court first struck down state legislation distinguishing the rights of the sexes as a violation of that clause. As in the privacy cases, so in sex discrimination the Court moved from a 1961 case deferring to legislative judgment in presumptively excusing women from jury service to a 1971 case in which a legislative presumption preferring a male to a female executor of an estate failed to meet the standard of rationality, which is the lowest threshold of equal protection review.[22] In every case, whether the issue was jury service or military benefits, the statutory scheme in question could be easily explained by the purpose of recognizing or reinforcing the traditional order of family life; if that purpose were legitimate, the scheme would easily pass rationality review, and if the family mattered as it once did to the law, the statute would pass the level of heightened scrutiny established for sex discrimination in *Craig v. Boren.*[23] The case of *Frontiero v. Richardson* in 1973, in which the Court came within one vote of enacting the Equal Rights Amendment then before the states, is typical. The statute presumed a serviceman's wife to be his dependent but required an administrative showing that the husband (in this case, a full-time student receiving veteran's benefits himself) was the dependent of his servicewoman wife. Only on the theory that a wife has an equal right to be her husband's provider could this statute be struck, but the plurality, through Justice Brennan, took the occasion to ridicule Justice Bradley's "romantic paternalism" as engendering "gross, stereotypical distinctions . . . [making] the position of women . . . comparable to that of blacks under the pre–Civil War slave codes."[24]

Ruth Bader Ginsburg argued *Frontiero* for the American Civil Liberties Union, and she took the point of view adopted by Justice Brennan in that case and expounded it herself with authority in the 1996 case of *United States v. Virginia,* forbidding the Virginia Military Institute (VMI) from operating as a school only for men.[25] If you begin from the presumption of interchangeability of the sexes, excluding women from a unique and uniquely successful state military institution is simply discriminatory. If you suppose that men and women fulfill fundamentally different roles in the family and thus in society, the all-male program is perfectly intelligible, as is the impossibility of admitting women without undoing the adversarial method or the code of chivalry with which it is intertwined. When the court of appeals found that "female participation in VMI's adversative training 'would destroy . . . any sense of decency that still permeates the relationship between the sexes,'"[26] it spoke the language of traditional common sense, but in an idiom now forbidden in contemporary constitutional law. The "skeptical scrutiny" Justice Ginsburg applied in the case rejected out of hand any argument based on society's effort to reinforce its patterns or its order; once it was determined that "the educational opportunities provided by VMI . . . deny . . . women 'capable of all of the *individual* activities required of VMI cadets,'" the case was closed.[27] The sovereign self demands protection by the sovereign state, and the intermediary institutions in society—family, school, business, and soon perhaps church as well—must yield, whatever their traditions or their contribution to the happiness of ordinary women and men.

The constitutional dismantling of the traditional family—or, more precisely, of the legal basis of the traditional family—would have been unimaginable had common-law modes of reasoning retained their vigor and reputation. Of course, such counterfactuals in historical analysis have little real meaning, but they may have some use, at least in posing questions. My question is whether legal space can be carved out of the current oppressively egalitarian and libertarian constitutional regime for traditional institutions, from the courtly gesture to the state-run military academy, by appeal only to the doctrine of legislative choice, as Justice Scalia, in his dissent in *United States v. Virginia* and in other opinions, seems to think.[28] Traditional institutions were understood traditionally not as mere legislative choices but as embedded in or dependent on common law, an unwritten law that was partly traditional but also partly natural; legislative choice might declare or revise the tradition, but it could not re-create it. For common law, the family was paradigmatic, since any family governs itself, if not arbitrarily, then by unwritten rules. That some today see the traditional family as an arbitrary monarchy may be due in part to the invisibility to the contemporary legal mind of unwritten law. That traditional patterns of family life persist and the callings of wife and mother are still heard above the din of contempt from the legal establishment perhaps testify to unwritten law's persistent voice.

CHAPTER 6

Peremptory Challenge

African Americans, the Jury, and
the Constitutionalism of Common Law

The *Batson* Cases and the Marshall-Thomas Dispute

In the 1986 case of *Batson v. Kentucky*,[1] when the U.S. Supreme Court condemned a prosecutor's use of peremptory challenges to remove black jurors in the trial of a black defendant, Justice Thurgood Marshall wrote a concurring opinion in which he called for, or perhaps predicted, complete abolition of the peremptory device. The opinion of the Court by Justice Powell tried its best at once to enforce the Fourteenth Amendment's ban on state-sponsored discrimination and to preserve the historical right of the parties in a legal case not only to disqualify all potential jurors from the venire who can be shown to harbor prejudice but also to strike at will a certain number of veniremen without assigning cause. Both objectives had been endorsed in *Swain v. Alabama*,[2] the Court's previous encounter with the issue some twenty-one years before, and Powell's carefully crafted opinion purported to modify *Swain* only by adjusting the evidentiary burden in accord with intervening equal protection precedents. Nevertheless, the Court clearly recognized that the implication of the shift was the reversal of the presumption, so whereas *Swain* had left a prosecutor free to remove black jurors unless the defendant could establish that the motive was to discriminate on the grounds of race, *Batson* effectively required that a prosecutor who employed a peremptory challenge to reject a black juror prove to the trial judge that the juror's race was not the reason for his or her removal. Justice Marshall joined and complimented the Court's opinion, but he made it clear that he thought the opinion did not go far enough "toward eliminating the shameful practice of racial discrimination in the selection of juries." He pointed out, "That goal can be accomplished only by eliminating peremptory challenges entirely." And because the criminal justice system requires balance, this meant eliminating challenges not only by the government but also by the accused.[3] Though Marshall's concurrence stresses the likely ineffectiveness of the Court's compromise in suppressing discrimination, it was reinforced by the logical difficulty noted in Chief Justice Burger's dissent, namely, how a challenge can still be called peremptory if, upon objection, the party must assign to it a legitimate cause.[4]

The subsequent history of the *Batson* doctrine forms what could be a textbook study of how, through changes in Court personnel and through the circumstances of particular cases, a doctrine can evolve in a direction that was resisted in its first appearance. In 1990 the Court declined the invitation of a white defendant to forbid prosecutorial use of peremptory challenges to remove blacks from his jury on the theory that the Sixth Amendment's guarantee of an impartial jury entitled him to a panel that was a representative cross section of the community. Writing for a five-to-four Court, Justice Scalia interpreted the Sixth Amendment as permitting the historic peremptory challenge as a means to secure impartiality, without regard to cross-sectional characterisics, and he distinguished *Batson* as establishing an exception on equal protection grounds for defendants claiming racial discrimination against themselves.[5] The following year, however, a white defendant whose prosecutor had used peremptory challenges to strike black veniremen succeeded in getting his conviction reversed, relying in his argument on the Equal Protection Clause. The same term, in *Edmonson v. Leesville Concrete,* the Court extended the *Batson* rule to civil cases, which, since neither party was a governmental body, meant interpreting state action quite broadly and, incidentally, applying the ban on alleged race-based peremptory challenges to both sides.[6] With these precedents in place, it came as no surprise that in 1992, in *Georgia v. McCollum,* the Court turned the *Batson* rule against criminal defendants—three whites, charged with assault and battery in the beating of a black couple, who had used their peremptory challenges to remove blacks from the jury.[7] And the Court sustained an equal protection complaint against the state's use of peremptory challenges to exclude members of the defendant's sex—here, in paternity proceedings[8]—extending the *Batson* scheme beyond the racial context. This development, if not entirely fulfilling Marshall's goal of the outright abolition of peremptory challenges, at least validates Burger's prediction in his *Batson* dissent of their eventual extinction.

Justice Clarence Thomas, Marshall's successor on the Court, concurred in *Georgia v. McCollum*—he thought that the result was mandated logically by the Court's decision in *Edmonson*—but he wrote separately "to express my dissatisfaction with our continuing attempts to use the Constitution to regulate peremptory challenges." Like nearly every modern justice who has written on race and the jury, he invoked the precedent of *Strauder v. West Virginia,* the 1880 case in which the Court for the first time reversed a conviction because of the exclusion of blacks, by state law, from jury service. But in a striking departure from earlier dicta, Thomas claimed that *Batson* and the line of cases following from it betrayed *Strauder* rather than, as their authors had asserted, fulfilling it. For Thomas, "that conscious and unconscious prejudice persists in our society and that it may influence some juries" is a reason to preserve the peremptory challenge intact, not an occasion for its abandonment and replacement by judicial monitoring, which would at most ensure in jurors and other parties appearing in court outwardly correct behavior in matters pertaining to race. "I am certain," he wrote, "that black criminal defendants will rue the day that this court ventured down this road that inexorably will lead to the elimination of peremptory strikes."[9]

The opposing perspectives of the only two African Americans to sit on the Supreme Court will surprise no one who has observed the Court or American politics in recent years, but it would be superficial, not to mention condescending, to dismiss their disagreement as a reflex of ideological posture. For one thing, in their assessment of the persistence of racial prejudice in America and of the fact that it marks our system of criminal justice, they substantially agree, and both express this view with the authority that comes from experience. Moreover, neither is satisfied with the compromise, worked out by the Court majority, of carving out exceptions to the peremptory challenge; instead, each seeks a crisp and authoritative rule. In the discussion that follows, I do not explore the differences between Justices Marshall and Thomas in particular detail, nor do I systematically develop an analysis of the changes in personnel and position that characterize the peremptory challenge cases. But I do suggest that the disagreement on the Court concerning this matter reflects a larger pattern in American constitutionalism: the tension between the common-law heritage of that constitutionalism on the one hand, and its modern interpretation in the light of liberal political theory on the other. Since the liberal influence is better known and, in the contemporary era, undeniable, I concentrate where I am at any rate obliged to begin, with attention to the jury at common law.

The Common-Law Jury, the Constitution, and the Peremptory Challenge

The jury may not be the most ancient institution of the common law, but it is surely among its most distinctive. William Blackstone repeated the traditional account of its origins in the fog of pre-Norman England, but modern historians date the trial or petit jury to the thirteenth century, the catalyst for its establishment having been the decree of the Lateran Council in 1215 forbidding clerical participation in trial by ordeal. (The inquest or grand jury is apparently somewhat older, having grown with the rise of royal courts in the centuries following the Conquest.) By 1600, many of its now-familiar characteristics were well settled: jurors sat alongside a judge, who was responsible for administering the trial and giving them their charge; juries sat in civil as well as criminal cases; though there were means for punishing false or tainted verdicts, juries had in practice substantial leeway to render a "verdict according to conscience" and thus could nullify the effect of unpopular laws by returning a verdict of "not guilty"; and in the selection of jurors, criminal defendants could challenge and remove jurors both for cause and peremptorily, while the crown in criminal prosecutions and the parties in civil disputes were also given various means, dependent on the number of veniremen the sheriff was able to produce, to remove jurors. To submit one's case to the jury was, in the formula of common law, to put oneself upon "the country," and the jurors were said to be "twelve free and lawful men" or "twelve good men and true."[10]

The American colonists brought the jury with them from England, along with the common law. In fact, historians have argued, the American jury in colonial times surpassed its English counterpart in authority, partly because eighteenth-century English judges were developing ways to limit juries, and partly because the paucity of printed legal sources and the inaccessibility of the courts in Westminster encouraged the colonial jury to determine not only the facts of the case but also the governing law.[11] The best-known instance of the power of colonial juries to settle the law is probably the seditious libel trial of Peter Zenger, whose acquittal signaled the legitimacy of truth as a defense in libel cases. Among the complaints lodged against the Parliament and the king in the struggle that led to the Revolution were their inroads against the right to trial by jury; this was protested in the Declaration of the Stamp Act Congress, the Virginia Resolves of 1769, the Declaration and Resolves of the First Continental Congress, and the Second Congress's Declaration of the Causes and Necessities of Taking Up Arms, as well as in the Declaration of Independence.[12] Naturally, the first state constitutions carried guarantees of the right to a jury trial.[13]

The place of the right to a trial by jury in the Constitution of 1787 is a matter of interest to judges interpreting that document today, and it is not a simple tale. Article III, section 2, clause 3, of the Constitution guarantees the right, as follows: "The Trial of all Crimes, except in Cases of Impeachment, shall be by Jury; and such Trial shall be held in the State where the said Crimes shall have been committed; but when not committed within any State, the Trial shall be at such Place or Places as the Congress may by Law have directed." To the Anti-Federalists, this clause was not specific enough concerning the criminal jury and, by its silence concerning the civil jury, seemed to portend its abandonment in federal law. Hence, the Sixth and Seventh Amendments:

> In all criminal prosecutions, the accused shall enjoy the right to a speedy and public trial, by an impartial jury of the State and district wherein the crime shall have been committed; which district shall have been previously ascertained by law, and to be informed of the nature and cause of the accusation; to be confronted with the witnesses against him; to have compulsory process for obtaining witnesses in his favor, and to have the assistance of counsel for his defence.

> In Suits at common law, where the value in controversy shall exceed twenty dollars, the right of trial by jury shall be preserved, and no fact tried by a jury shall be otherwise re-examined in any Court of the United States, than according to the rules of the common law.

It must be admitted that the omission of the civil jury in the Philadelphia document was probably no accident; Hamilton defends its absence in *The Federalist* Number 83, doubting the importance of the civil jury for liberty. Besides, as the Anti-Federalists probably sensed, the necessarily local character of the jury cut against the grain of every other institution the Constitution established. Several of the procedures enumerated in the Sixth Amendment were unknown to the ancient common law, having been established by parliamentary statute in the seventeenth or eighteenth century, but the jury itself and the vicinage requirement were long settled. In the Seventh Amendment, the common law is made the explicit point of reference, even to the point of open incorporation of some of its unwritten rules.

The federal constitutional law of the jury could probably fill a volume, even exclusive of the cases pertaining in one way or another to race. Modern students are perhaps most familiar with the decisions from the late Warren and the Burger eras, incorporating the jury right into the Fourteenth Amendment and thus applying it to the states, but allowing juries smaller than twelve or nonunanimous verdicts in state courts.[14] Numerous earlier cases raised matters of federal law concerning the jury, including the question of peremptory challenges. From the start, Blackstone's account was taken as the authoritative rendering of English common law at the time of the Founding: The criminal defendant was to be allowed thirty-five peremptory challenges when tried for treason and twenty when on trial for other felonies; the crown, as a result of a statute passed in the early 1300s, was allowed no challenges that were not for cause, but the prosecutor was by custom allowed to ask veniremen to stand aside without assigning cause, and they would be excused from serving unless they were needed to achieve a jury of twelve. Blackstone's account of the reasons behind the right has likewise been a common point of reference, and is worth quoting at length:

> In criminal cases, or at least in capital ones, there is, *in favorem vitae,* allowed to the prisoner an arbitrary and capricious species of challenge to a certain number of jurors, without shewing any cause at all; which is called a *peremptory* challenge: a provision full of that tenderness and humanity to prisoners, for which our English laws are justly famous. This is grounded on two reasons: 1. As every one must be sensible, what sudden impressions and unaccountable prejudices we are apt to conceive upon the bare looks and gestures of another; and how necessary it is, that a prisoner (when put to defend his life) should have a good opinion of his jury, the want of which might totally disconcert him; the law wills not that he should be tried by any one man against whom he has conceived a prejudice, even without being able to assign a reason for such his dislike. 2. Because, upon challenges for cause shewn, if the reason assigned be proved insufficient to set aside the juror, perhaps the bare questioning his indifference may sometimes provoke a resentment; to prevent all ill consequences from which, the prisoner is still at liberty, if he pleases, peremptorily to set him aside.[15]

In 1790, Congress by statute adopted the English numbers for challenges by defendants, with subsequent statutes generally settling on twenty peremptory challenges in capital cases and ten in others. Justice Story's opinion in *United States v. Marchant* discussed peremptory challenges in the context of whether criminal suspects could be tried jointly against their wishes, the ground of the complaint being that one defendant in a joint trial might wish to retain a juror that another defendant challenged. Story ruled against the claim, since "the right of peremptory challenge is not, of itself, a right to select, but a right to reject jurors"; Story reinforced the conclusion that the defendant has no right to select jurors by finding that the crown's right to ask jurors to stand aside was a "qualified and conditional exercise of the same right" of peremptory challenge.[16] The implication of this last point is that, for Story, the common-law right of the government to set aside jurors in criminal cases is incorporated in federal law, if not through the Sixth Amendment, at least through congressional statute. He notes in passing, however, a diversity at the state level on the question of government peremptory challenges. An 1840 statute directing federal courts to constitute juries according to the law of the state in which they sit obviously complicated the matter, and in 1856, the Court held that although the 1790 specification of defendants' peremptory challenges survived the 1840 act, the implication of a corresponding qualified right in the prosecutor did not; its existence was now to be determined by the applicable law of the state.[17]

In 1865, Congress gave the government five peremptory challenges when the defendant had twenty, and two when the defendant had ten. Perhaps in response, strong dicta in favor of the defendant's peremptory right appeared some years later in *Lewis v. United States:* "The right of challenge comes from the common law with the trial by jury itself, and has always been held essential to the fairness of trial by jury." That case involved whether challenges could be made by separate lists given to the government and the accused when the record did not show that the defendant was present as the challenges were made. The Court decided in the defendant's favor, holding that he had a right to inspect his potential jurors face-to-face.[18] But in *Stilson v. United States,* a criminal prosecution for conspiracy to violate the World War I Espionage Act, the Supreme Court was faced with a constitutional challenge to the provision of the 1865 statute that treated multiple defendants as a single party in apportioning peremptory challenges. The Court upheld the statute, ruling: "There is nothing in the Constitution of the United States which requires the Congress to grant peremptory challenges to defendants in criminal cases; trial by an impartial jury is all that is secured. The number of challenges is left to be regulated by the common law or the enactments of Congress."[19] Without regard to the dicta in *Lewis* or to the authority of Story's opinion in *United States v. Marchant,* both of which were decided implicitly as matters of federal common law, the Court treated the peremptory challenge simply as "a privilege granted by the legislative authority," which therefore "must be taken with the limitations placed upon the manner of its exercise."[20]

Before turning to the cases involving the jury and race, one other decision deserves mention. In the 1930 case of *Patton v. United States,* the Court ruled that it was the defendant's right to waive a jury trial and that such a waiver did not result in a violation of the constitutional mandate that "The Trial of all Crimes . . . shall be by Jury." Reading this passage as invoking the same "right to . . . trial by . . . jury" mentioned in the Sixth Amendment, Justice Sutherland noted that the courts of different states had decided the question in different ways as a matter of state law, but he found greater force in the argument that since the defendant can waive his right to trial altogether by pleading guilty, he can take the lesser step of waiving a jury trial. He rejected the claim that as a matter of public policy, the people have an interest in ensuring a jury trial that can override any right of the defendant to waive a jury.[21] For our purposes, the opinion is of interest on two counts. First, the jury trial is defined as a right to which the defendant is entitled, not as a process that the state can impose. Second, Sutherland's reasoning contains an important paradox, for while he "demonstrate[s] the unassailable integrity of the establishment of trial by jury in all its parts, and make[s] clear that a destruction of one of the essential elements has the effect of abridging the right in contravention of the Constitution," he also acknowledges that in English common law, the right to trial by jury could not be waived.[22] Citing the maxim "It is contrary to the spirit of the common law itself to apply a rule founded on a particular reason to a law when that reason utterly fails—*cessante ratione legis, cessat ipsa lex*"—Sutherland found that the disallowance of waiver at common law depended on several now-abandoned conditions of the ancient common law: "the accused could not testify in his own behalf; in felonies he was not allowed counsel . . . ; and conviction of crime worked an attaint and forfeiture of official titles of inheritance," thus implicating third parties whose own rights a defendant could not be presumed to waive. He concluded: "These conditions have ceased to exist, and with their disappearance justification for the old rule no longer rests on a substantial basis."[23] The right to trial by jury is a right of the accused, but the form of the jury, though largely fixed, can in some particulars be altered by the course of reasoning characteristic of common law.

Race and the Jury: The Early Years

It was one of the glories of English law, wrote Blackstone in 1765, that slavery was unknown to it: "this spirit of liberty is so deeply implanted in our constitution, and rooted even in our very soil, that a slave or a negro, the moment he lands in England, falls under the protection of the laws, and with regard to all natural rights becomes *eo instanti* a freeman."[24] He had behind him the authority of *Smith v. Gould,* in which the court had written: "the common law takes no notice of negroes being different from other men. By the common law no man can have a property in another, but in special cases, as in a villain, but even in him not to kill him: so in captives took in war, but the taker cannot kill them, but may sell them to ransom them: there is no such thing as a slave by the law of England."[25] This suggests not only that the common law conferred liberty but that it was, to use Justice Harlan's later phrase, color-blind. In 1772, Lord Mansfield's opinion in *Somerset v. Stewart* affirmed this view, noting that slavery was "so odious, that nothing can be suffered to support it but positive law."[26] Generally accepted as law in America, the *Somerset* doctrine kept common law relatively immune to the peculiar institution, requiring its establishment and regulation by statute. When slavery was abolished by the Thirteenth Amendment and its incidents in law and politics ensured against in the Fourteenth and Fifteenth, respectively, it was to be expected that the old policy of the common law would reappear.

This helps explain the 1880 case of *Strauder v. West Virginia* and its companions, which to the twentieth-century mind seemed to be in sharp contrast to the Court's decision three years later striking down the equal accommodations provisions of the Civil Rights Act of 1875, not to mention their decision upholding segregation the following decade in *Plessy v. Ferguson.*[27] As I noted at the outset, the Court in *Strauder* overturned the conviction of a black defendant on the grounds that West Virginia law had excluded blacks from the venire. The Court used sweeping language frequently quoted in modern cases—that the Fourteenth Amendment established for blacks "a right to exemption from unfriendly legislation against them distinctively as colored"—but it also paid particular attention to the special character of the institution in dispute:

> The very fact that colored people are singled out and expressly denied by a statute all right to participate in the administration of the law, as jurors, because of their color, though they are citizens, and may be in other respects fully qualified, is practically a brand upon them, affixed by law, an assertion of their inferiority, and a stimulant to that race prejudice which is an impediment to securing to individuals of the race that equal justice which the law aims to secure to all others. . . . The very idea of a jury is a body of men composed of the peers or equals of the person whose rights it is selected or summoned to determine; that is, of his neighbors, fellows, associates, persons having the same legal status in society as that which he holds.

After a quotation from Blackstone, there follows the passage quoted by Justice Thomas in *McCollum,* acknowledging "that prejudices often exist against particular classes in the community, which often sway the judgment of jurors," and marking the command of the Fourteenth Amendment as the remedy against this mischief—thus declaring unconstitutional the West Virginia law. Before proceeding to uphold a provision of the Civil Rights Act that allowed removal of a case to federal court when civil rights are denied in a state tribunal, the Court added the following qualification:

> We do not say that within the limits from which it is not excluded by the amendment a State may not prescribe the qualifications of its jurors, and in so doing make discriminations. It may confine the selection to males, to freeholders, to citizens, to persons within certain ages, or to persons having educational qualifications. We do not believe the Fourteenth Amendment was ever intended to prohibit this. . . . Its aim was against discrimination because of race or color.[28]

Strauder's companion cases, *Virginia v. Rives* and *Ex parte Virginia,* make clearer what the Court was and was not holding.[29] In the first, the Court rejected a request for removal to federal court of a Virginia murder trial of two blacks who, alleging the existence of racial prejudice against them, sought a jury one-third of whose members belonged to their race. Although the case was disposed of on the technical question—removal was not appropriate because Virginia *law* did not discriminate against blacks, and error in practice could be reviewed on appeal—the Court seemed clearly indisposed to mandate racial balance on particular juries. In *Ex parte Virginia,* by contrast, it upheld federal criminal proceedings under civil rights law against a Virginia county judge accused of excluding all blacks from the jury list he was charged by state law with devising. As the Court put the matter in relation to whites in *Strauder,* "every . . . man is entitled to a trial by a jury selected from persons of his own race or color, or, rather, selected without discrimination against his color."[30]

Justice Field, joined by Justice Clifford, wrote separately in each case, concurring in *Rives* but dissenting in *Strauder* and *Ex parte Virginia.* The *Rives* concurrence makes clear his own theory of the Fourteenth Amendment: it reaches only discriminatory legislation, not the acts of state officials, except insofar as the latter are governed by state law. In the *Ex parte Virginia* dissent, which he also applied to *Strauder,* Field explained the fallacy he saw in the Court's reasoning as a failure to distinguish political from civil rights, as well as a willingness to trample on the rights of the states, which in his view, except for the new prohibition on race-directed legislation, were not altered from the original federal plan by the amendments. The right to sit on a jury was a political right, to his mind, and thus its assignment, like that of all officeholding, should be left to the discretion of the states. Indeed, he saw the Fifteenth Amendment's silence on jury participation as significant, concluding that the only political right guaranteed was the right to vote, with the vote then trusted to secure all else.[31] The majority, by contrast, did not draw a distinction between political and civil rights, moving quietly, as the preceding quotations show, between the rights of jurors to participate and the rights of the accused.

Modern cases on race and the jury begin with *Norris v. Alabama,* one of the Scottsboro cases. Here and in a series of decisions over the next several decades, the Court threw out convictions when they were convinced that the process by which jurors had been called was systematically discriminatory against blacks.[32] Although the Court came to show less sympathy than the *Strauder* Court toward apparently neutral qualifications that had a disproportionate effect in excluding blacks from the jury pool—no doubt the long experience with devices used to restrict black suffrage was not lost on the justices—the modern Court nevertheless seemed committed to the same end as the Court in *Strauder*, namely, that blacks not be excluded from the pool of available jurors and thereby from the venire. The Court's attention to the venire rather than to the actual jury seems intended to avoid any infringement of the traditional practices whereby veniremen were reduced to juries, but the eventual irony is that focusing on the venire turned the justices' attention toward the right to sit on a jury, already evident in *Strauder* dicta, and away from the right of the accused to a jury that was, if not of his choosing, at least not imposed on him without some exercise of choice on his part.

From *Swain* to *Batson*

The preceding discussion of the peremptory challenge and of the Court's early opinions demanding the absence of racial discrimination in the selection of veniremen shows the two principles clearly on a collision course. The race cases aimed to remove race prejudice as a cause for disqualifying jurors, but the peremptory challenge was, in Blackstone's words, "arbitrary and capricious," its usefulness consisting precisely in the license it allowed to a defendant even, or especially, when he was on trial for his life. In *Swain v. Alabama,* the two principles indeed collided, and Justice White's opinion of the Court sought to have it both ways, allowing the peremptory challenge to win in the case at hand while reserving the racial claim for a better record. To his credit, White did not shy away from admitting the arbitrary character of the peremptory challenge:

> The essential nature of the peremptory challenge is that it is one exercised without a reason stated, without inquiry and without being subject to the court's control. . . . It is . . . frequently exercised on grounds normally thought irrelevant to legal proceedings or official action, namely, the race, religion, nationality, occupation or affiliations of people summoned for jury duty. . . . In the quest for an impartial and qualified jury, Negro and white, Protestant and Catholic, are alike subject to being challenged without cause.

White recognized that "to subject the prosecutor's challenge in any particular case to the demands and traditional standards of the Equal Protection Clause would entail a radical change in the nature and operation of the challenge," since a challenge "open to examination" would by definition no longer be peremptory. He described the purpose of the peremptory challenge as "not only to eliminate extremes of partiality on both sides, but to assure the parties that the jurors before whom they try the case will decide on the basis of the evidence placed before them, and not otherwise." Thus, White upheld the right of challenge in the particular case before him, where there was, to the Court's mind, no adequate showing of systematic racial discrimination in its use.[33]

The final section of the *Swain* opinion acknowledged that the claim that the Talladega County prosecutor had used the peremptory challenge systematically to exclude blacks "raises a different issue and it may well require a different answer." In *Batson v. Kentucky,* that issue was brought to the fore, and the different answer was rendered. Because equal protection standards had changed in the interim to shift the burden of proof when black underrepresentation could be documented, and, as Justice White noted in his concurrence, because *Swain* "should have warned prosecutors that using peremptories to exclude blacks on the assumption that no black juror could fairly judge a black defendant would violate the Equal Protection Clause," the Court altered the balance between the two rights, allowing peremptory challenges themselves to be challenged for discriminatory intent.[34] Quoting extensively from *Strauder* at the outset of his opinion and finding that "while decisions of this Court have been concerned largely with discrimination during the selection of the venire, the principles announced there also forbid discrimination on account of race in selection of the petit jury," Powell concluded:

> The reality of the practice, amply reflected in many state- and federal-court opinions, shows that the challenge may be, and unfortunately at times has been, used to discriminate against black jurors. By requiring trial courts to be sensitive to the racially discriminatory use of peremptory challenges, our decision enforces the mandate of equal protection and furthers the ends of justice.[35]

Powell's opinion in *Batson* might seem to follow in the tradition of Sutherland's rationalization of the ancient common law in *Patton,* but an important difference should be noted. Whereas Sutherland paid attention to the niceties of form in the jury process, adjusting the old rule only in the light of established procedural innovations, Powell turned from the form to the end, the "reality," the apparent result, replacing the formal rule with a call for judicial sensitivity. In his dissent, then-Justice Rehnquist quoted the passage from *Swain* explicitly permitting peremptory challenges for undefended racial suspicions, adding, "there is simply nothing 'unequal' about the State's using its peremptory challenges to strike blacks from the jury in cases involving black defendants, so long as such challenges are also used to exclude whites in cases involving white defendants, Hispanics in cases involving Hispanic defendants, Asians in cases involving Asian defendants, and so on."[36] But the reminder fell on deaf ears. That the peremptory challenge survived unimpaired for so long, despite having been denied constitutional status since *Stilson,* while the Equal Protection Clause is obviously a constitutional command, is testimony to the authority of common law in our constitutional system, especially when the matter at hand is related to a criminal trial. That the reasons once given in its defense now seem so inadequate to the modern sensibility suggests the frailty of the common-law way of thinking in the contemporary mind.

After *Batson:* Community Claims over Defendant Rights

As noted earlier, Justice Scalia's opinion in *Holland v. Illinois* seemed to breathe life back into the peremptory challenge. Without overruling *Stilson,* it anchored the peremptory challenge in the Sixth Amendment right to an impartial jury and rejected the claim that that right includes a command that the jury mirror a cross section of the community where the crime took place. But Scalia could gain a majority only because the petitioner in the case rested his claim exclusively on the Sixth Amendment, precluding any reliance on the Fourteenth. The following term, when a similar case was presented with the Fourteenth Amendment claim properly raised, the Court did not hesitate to extend the *Batson* rule to state challenges of blacks in a case involving a white defendant, despite explicit language in *Batson* requiring a defendant objecting to the use of a peremptory challenge to "show that he is a member of a cognizable racial group."[37] Justice Kennedy's opinion emphasized not the defendant's right to a fair trial but the jurors' right to judge: "The opportunity for ordinary citizens to participate in the administration of justice has long been recognized as one of the principal justifications for retaining the jury system," he wrote. He went on to quote Tocqueville on the political value of the jury, including even Tocqueville's qualification, "I do not know whether the jury is useful to those who are in litigation; but I am certain it is highly beneficial to those who decide the litigation"[38]—as though a defendant facing life imprisonment had in mind to vindicate the benefits that would flow to his judges without considering whether his own interest was thereby served. The consequences for the doctrine of third-party standing were among the objections in Justice Scalia's dissent.

The clear shift in focus between *Holland* and *Powers* from the defendant's rights to the community's participation prepared the judgment in *Edmonson v. Leesville Concrete Co.,* where the right to object on racial grounds to peremptory strikes was extended to civil litigants. Again speaking through Justice Kennedy, the Court was here obliged to extend the concept of state action—since the basis of the claim was, after all, the Fourteenth Amendment—to include as state actors both the parties to a civil dispute and the jurors themselves. The judge, "who beyond all question is a state actor," is the one who actually excuses the jurors to whom the parties object, while the jury's duties to make final determinations of fact, to weigh the gravity of civil wrongs, and by their findings to preclude later dispute "are traditional functions of government, not of a select, private group beyond the reach of the Constitution." Indeed, pursuing the Tocquevillian analysis without further citation and with the modern rather than the Tocquevillian citizen in mind, Justice Kennedy remarked that "the quiet rationality of the courtroom makes it an appropriate place to confront race-based fears or hostility by means other than the use of offensive stereotypes." As for the old common-law rationale, it was openly overridden: "It may be true that the role of litigants in determining the jury's composition provides one reason for wide acceptance of the jury system and of its verdicts. But if race stereotypes are the price for acceptance of a jury panel as fair, the price is too high to meet the standard of the Constitution."[39]

The logic of the step from *Powers* to *Edmonson* is clear, once one accepts that the rights of the litigants in the matter of jury composition are secondary to the rights of jurors to be impaneled without regard to race. What went unnoticed by the Court, perhaps precisely because at issue was a civil dispute between two private parties, was that in *Edmonson,* the objection to the use of peremptory challenges was allowed for the first time against such challenges by a defendant. In *Georgia v. McCollum,* scrutiny of criminal defendants' peremptory challenges was upheld, generating Justice Thomas's objections quoted at the outset of this chapter, as well as dissents from Justices O'Connor and Scalia, with the latter commenting on the absurdity of holding "[a] criminal defendant, in the process of defending himself against the state, . . . to be acting on behalf of the state."[40] Here, Justice White's willingness back in *Swain* to equate prosecutorial peremptory challenges, which had been qualified at common law, with those of defendants, which had been absolute,[41] now serves not to shore up the prosecutor's right but to dismantle the defendant's. Whether the peremptory challenge will survive in any form remains an open question. In the case anticipated by Justice Thomas, in which the state objects to a black defendant's use of the peremptory challenge against a white juror he suspects of prejudice, it is hard to see how the Court could do anything but sustain the objection. Extension of the *Batson* rule to the use of the peremptory challenge to exclude members of one sex, which occurred in the1994 case *J.E.B. v. Alabama ex rel T.B.,* was hardly a surprise, given the Court's 1975 decision in *Taylor v. Louisiana,* striking down a law that made women less likely to be called for jury duty.[42] It is hard to imagine any class that now qualifies for heightened scrutiny under the Equal Protection Clause being immune to having their right to serve on juries invoked by defendants eager to find some grounds to have their convictions reversed. At that point, the peremptory challenge, if not quite dead, will certainly have been retired.

What is lost with the end of the peremptory challenge? A lawyer would be better able to predict the effect on the courtroom: the peremptory challenges not risked, the trivialization of challenges for cause, and the like. My concern in conclusion is with the larger effect on our way of thinking about law. The modern discomfort in the face of an arbitrary challenge—that is, a challenge to which no cause is expressly assigned—belongs to the general trend toward rationalization in the law, but it also belongs to the gradual weakening of respect for individual consent. It was never strictly a dictate of reason that the defendant have some role in choosing his or her judges, since pure reason would rather give judgment to a rational person; it was never strictly a dictate of reason that, granted some role in the choice, the defendant should be able to choose, albeit by exclusion, without giving a reason adequate to convince the rational authority in charge. But neither is it strictly according to reason that jurors be permitted to give their verdicts without having to render *their* reasons, much less that those verdicts be unreviewable. The fabric of the law is full of moments when an absolute though circumscribed prerogative is allowed. This is due in part to the necessity of finality in human affairs: not every question can be debated endlessly in practice, though many can and indeed must in theory. But it is also due to the genius of our own law, and especially to its common-law heritage, with its tender concern for the individual's conscience and dignity (think here of the privilege against self-incrimination) and its subtle insurance that such prerogatives are spread throughout the law and thus throughout society, instead of being concentrated, as the logic of modern rationalism always has it, in the reason of some sovereign, whether a representative assembly, a democratic majority, or an unelected judge. When one is sure of the presence of a wrong, such as racial prejudice, the temptation to seek its eradication at whatever cost to constitutional forms seems irresistible. But if it happens that, after years of sustained effort, the prejudice itself does not disappear but seems to be growing, it is reasonable to wonder whether our chosen instruments are adequate to the task. In particular, one might consider whether settled prejudice can be countered more effectively by other men's reasons or by allowing, at some risk of its advancement, its assertion, thereby forcing it to stand on its own authority or to listen to the voice of reason from within. It would be foolish to see in the demise of the peremptory challenge the end of our constitutional order. But neither constitutionalism nor racial harmony will be served by the steady erosion in the law of individual responsibility for reflection and choice.

CHAPTER 7

The Judicial Science of Politics

Or Why Taxation without Representation Is Constitutional
and Party Discipline Is Not

Like men and women, or—as one used to be able to say, when subtle differences too had standing—like the English and the French, law and politics are at once closely related and persistently at odds. Each sees itself differently than the other sees it, and differently than it sees the other. The law presents itself as a structure of rational justice, while it sees in politics something less rational and less ordered, indeed arbitrary, unpredictable, and subject to force. Politics, by contrast, sees in law a rigid structure that is not without arbitrariness or even irrationality, while it sees itself as promising a more direct avenue to the achievement of public good. These crisscrossing perspectives of law and politics, or maybe one should say of lawyers and politicians, do not rule out the possibility that one side will try to collapse the other into itself—for instance, when law is defined as the command of the (political) sovereign, or when political life is narrowly constricted in the name of the rule of law. Nor do I deny that there are some, especially in the present, who would collapse the two perspectives into a single one different from either, for instance, the perspective of policy and administration. But I do mean to suggest that the dual perspective of law and politics is deeply rooted in our political and legal culture—manifesting itself, for example, in Plato's separate dialogues on the *Republic* and the *Laws* or in the modern doctrine of the separation of powers—and that any account of American constitutionalism that is oblivious to this duality is apt to be seriously flawed.

In this chapter, I turn my attention to what I have called in its title "the judicial science of politics," by which I mean the understanding of politics evinced in much contemporary judicial doctrine. If that title is not entirely free of sarcasm, it is because I hope to show the inadequacy of the contemporary perspective it names, not because I think that some modern political science of judging has made the serious study of judicial doctrine anachronistic. In the past, the judicial perspective on politics might have been studied by attention to what was called the "political question doctrine," but despite a brief appearance in the mid-1990s, that doctrine has generally been eclipsed, to the point that it seems not to have entered the discussion when the Supreme Court effectively determined the winner of the 2000 presidential election.[1] I have chosen for illustration two cases decided by the Supreme Court in 1990, by identical majorities—one involving a judicially ordered tax, the other a state system of political patronage. Neither case was especially new in the sense that it was entirely lacking in supporting precedent, but neither case could be decided without a significant extension of existing precedent. And in each case the opinion of the Court was met by an opposing opinion—in one instance, technically a concurrence; in the other, a dissent—from the four judges appointed or promoted by President Reagan. I discuss each case in turn, then try to discern from their commonalities the political perspectives of both the majority and the minority on the Court at the time. Personnel on the Court have changed significantly since then, but the rules laid down remain the law, even though in some respects the justices have recently shown greater sensitivity to what distinguishes their function from that of what used to be called the "political branches."

Missouri v. Jenkins: Desegregation Remedies and Judicial Taxation

Missouri v. Jenkins is one of the numerous school desegregation cases pursued in the federal courts over the last several decades.[2] Like many of its kind, it has come before the Supreme Court several times for the resolution of different questions, all the while being continued in the docket of the district court where the suit was initiated, as remedial decrees are developed and revised and their implementation is supervised by the presiding judge. Although the complexity of these cases and the range of their consequences must not be underestimated, neither should their paradigmatic status for the modern exercise of judicial power be overlooked. To understand the particular issue in the 1990 opinion in *Jenkins,* it is not necessary to examine in detail the Court's development of equitable remedies in school desegregation cases, but to set the context for a reading of the *Jenkins* opinions, a brief review is in order.

Brown v. Board of Education and its companions, decided in 1954, held that racially segregated public schools violated the Equal Protection Clause of the Fourteenth Amendment, but in retrospect, that initial judgment looks easy in comparison to the decisions that followed.[3] In the 1954 decision, the Court ordered reargument on the question of what remedy should be devised to enforce the ruling, and the following year it established its approach: not to formulate a simple injunction, for instance, ordering race-blind neighborhood school districts, but to remand the cases to the district courts. The district courts, "guided by equitable principles," would then fashion decrees that recognized that "school authorities have the primary responsibility for elucidating, assessing, and solving [various local school] problems"; at the same time, those decrees would ensure "good faith implementation of the governing constitutional principles," that is, would ensure that students were admitted "to public schools on a racially nondiscriminatory basis with all deliberate speed."[4] As recalcitrance was widespread and voluntary compliance relatively rare, desegregation cases were brought in numerous jurisdictions and continued in several of the original districts. Rarely did appeal of the decrees reach the Supreme Court in the first decade after *Brown II*. The most prominent exceptions in those early years were *Cooper v. Aaron*, which involved desegregation in Little Rock, Arkansas,[5] and *Griffin v. Prince Edward County School Board*, in which the Court upheld a district court decree that forbade the closing of the public schools in a Virginia county and the use of state funds to make tuition grants to white pupils attending "private" schools established by a special "Foundation."[6]

In the 1968 case of *Green v. New Kent County School Board*, the Supreme Court effectively put an end to the first phase of court-ordered desegregation by declaring inadequate the "freedom of choice" plans that had proved to be a common expedient. With evident impatience, the Court announced that "racial identification of the system's schools" must be erased, since "the transition to a unitary, nonracial system of public education was and is the ultimate end to be brought about."[7] Apparently, the decision in *Green* signaled to the district courts a clearer or perhaps a more expansive standard than *Brown*, for they began fashioning complex remedial decrees for the reordering of segregated school districts, including the busing of schoolchildren to achieve a sort of racial balance in schools districtwide, a measure upheld by the Supreme Court in *Swann v. Charlotte-Mecklenburg Board of Education* in 1971.[8] In the years that followed, cases came to the Court from northern states as well, where state-sponsored racial discrimination, though not established by Jim Crow laws, was imputed to actions such as the drawing of school district lines or the placement of new schools with the evident aim of maintaining or promoting racial separation.[9] On the whole, the Court upheld the lower court decrees, granting wide equitable discretion as long as certain basic principles were observed:

> The nature of the desegregation remedy is to be determined by the nature and scope of the constitutional violation . . . [;] the decree must indeed be *remedial* in nature, that is, it must be designed as nearly as possible "to restore the victims of discriminatory conduct to the positions they would have occupied in the absence of such conduct" . . . [; and] the federal courts in devising a remedy must take into account the interests of state and local authorities in managing their own affairs, consistent with the Constitution.[10]

The most prominent exception to general acceptance of lower court discretion was the Court's refusal to approve remedies that crossed school district lines when no interdistrict violation had been shown—an exception of no small practical importance, as "white flight" to suburban jurisdictions left many central-city school districts with relatively little racial diversity to mix.[11]

The grant of certiorari in *Missouri v. Jenkins* at the time was limited to consideration of the district court's order for financing the remedial plan developed in conjunction with the local educational authority, the Kansas City, Missouri, School District (KCMSD), but some attention to the plan itself is necessary, at least for understanding the Court minority's concurrence. The suit began in 1977 as a complaint against the state of Missouri filed by a group of students together with the KCMSD, alleging that the state operated a segregated interdistrict school system. The district court realigned the parties to the case, treating the KCMSD as a defendant, and after several years of litigation, it held the KCMSD and the state liable for having run segregated schools within Kansas City, although no interdistrict violations were found. Together with the KCMSD, the district court devised an ambitious remedial decree that would eventually transform every high school, every middle school, and half the elementary schools in the city into "magnet schools" that would include such facilities as a planetarium, a twenty-five-acre farm, broadcast radio and television studios, an art gallery, and the like. According to the concurrence, the aim was "to make a magnet of the district as a whole. The hope was to draw new non-minority students from outside the district."[12] Needless to say, an immediate issue was how the cost of the desegregation decree was to be paid. After some correction of the original findings in the Eighth Circuit Court of Appeals, the district court held the state of Missouri and the KCMSD comparatively at fault for past violations in the proportion 75 percent and 25 percent, respectively, and "ordered them to share the cost of the desegregation remedy in that proportion."[13]

It soon became clear that the KCMSD could not raise the funds necessary to pay even its limited portion of the liability, given the projected cost of the remedy, and this precipitated the district court action at issue before the Supreme Court. The Missouri Constitution and several statutes limit the taxing authority of the KCMSD. Most to the point, local property taxes are limited to $1.25 per $100 of assessed valuation, unless a majority of the voters in the district approves a higher amount, up to $3.25 per $100; to raise property taxes above this amount requires two-thirds approval of district voters. In the first stages of devising the remedy, before the proportions of state and local funding had been settled, the district court ordered the KCMSD to submit a tax increase to the voters, which it did, but the voters defeated the plan. In 1987, after settling the proportion and expanding the remedy to the extent described above, the district court ordered that the state tax limitations be suspended and that the KCMSD property tax be raised from $2.05 to $4.00 per $100 assessed valuation through the 1991–1992 fiscal year. In support of this admittedly extraordinary remedy, the district court cited the Supreme Court's 1964 decision in *Griffin,* the case in which a county had closed its public schools to avoid integration, particularly this sentence: "the District Court may, if necessary to prevent further racial discrimination, require the Supervisors to exercise the power that is theirs to levy taxes to raise funds adequate to reopen, operate, and maintain without racial discrimination a public school system in Prince Edward County like that operated in other counties in Virginia."[14] The court of appeals in *Jenkins* let stand the district court's property tax order, struck down a simultaneous 1.5 percent surcharge on the state income tax it had ordered, and advised the district court that in the future it could take the less drastic step of merely enjoining operation of the state tax limits and then ordering the KCMSD to raise taxes to whatever level it needed.

The Supreme Court was faced only with the property tax issue and a technical matter of appellate procedure, the latter of which it settled unanimously. In an opinion by Justice White, the Supreme Court supported the court of appeals' determination of the proper course to be taken in the future but reversed that court's decision insofar as it allowed the original property tax order to stand. Citing not the Constitution but "principles of federal/state comity," as had the circuit court in its approved advice, Justice White held that a direct judicial taxation order was too severe a step, given the availability of less drastic means, namely, ordering the KCMSD to find sufficient tax revenues while suspending state laws that got in the way. He did reach the question of the constitutionality of the less drastic order, however, dismissing the Tenth Amendment claim of state sovereignty as sufficiently answered by the Fourteenth Amendment command of equal protection and asserting that "a court order directing a local government body to levy its own taxes is plainly a judicial act within the power of a federal court." In support of this last proposition, he cited *Griffin,* as had the district court, and he placed *Griffin* in "a long and venerable line of cases in which this Court held that federal courts could issue the writ of mandamus to compel local government bodies to levy taxes adequate to satisfy their debt obligations." To the objection that the earlier cases, all from the nineteenth century or the first decade of the twentieth, had involved mandamus to order the exercise of authority granted, not withheld, by state law, White noted that in one of the early cases a state statute limiting local taxation had indeed been set aside as an impairment of the obligation of contract, the statute in question having been passed after the bonds were issued. "It is therefore clear that a local government with taxing authority may be ordered to levy taxes in excess of the limit set by state statute where there is reason based in the Constitution for not observing the statutory limitation." Once, such reason was the Contract Clause; now it is the Equal Protection Clause. "To hold otherwise would fail to take account of the obligations of local government, under the Supremacy Clause, to fulfill the requirements that the Constitution imposes on them."[15]

Since the Supreme Court reversed that part of the circuit court's decision that allowed the district court's property tax order to stand, Justice Kennedy's separate opinion was technically a concurrence in the judgment, but he took sharp issue with White's affirming the circuit court's suggested modification for the future. For starters, Kennedy found consideration of the matter premature: advice for the future is, strictly speaking, dictum in a court opinion, and the importance of speaking strictly within the judicial role is the starting point of his argument. Moreover, as he explained later in his opinion, Kennedy thought that the whole consideration of the tax order was unnecessary, since the sweeping scope of the decree suggested that a less drastic, and thus more affordable, remedy could have been found. Still, because certiorari had been granted only on the taxation issue, not on the question of the appropriateness of the remedial program, and because the majority had spoken at length about the appropriate sort of taxation order for a district court to issue, the minority felt obliged to respond on that point.

The concurrence attempts to limit its argument to the facts of the case at hand, but it does establish, by reference to statements at the time of the Founding and to subsequent cases, many of recent vintage, that the principle of "no taxation without representation" makes clear that the power to tax has always been considered a legislative function. Moreover, by analyzing the structure of adjudication, in particular the identity of the parties before the court, Kennedy shows that due process itself forbids judicially imposed taxation, since taxpayers may be denied even a formal hearing before a judge considering a tax hike, not to mention the power to consent. In fact, the opinion is quite understated on the point of how deeply the principle of consent to taxation runs in the American political tradition, omitting mention of the role of consent to taxation in the rise of parliamentary authority in Great Britain, the centrality of disputes over taxation in the American Revolution, and the importance of tax disputes (for instance, over the tariff) in the course of American politics for the previous 200 years. White's majority opinion admits in passing that judicially imposed taxation is an extraordinary remedy, but he implicitly allows his reservations to be counterbalanced by the demands of equity in a desegregation case. Kennedy's response, by contrast, is categorical: "The power of taxation is one that the federal judiciary does not possess." To White's invocation of the Supremacy Clause, Kennedy responds, "the fundamental point [is] that the judiciary is not free to exercise all federal power; it may exercise only the judicial power."[16]

In reference to the particular case, Kennedy insists that the older, "long and venerable line of cases" is on the whole inapposite. Describing as vague the Court's broad interpretation of the cases as establishing a judicial power to order taxation "where there is a reason based in the Constitution," he anchors the municipal debt cases squarely within the province of the Contract Clause; he considers more to the point here several cases that the Court had treated as exceptions, cases in which earlier Courts had found themselves unable to grant relief because of the absence of officers against whom mandamus could issue.[17] According to Kennedy, because the power of taxation is an attribute of sovereignty, possessed by local government only as a consequence of a grant from the state, the KCMSD had no independent authority to tax that could be restored by the suspension of the state constitutional and statutory limits on taxation. Absent a challenge to the federal constitutionality of those limits—and in this case, there was no such challenge, and apparently no evidence on the record that the limits had been enacted to avoid desegregation—they are valid law, he would have held. The federal judiciary acts as much beyond its power in suppressing them and

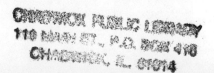

ordering a local authority to pass a tax (as the circuit court recommended) as it does in suppressing state limits and directly ordering a tax (as the district court did). As for the Court's use of *Griffin,* Kennedy describes the critical sentence as "dicta" and emphasizes that it did not expand the powers of the Prince Edward County supervisors; it only commanded that they exercise "the power *that is theirs* to levy taxes." Moreover, in the 1977 *Milliken* case, where the Court upheld a lower court's desegregation order that included (as does an implicitly affirmed portion of the order in *Jenkins*) a requirement that the state pay a portion of the cost, the Court had stressed that it "neither attempted to restructure local governmental entities nor to mandate a particular method or structure of state or local financing." Justice Kennedy would have the majority here maintain a similar restraint.[18]

The opinions in *Missouri v. Jenkins* reveal, I think, two quite different understandings of the scope and character of judicial authority, at least in the exercise of equity powers. For the majority, while local authority remains a value to weigh in the balance, federal courts must face no firm or formal limits in administering the remedies they find appropriate to repair constitutional violations. The means of power must be as extensive as the ends they seek, and although judicial prudence or discretion might counsel restraint when judges face insurmountable political opposition, there is nothing in the nature of judicial authority itself that binds it from reaching for the means it needs. The minority, by contrast, reads judicial power more strictly, not by counseling political prudence but by urging attention to the distinctive forms of the judicial task. This becomes apparent not only in the conclusion that taxation is ordinarily a legislative matter, with judicial involvement limited to situations in which mandamus is ordered to fulfill the obligation of debt, but also in Justice Kennedy's reasoning at every step. As even the preceding summary of his opinion illustrates, he repeatedly calls attention to the particularities of the case at hand and insists that the principles enunciated by the Court be limited to what are needed to resolve the instant case: first in criticizing the Court's description of the circuit court's "modification" of the original order by insisting on the distinction between holding and dictum, then in urging that attention not be focused on the abstract constitutional question of taxation apart from scrutiny of the extent of the remedy commanded. To the administrator with a policy mission, adequate means are implied in the end to be accomplished, but to the minority, even in the most administrative aspect of the judicial function (the fashioning of complex remedies under the principles of equity) and in what the Court has long treated as its most compelling constitutional policy (school desegregation), it remains imperative that federal courts limit themselves to specifically judicial modes of analysis and decree.

Rutan v. Republican Party of Illinois: Party Patronage

In contrast to *Jenkins,* where the basic constitutional question under the Fourteenth Amendment was long settled and the dispute concerned the remedial powers of the courts, *Rutan v. Republican Party of Illinois* involved a more straightforward claim of constitutional right against state practice, although the context of the case was seen by the Court as specific to modern governance, since it involved the state's relation to its employees in an age when an extensive proportion of the population is employed in some form or another by government.

In 1980, Governor Thompson of Illinois, a Republican, established a freeze on government hiring that affected about 60,000 state workers; exceptions could be granted only by the governor, and the Governor's Office of Personnel established a more or less routine process for granting exceptions, which apparently required Republican Party sponsorship of any application for new hiring, promotion, transfer, or recall after a layoff. The petitioners in *Rutan* included a rehabilitation counselor who had been repeatedly denied promotion; a road equipment operator denied a transfer closer to his home; a laid-off garage worker who had not been recalled when his colleagues were; a dietary manager, also laid off, recalled only to a lower-paying job; and a man whose application to be a state prison guard had repeatedly been denied. Each of the five alleged that he or she had been denied promotion, transfer, recall, or hire for not being a member of the Republican Party, not working for Republican campaigns, not voting in the Republican primary, or not securing the support of local Republican Party officials; the dietary manager who was rehired, albeit at a lower wage, had finally secured a Republican patron. The Supreme Court, in an opinion by Justice Brennan, ordered that relief be granted in every case: running a party patronage system for "low-level public employees" violates their First Amendment rights.[19]

There was no dispute between the majority and the dissenters, who spoke through Justice Scalia, as to the applicable precedents in the case, although the dissent was sweeping enough to challenge not only their extension but also their validity. The first precedent, *Elrod v. Burns,* had been decided in 1976 by a plurality opinion, also authored by Justice Brennan; the second, *Branti v. Finkel,* followed in 1980, this time with an opinion by Justice Stevens, who, while a circuit court judge, had authored an opinion in a case contemporary with *Elrod* that had been quoted in Brennan's *Elrod* opinion.[20] Both cases involved patronage dismissals, and both held them to be a violation of the First Amendment rights to free speech and free association, guaranteed against state infringement by incorporation in the Fourteenth Amendment. In neither instance were the ruling justices moved by the fact that the complaining employees had originally gotten their jobs through patronage, nor by their employers' claim that everyone understood the operation of the patronage system and thus had no reason to expect continued employment when a new party came to power. In both cases it was recognized that elected officials could legitimately appoint a few aides, although the criteria of allowability were unsettled: in *Elrod,* it was suggested that policy-making or confidential employees might be exempt; in *Branti,* Justice Stevens proposed more narrowly that "the question is whether the hiring authority can demonstrate that party affiliation is an appropriate requirement for the effective performance of the public office involved."[21] More precisely, since the only issue in both cases was dismissal, elected officials were allowed to dismiss only a few of their predecessors' aides, although the opinions' general disdain for patronage practice of any kind beyond an inner circle seemed poised for the extension sought in *Rutan.*

To speak of *Elrod* and *Branti* as the two clear precedents whose reach was at issue in *Rutan* is not, however, to suggest that they were themselves fashioned out of whole cloth. In both the earlier opinions, the justices drew on two lines of precedent whose intersection produced the admittedly novel result. First, and most ironically, both cases made appeal to the 1947 case *United Public Workers v. Mitchell* and to its recent reaffirmance, in which the Court upheld the constitutionality of the federal Hatch Act.[22] The irony, of course, is that the Hatch Act itself had placed strict limits on the political activities of federal workers of all stripes, in the name of ensuring a strictly professional, nonpartisan civil service. In the patronage cases, the same judicial test—weighing governmental interest against workers' First Amendment claims—yielded an apparently opposite ledger, as government interests in effectiveness, efficiency, loyalty, and the democratic process were ruled inadequate, but again with a nonpartisan (or perhaps a multipartisan) civil service as the end result.[23] The second line of cases concerned the dismissal of government employees, in particular teachers and professors, for political activities or membership not in the major parties but in smaller, unorthodox associations, such as the NAACP or the Communist Party.[24] Most useful to the Court in both *Elrod* and *Branti* were a couple of sentences from a 1972 case, *Perry v. Sindermann,* in which the Court held that nonrenewal of the contract of an untenured college professor could violate the First Amendment if the only grounds for nonrenewal were his political activities: "this Court has made clear that even though a person has no 'right' to a valuable governmental benefit and even though the government may deny him the benefit for any number of reasons, there are some reasons upon which the government may not rely. It may not deny a benefit to a person on a basis that infringes his constitutionally protected interests— especially his interest in freedom of speech."[25] Thus, applying the *Mitchell* balancing test with the new weighting of interests implied in the cases that rebuked teachers' dismissals in the name of the First Amendment, the Court—still in the context of dismissals, but now involving sheriff's deputies and bailiffs (*Elrod*) or assistant public defenders (*Branti*)—held that dismissal, even of patronage appointees, for no reason other than political affiliation was an unconstitutional coercive burden on the freedom of political activity and belief.

The logic in *Elrod* and *Branti*—especially the dismissive treatment of Justice Powell's dissenting argument in both cases that patronage often served the democratic process by maintaining active and thus politically accountable parties—made clear the likely result in *Rutan,* provided the same majority held.[26] Not surprisingly, then, Justice Brennan's *Rutan* opinion is brief and to the point. Since conditioning employment on the support of the dominant party places a burden on First Amendment rights to freedom of belief and association, the government must show that the patronage practices in question are the least restrictive means to promote its interests. This it clearly failed to do in every case: "A government's interest in securing effective employees can be met by discharging, demoting, or transferring staffmembers whose work is deficient." As for its interest in the democratic process, political scientists have shown that "political parties have already survived the substantial decline in patronage employment practices in this century," and besides, "patronage decidedly impairs the elective process by discouraging free political expression by public employees." To the claim that the burdens involved here were insubstantial compared with the dismissals at issue in the earlier cases, Brennan responds that they were sufficient to coerce belief: being denied a promotion, a transfer, rehiring after a layoff, or even a new job in "occupations where the government is a major (or the only) source of employment" can be enough to induce someone to modify his or her beliefs so that the burden is lifted.[27] Finding Brennan's opinion, which he joined, a little too curt to answer the challenge in the dissent, Justice Stevens, the *Branti* author, adds a concurring opinion, quoting at some length the opinion he wrote as a circuit court judge almost twenty years before and insisting that the putative interest in maintaining political parties is not a public interest: "The only systemic consideration permissible in these circumstances is not that of the controlling party, but that of the aggregate of burdened individuals."[28]

Justice Scalia's dissent in *Rutan* is ambitious in its range, and for good reason, since the swath of the Court's decision is potentially quite wide and its direction well established. His opening paragraph provides a sample of its flavor:

> Today the Court establishes the constitutional principle that party membership is not a permissible factor in the dispensation of government jobs, except those jobs for the performance of which party affiliation is an "appropriate requirement." . . . It is hard to say precisely (or even generally) what that exception means, but if there is any category of jobs for whose performance party affiliation is not an appropriate requirement, it is the job of being a judge, where partisanship is not only unneeded but positively undesirable. It is, however, rare that a federal administration of one party will appoint a judge from another party. And it has always been rare. See *Marbury v. Madison,* 1 Cranch 137 (1803). Thus, the new principle that the Court today announces will be enforced by a corps of judges (the Members of this Court included) who overwhelmingly owe their office to its violation. Something must be wrong here, and I suggest it is the Court.

The burden of his argument is not to insist that patronage practices themselves gain constitutional protection but to leave to political institutions "the choice between patronage and the merit principle—or, to be more realistic about it, the choice between the desirable mix of merit and patronage principles in widely varying federal, state, and local political contexts."[29] He begins with a brief explanation of how he would dispatch the case on his own legal principles; offers a long central section in which he applies a "balancing" test similar to what the Court employs, but with opposite results, not only in the instant case but also in *Elrod* and *Branti;* and concludes with a brief suggestion how, even if the two precedents must stand, their reach could be limited by noting the much lesser burden involved in not getting the job you want than in losing the one you have. Since this last point is but a last recourse, I concentrate my summary on the first two sections of his dissent.

Although he is joined in the first section only by Chief Justice Rehnquist and Justice Kennedy, Justice Scalia's opening recommendation reveals the sort of jurisprudence with which he would replace the numerous "balancing" tests common on the Court for about a generation and characteristic of the mentality of "bureaucratic rationalism" described by Professor Robert Nagel.[30] Scalia starts with the premise that the demands the Constitution makes on government in its capacity as employer are different from those it makes on government in its general lawmaking capacity, and he supports this claim with a number of authorities, including the Hatch Act cases. He then moves on to consider what the Constitution has to say about government employees in relation to patronage practices and finds the matter easy to resolve:

> The provisions of the Bill of Rights were designed to restrain transient majorities from impairing long-recognized political liberties. They did not create by implication novel individual rights overturning accepted political norms. Thus, when a practice not expressly prohibited by the text of the Bill of Rights bears the endorsement of a long tradition of open, widespread, and unchallenged use that dates back to the beginning of the Republic, we have no proper basis for striking it down.

American constitutionalism is not an abstract theory sublimated in an attempt to articulate a simplistic consistency from among a rich variety of principles, rules, laws, and practices. Rather, it is anchored, like the old common law from which it descends, in authoritative traditions: "such traditions are themselves the stuff out of which the Court's principles are to be formed. They are, in these uncertain areas, the very points of reference by which the legitimacy or illegitimacy of other practices are to be figured out."[31] Thus, the practice of patronage, shown by Justice Powell in his *Elrod* dissent to be as old as the Republic, cannot possibly fall before a provision of the Constitution made in full awareness of its existence and with no evident purpose to displace it.

Scalia adds an extra colleague, Justice O'Connor, when he writes within the framework of "balancing." First, he challenges the majority's assertion that restrictions on the speech of government employees must survive the same "strict scrutiny" test as restrictions on the citizenry at large. Citing a number of precedents, including the Hatch Act cases and even *Perry v. Sindermann,* he suggests that the Court's holdings are better explained, and often explicitly defended, in terms of a less exacting test, which he proposes to formulate as follows: "can the governmental advantages of this employment practice reasonably be deemed to outweigh its 'coercive' effects?"[32] Then he proceeds to explain how a plausible case could be made by responsible policy makers that the values of party patronage deserve ample weight on the balancing scales, drawing deftly on political science literature to refute the majority's "naive vision of politics and . . . inadequate appreciation of the systemic effects of patronage in promoting political stability and facilitating the social and political integration of previously powerless groups," and citing again Powell's similar account in his *Elrod* dissent. Scalia adds his own observations on political developments since that case was decided in 1976, including the continued decline in party loyalty, reflected in the chronic division of the political branches of the federal government between the parties and in the very high rate at which incumbents of whatever party have been returned to office in recent years. Against the arguable benefits of the patronage system, the alleged "coercion" is nothing but an "inducement":

> Corruption and inefficiency, rather than abridgement of liberty, have been the major criticisms leading to enactment of the civil-service laws—for the very good reason that the patronage system does not have as harsh an effect upon conscience, expression, and association as the Court suggests. . . . [I]t is the nature of the pragmatic, patronage-based, two-party system to build alliances and to suppress rather than foster ideological tests for participation in the division of political "spoils."[33]

The proper balance thus struck, Scalia turns the knife in what remains of *Elrod* and *Branti* by showing, with reference to more than a dozen lower court decisions seeking to apply their mandate, the essential lack of clarity in the criteria they recommend to distinguish between acceptable and unacceptable patronage positions: "Once we reject as the criterion a long political tradition showing that party-based employment is entirely permissible, yet are unwilling (as any reasonable person must be) to replace it with the principle that party-based employment is entirely impermissible, we have left the realm of law and entered the domain of political science, seeking to ascertain when and where the undoubted benefits of political hiring and firing are worth its undoubted costs."[34]

Whether or not we are prepared to meet that last task, it seems to me that political scientists will not deny the superior understanding of the role of political parties evinced in Scalia's dissent in comparison to the majority opinion, whatever we think of his own political affiliation off the bench or his other decisions on it. How this majority conception could develop, and what these different perspectives imply for our study of the American judiciary and of American constitutionalism more generally, are topics for reflection in my concluding remarks.

Constitutionalism and Judicial Politics Today

In an article in the *Harvard Law Review* titled "Constitutionalism after the New Deal," Professor Cass Sunstein of the University of Chicago describes the three principal tenets of the New Deal program of constitutional reform and how they have fared up to the present. Though unwritten, in the sense that it involved no constitutional amendments, the "constitutional revolution" sought by the New Deal had as its program, according to Sunstein, the modification of the rigid system of separation of powers, with greater concentration of political authority in the president and more responsibility for the actual tasks of governance in professional and independent administrators; the abolition of "common-law baselines" in the definition of rights and their replacement with personal rights to distributed government benefits; and the replacement of the old "dual federalism" with a cooperative model that would concentrate authority in the federal government to attack problems of increasingly national scope.[35] Sunstein's point is to assess the success of this program, especially in light of subsequent developments in administrative law and practice. Put simply, he finds room for revising the New Deal antipathy to the separation of powers by preserving the theory's dynamic of "checks and balances," without undue attachment to its specific forms; he regrets the persistence in law of common-law baselines and urges continued effort to transcend them; and, without compromising federal preeminence, he calls for renewed attention to local participation. But for our purposes here, it is worth remarking that the mentality he sketches—even, or perhaps especially, in its perfected form—seems to characterize the mindset of the Court majorities in both cases examined here. In both cases, a certain impatience with the old forms of separation of powers is implicit, at least with any aspect of those forms that might impede the rational administration of judicial policy; one sees this especially in the *Jenkins* case, of course, but it is also implicit in the *Rutan* majority's tacit assumption that the question of how to structure the executive branch is in no sense a "political question" for whose resolution judicial reason is not competent.[36] In dismissing Justice Scalia's concerns about unchallenged political traditions in

Rutan, the majority implicitly rejects what Sunstein calls common-law base-lines in favor of abstract personal rights—rights characterized in individualistic terms but better designed for use by the frustrated denizens of the impersonal modern world of complex organizations than by men and women situated in a world of common understandings and practiced in the art of compromise. Likewise, in *Jenkins,* the traditional right to consent to taxation is given short shrift in comparison to the modern project of developing a racially integrated system of public education. Finally, both cases involve the plenary exercise of federal judicial authority to restructure state or local institutions—in *Rutan,* with no concern expressed for residual state sovereignty, and in *Jenkins,* with a bow to federal-state comity but in fact with an alliance of federal judicial authority and a local governing body against state restrictions.

The modern rationalism characteristic of each phase of what Sunstein calls the "New Deal Reformation" is evident as well in the majority opinions in each case. I commented earlier in reference to *Jenkins* that its commands depict the attitude of an administrator faced with a policy to implement rather than any form of thought or action peculiar to the judiciary. One sees something of the same tendency in the majority's approach in *Rutan,* both in the balancing method itself, which is the emblem of administrative reason, and in the insistence on isolating the particular burdens and benefits of hiring practices while eschewing systemic considerations. Indeed, the typical standpoint in the modern exercise of judicial review—that of judges who pronounce on a constitutional question abstractly, as if the courts themselves were not constituted bodies but oracles of the supreme Constitution, and as if the cases brought before them were only vehicles for larger issues—is present in both cases: in *Jenkins,* where the Fourteenth Amendment is personified by the superintending judge, and in *Rutan,* where the justices ignore, as Scalia points out, the patronage element in their own appointment. For political scientists whose premise of research is that judges are policy makers, these last remarks will produce a sort of bafflement. My point is simply to suggest that that premise itself is part of the mentality at issue and thus is, in a way, invisible, or at least easily overlooked, from within.

The alternative approach suggested by the opinions of Justice Kennedy in *Jenkins* and Justice Scalia in *Rutan* is more in harmony with a common-law approach to constitutionalism. To describe this approach as an alternative theory of judging would be a mistake, as it is characterized in part by a skepticism toward theoretical syntheses, but likewise, it would be misleading to treat it as merely the ad hoc exercise of political prudence.[37] One would do better to characterize it as the attempt to maintain, in constitutional cases, the forms of reasoning and of judgment characteristic of the common-law judge. In our two cases here, this attitude appears most clearly in Justice Kennedy's constant attention to the particulars of the case at hand in *Jenkins*, his reluctance to speak abstractly beyond what the facts warrant, and his precise reading of established legal rules. In Justice Scalia's opinion, one sees the mind of the common law at work in his turn to tradition as an aid in interpreting statutes and as an authority in its own right, as well as in his tendency to read past precedents strictly, looking to the results to find the rule rather than to dicta to repeat a doctrine.

To say of a consciously revived common-law constitutionalism that it aims to undo the "constitutional revolution" of the 1930s and effect a return to the constitutionalized laissez-faire of the "nine old men" would also be a mistake, for two reasons. In the first place, there is a reluctance among judicial conservatives to reembark on the sort of judicial review practiced by the Court in the early part of the twentieth century—despite the urgings of some observers in the legal academy—because of a sense that the common law and the Constitution were stretched by those earlier judges beyond their proper bounds. It is not that they see in judicial restraint a command of intellectual abstinence, nor that they fail to recognize that there are real guarantees of certain forms of property in the Constitution; rather, they heed Holmes's adage and doubt that the Constitution means to enact any particular social or economic or even political theory. In the second place, and perhaps more importantly, we need to recognize the limits of the "constitutional revolution" itself. As even an ardent proponent like Sunstein admits, the forms and categories of common law in many respects survived the "revolution"; in fact, as Sunstein does not say, in some respects they were strengthened in its aftermath. I refer here not only to the law of property, as Sunstein does, but also to the many personal liberties connected to due process that had their undisputed origin in common law, even if they were at one point ignored by purported reformers and later expanded by libertarian activists almost beyond recognition. Moreover, though it might have become academic orthodoxy that judges should be viewed realistically as policy makers in robes, when a judge takes this view of himself or herself in the performance of the judicial function, he or she becomes a cynic, not a realist. Thus, it is not surprising that an older understanding of the integrity of judging persisted, at least among judges whose experience with the varied texture of the law left them skeptical of reformist theory or whose character made them reluctant to replace impartiality with a political program, however well meant.

I noted at the outset that the four justices who joined in both *Jenkins* and *Rutan* to oppose the Court majority were the four appointed or promoted by President Reagan. If what they seek is a revived common-law constitutionalism, is it then a political program in judicial dress, designed to further conservative causes? At one level, of course, any common aim that is controversial can be said to be political; in this way, one could certainly say that there was a political project implicit in Roosevelt's appointment of Supreme Court justices, since all were known to be friendly to the New Deal and thus unlikely to revive the recently abandoned doctrines that had thwarted the New Deal in its early years. But it is well known that Roosevelt's appointees, liberals all, were deeply and bitterly divided, even among themselves, before their tenures on the Court were complete. With the addition of Justice Thomas, the Reagan justices have formed a steady bloc in the related issue of state sovereign immunity, but the political implications are not so easy to characterize, because some states are governed by one party, some by the other, and occasionally a governor is elected by a third. Even in the cases discussed here, the political implications of judicial doctrines are not self-evident. This may be less true in the matter of school desegregation, where liberal and conservative positions are commonly recognizable, even if solutions are exasperatingly elusive. But in the matter of political patronage, what serves one party can as easily serve the other.[38] Constitutionalism, in other words, is not without its own sort of politics, but only by suspending the assumption that it coincides with partisan policy alternatives will that politics be visible, much less understood.

CHAPTER 8

Commerce, Property, and Police

The police power of the states was, for many years before 1937, the hinge on which much federal constitutional law turned. On the one side, the term *police power* referred to the power alluded to in the Tenth Amendment that was reserved to the states because it was not delegated to Congress. It was general, undefined, and unenumerated—or rather, its enumerations were not exclusive and varied from case to case—and it could even run concurrently with the powers of Congress, unless there was an unavoidable conflict between the exercise of the two. On the other side, a doctrine developed in the nineteenth century that gave constitutional protection to certain property rights against purported exercises of the police power, a doctrine that originated in the states and was then applied in federal courts after ratification of the Fourteenth Amendment. Precisely because the police power was premised, at least in part, on protecting people from others' harmful uses of their property, it could not be invoked to allow legislatures to interfere with legitimate property rights.[1] To switch metaphors, as a matter of federal constitutional law, the police power stood poised between the Commerce Clause and the Due Process Clause, the latter as the floor below it, the former as the ceiling above. It is no accident that both floor and ceiling collapsed within a few weeks of each other in 1937, nor that the contemporary Supreme Court is modestly rebuilding them both.

The question of the reach of the federal commerce power and the question of "constitutional limitations" on the power of government in the name of property rights—the questions surrounding the police power—were the central issues of American constitutional law in its first century and a half. Their displacement in the "constitutional revolution" of 1937 by a Court eager to avoid defining or limiting Congress's role in regulating the nation's economy—indeed, to endorse New Deal innovation in macroeconomic management—is the first main event in the orthodox liberal account of twentieth-century constitutionalism, and it prepared the way for the second main event, the Supreme Court's decision to take the lead in ending racial segregation. In recent years, however, scholarship has revisited that earlier jurisprudence, or at least its due process dimension, finding it more coherent than the Progressives and their liberal successors had supposed. When protecting "liberty of contract" under the Due Process Clause of the Fourteenth Amendment, the justices meant to stave off "class legislation" that gave special legal privileges to particular groups of citizens. This concern originated in the Jacksonians' opposition to state-granted special privileges, most evident in the controversy over the National Bank, and it led to a notion of equal entrepreneurial rights—progressive in its own time, if anachronistic later on.[2] Moreover, as has long been noted, in the period between the Civil War and 1935, the Court often voted to uphold state legislation against due process challenges and federal legislation against challenges based on a narrow reading of the Commerce Clause; to read the whole era as exemplified by the decisions of 1935 and 1936 is widely understood to be mistaken.[3] Indeed, a complex jurisprudence of the police and commerce powers developed in the nineteenth and early twentieth centuries, only to be discarded in 1937 and the years that followed when the Court, as it were, cut the Gordian knot.

No one doubts that the common law played a significant role in that earlier jurisprudence. Until 1891, this was entirely to be expected, since the Supreme Court justices spent a substantial part of their time sitting on federal circuit courts in the several states, hearing cases arising under their diversity jurisdiction but involving principally, and sometimes exclusively, state law.[4] Here, common law was always present, if only in the background to statutes, and the doctrine of federal or general common law established in *Swift v. Tyson*[5]—and not swept away until the jurisprudential revolution of the late 1930s—further ensured that questions of contract, tort, and all the various instrumentalities and consequences of interstate commerce were a constant part of the justices' business. Institutionally, it is probably no accident that the Court developed stricter limits on legislative power when the justices became a panel sitting exclusively in Washington, D.C. My concern here, however, is with the influence of common law and the common-law way of thinking on the classical, and then for sixty years discredited, jurisprudence of state police power in relation to property rights on the one hand and to the commerce power of the federal government on the other, as well as with the role of common law in the revived jurisprudence of property rights and federal power that has appeared in the last decade and a half. Nothing would surprise the "constitutional revolutionaries" more than the fact that, before the twentieth century was over, free-market economics would regain academic respectability and even dominance, would contribute to the collapse of international communism, and would be embraced—enthusiastically or grudgingly—by the two major parties. Nothing would surprise them less than that such a development would influence the constitutional jurisprudence of American courts.

Common Law, Property, and Police

The common law of property, which most landed property in the United States still depends on, in one way or another, is older than the writings of John Locke.[6] This is important to remember, since it is often wrongly assumed that the common law before 1937 was merely an instrument of capitalist development. To be sure, nineteenth-century common law incorporates Lockean insights as it facilitates a Lockean economy, but the ancient doctrines surrounding estates in land rest on a medieval, not a modern, frame of mind. Locke's contribution was to find the origin of property in human labor or, in contemporary terms, to see in human creativity the source of most wealth. Although Locke acknowledges the role of the positive rules of civil society in determining property once men have left what he calls the state of nature, property that originates in human labor has a claim under natural law, and that claim remains alive in society, since for Locke, the preservation of property is the end of government and the standard by which it can be held to account. The traditional way of thinking had been different: property consists of a distribution of things among households, made out of necessity for the sake of ensuring their proper care and use and of preventing the hostility sure to arise among people holding things in common. Christopher St. German, the sixteenth-century English common lawyer whose dialogue *Doctor and Student* was still treated as authoritative by the nineteenth-century American James Kent, described the common law of property as including the law of reason "secondary general," which forbids crimes against property such as trespass and theft, and the law of reason "secondary particular," based on the customs and statutes of England and woven together by judicial reason through a long line of cases into a reasonably coherent whole. The American understanding of property balanced the medieval view of property as distributed inheritance and the Lockean view of property as creative acquisition. The physical circumstances of the American continent gave Lockean acquisitiveness a certain impetus and gave Americans ready experience with the notion that the wealth of the whole develops through the privately rewarded efforts of individuals, but acquisition has little meaning if its fruits cannot be rendered secure.

The doctrine of the police power that developed in the nineteenth century can be found in germ in Blackstone, who masterfully assimilated Lockean insight to common-law tradition. It appears in the *Commentaries* not among the powers of Parliament, which are sovereign and comprehensive, but by implication in the catalogue of crimes against the public, specifically, "Of Offences against the Public Health, and the Public Police or Oeconomy."[7] Blackstone lists offenses as varied as bigamy, keeping disorderly inns, making fireworks, eavesdropping, and gaming, and he defines the whole category as follows:

> By the public police and oeconomy I mean the due regulation and domestic order of the kingdom: whereby the individuals of the state, like members of a well-governed family, are bound to conform their general behaviour to the rules of propriety, good neighbourhood, and good manners; and to be decent, industrious, and inoffensive in their respective stations. . . . Common nuisances are a species of offenses against the public order and oeconomical regimen of the state; being either the doing of a thing to the annoyance of the king's subjects, or the neglecting to do a thing which the common good requires.[8]

When coupled with laws protecting public health and linked to public justice, public peace, and public trade, discussed in the chapters immediately preceding, Blackstone's notion of public police already outlines a picture of a "well-regulated society" with ample authority to provide for the common good or, as William Novak called it in his book, "the people's welfare." Most of the laws at issue here are established by statute and so are not, strictly speaking, part of the common law, but it is clear that Blackstone finds nothing in them at odds with common law and plenty to endorse. At common law, the state could sue for public nuisances and individuals could sue for common nuisances, allowing not only satisfaction for harm done but also abatement of the nuisance itself.[9]

When, a century later, Thomas Cooley in his influential *Treatise on Constitutional Limitations* ventured a chapter on the police power, he offered a definition with clear Blackstonian overtones, though in a more individualistic key:

> The police of a State, in a comprehensive sense, embraces its system of internal regulation, by which it is sought not only to preserve the public order and to prevent offenses against the State, but also to establish for

the intercourse of citizen with citizen those rules of good manners and good neighborhood which are calculated to prevent a conflict of rights, and to insure to each the uninterrupted enjoyment of his own, so far as is reasonably consistent with a like enjoyment of rights by others.[10]

Still, one should not make too much of the collapse of common good into a calculation of what serves rights, for Cooley proceeds to quote at great length from Massachusetts Chief Justice Lemuel Shaw's decision in *Commonwealth v. Alger,* an 1851 case that nicely captures the crux of the relation of the police power and the common law. Shaw upheld a state law drawing a line in Boston harbor and forbidding docks to extend beyond it, despite the plaintiff's claim to own the land where the dock was built and his insistence that the dock did not obstruct navigation. Shaw recognized the claim to ownership after a review of Massachusetts law since colonial times, when by statute the legislature altered the boundary of ownership from the high-tide mark under common law to the low-tide mark. This explicitly saved the public rights to navigation and implicitly saved other rights of use (for example, fishing rights) that, under common law, would have been held by the king as a public trust and then passed to the state after independence. Nevertheless, Shaw asserted the power of the legislature to pass laws that more clearly define and protect common-law rights and duties:

Whenever there is a general right on the part of the public, and a general duty on the part of the land owner, or any other person, to respect that right, we think it competent for the legislature, by a specific enactment, to prescribe a precise, practical rule for declaring, establishing, and securing such right, and ensuring respect for it. . . . This principle of legislation is of great importance and extensive use, and lies at the foundation of most enactments of positive law, which define and punish *mala prohibita.* Things done may or may not be wrong in themselves, or necessarily injurious or punishable as such at common law; but laws are passed declaring them offenses, and making them punishable, because they tend to injurious consequences; but more especially for the sake of having a definite, known and authoritative rule which all can understand and obey.[11]

The police power, as expounded by the facts of the case, thus perfects the common law or adjusts it to the circumstances of a modern commercial society, but it begins from common-law rights and duties. This puts a gloss on the passage from the case that Cooley quotes:

We think it is a settled principle, growing out of the nature of well ordered civil society, that every holder of property, however absolute and unqualified may be his title, holds it under the implied liability that his use of it may be so regulated, that it shall not be injurious to the equal enjoyment of others having an equal right to the enjoyment of their property, nor injurious to the rights of the community. All property in this commonwealth, as well that in the interior as that bordering on tide waters, is derived directly or indirectly from the government, and held subject to those general regulations, which are necessary to the common good and general welfare. Rights of property, like all other social and conventional rights, are subject to such reasonable limitations in their enjoyment, as shall prevent them from being injurious, and to such reasonable restraints and regulations established by law, as the legislature, under the governing and controlling power vested in them by the constitution, may think necessary and expedient.[12]

Shaw goes on to distinguish this police power from the power of eminent domain, which entails compensation. The police power "is not an appropriation of the property to a public use, but the restraint of an injurious private use by the owner," he writes, admitting that the distinction is clearer in principle than in "the facts and circumstances of different cases." And he cites the common-law maxim, ubiquitous in early police-power cases, according to Novak, *sic utero tuo, ut alienum non laedas:* so use your own, as not to injure another's.

To this discussion of the police power as it emerged from common law must be added one note concerning the Americans' "peculiar institution." Common law was distinguished from its ancient and even medieval forebears in its attitude toward slavery: whereas they had admitted slavery on the same ground as property, as a necessity for civil life given human nature, it was the boast of the common lawyers that slavery was unknown at common law and that any slave setting foot on English soil was thereby freed. Whatever might have been said of England's serfdom or "villeinage," as it was called in the old common-law books, Sir Edward Coke already treated it as largely a thing of the past, and Sir William Murray, Blackstone's contemporary and friend, confirmed the rule of liberty just mentioned in *Somerset's Case* in 1772, a case well known to Americans. As a consequence, it became the American doctrine, announced in federal constitutional law by Justice Story in *Prigg v. Pennsylvania* but widely accepted before then, that since slavery was unknown at common law, it owed its existence and protection solely to written state statutes.[13] Insofar as the police power was sometimes said to encompass the whole legislative power of the states, it is hard not to wonder whether its enthusiasts may have had in mind its role in establishing the Black Codes. Even a friend of the common law such as Chief Justice Shaw could decide, just a couple years before *Commonwealth v. Alger,* that establishing and maintaining segregated schools for blacks in Boston was not an unreasonable exercise of the power granted to the Boston School Committee by the state legislature. And he reached this decision even though slavery had been declared void in the state some sixty years earlier as a violation of the same equality clause in the Massachusetts Constitution that was now deemed inadequate to override the right of a local authority, claiming reasonable necessity and expediency in executing its charge, to separate schoolchildren on account of their race.[14]

Constitutional Law and the Police Power: Commerce

The first thing to note about the police power in federal constitutional law is that although the power plays a central role in constitutional jurisprudence, from the point of view of the federal Constitution, it is unwritten. As mentioned earlier, it is alluded to in the Tenth Amendment, but the reference is declaratory, not defining. It is clear beyond argument that the legislative power of the states is not created or endowed by the Constitution; on the contrary, the states existed prior to the Constitution, and according to the orthodox understanding in the nineteenth century, the people of the states simply excepted out certain powers from the state governments and granted them to the federal government when that government was formed. Though alluded to in *Gibbons v. Ogden* as responsible for "that immense mass of legislation which controls everything within the territory of a State not surrendered to the General Government," the states' police power receives its first explicit mention in John Marshall's opinion in *Brown v. Maryland,* where it is acknowledged but is not thought to be a sufficient bar to federal commerce authority or an adequate excuse for a tax on imported goods. Although the states have the general power to tax property within their borders, Marshall strikes down a license tax on liquor importers, ruling that the sale of goods still in their "original package" remains a part of foreign commerce, explicitly authorized by federal statute, and thus the tax violates the constitutional prohibition on state import taxes. Settling the tax question by drawing a line between the federal commerce power and the state police power, Marshall frames one dimension of the police power in constitutional law from the start.[15]

Even in its mention in *Brown,* the author of the police power in federal law might be said to be Roger Taney, the lawyer for Maryland who defended the tax and Marshall's successor as chief justice. On the Court, Taney wasted no time asserting an important role for state legislative power (here, not explicitly called "police") in federal constitutional law in *Charles River Bridge v. Warren Bridge,* a case argued but not decided during Marshall's tenure. Over the vehement protest of Justice Story, who insisted that he was "stand[ing] upon the old law . . . seek[ing] for no new principles, but . . . apply[ing] such as are as old as the very rudiments of the common law," Taney held that a corporate charter granted by the Massachusetts legislature ought to be read strictly, as not to confer monopoly privileges without explicit terms, lest the constitutional prohibition on state impairment of contracts prevent the valid exercise of state legislative power:

> The object and end of all government is to promote the happiness and prosperity of the community by which it is established; and it can never be assumed, that the government intended to diminish its power of accomplishing the end for which it was created. And in a country like ours, free, active and enterprising, continually advancing in numbers and wealth, new channels of communication are daily found necessary, both for travel and trade, and are essential to the comfort, convenience and prosperity of the people. A state ought never to be presumed to surrender this power, because, like the taxing power, the whole community have an interest in preserving it undiminished.[16]

Though Taney makes no specific mention of the police power, the implication is clear, and in his opinion in the *License Cases* a few years later, he is explicit:

> What are the police powers of a State? They are nothing more or less than the powers of government inherent in every sovereignty to the extent of its dominions. And whether a State passes a quarantine law, or a law to punish offenses, or to establish courts of justice, or requiring certain instruments to be recorded, or to regulate commerce within its own limits, in every case it exercises the same powers; that is to say, the power of sovereignty, the power to govern men and things within the limits of its dominion.[17]

Of course, this is dictum, and although such sweeping pronouncements delight the historian with a point to prove, they are not law, at least in the traditional understanding. That distinction belongs to the precise holding in the case, and in the *License Cases,* Taney found that state law requiring a license to sell liquor at retail (that is, no longer in its original packaging) within a state was a valid exercise of the police power, not contradicted by a federal commercial law that permits the importation of liquor into the United States. The decision is a fractured one, with opinions given seriatim, but a few years later in *Cooley v. Board of Wardens,* the Court gathered a majority through Justice Curtis to uphold a broad understanding of the police power, allowing it to run concurrently with the commerce power of Congress, absent a direct conflict between statutes passed by Congress and those passed by a state.[18]

Constitutional Law and the Police Power: Property

Taney's opinion in the *License Cases* is cited in the alternative line of cases defining the police power, but this time in dissent. The critical case here is one from New York, *Wynehamer v. People,* decided in 1856 by a split vote in the state's highest court and argued seriatim in a complex series of opinions. The report of the case concludes with the judges' votes on several propositions, making clear its disposition: the New York State prohibition law is declared unconstitutional as to liquor already owned in the state, as a violation of the due process clause of the state constitution, and since the act does not distinguish between liquor already owned in the state and liquor that might be imported subsequent to the passage of the act, the whole statute must be declared unconstitutional, "although all the judges were of opinion that it would be competent for the legislature to pass such an act as the one under consideration (except as to some of the forms of proceeding to enforce it), provided such act should be plainly and distinctly prospective as to the property on which it should operate."[19] Critical to most of the opinions is the insistence that the right of property includes as a necessary incident the right to dispose of that property by sale. Most of the judges describe the legislative power in the broadest terms, its limitation by the court being possible only because of the explicit constitutional provision; but in defining what property means in that provision, they naturally turn to Blackstone and the common law.

Wynehamer is traditionally seen as the first "substantive due process" case, and since this is, or at least once was, the most discredited of constitutional doctrines, a word of caution is in order. Even today, people who should know better denounce substantive due process as a contradiction in terms, as if the distinction between it and the redundant "procedural due process" were not between terms devised precisely to discredit the one and promote the other. The phrase is never used by those who decide cases according to it, which is at least an indication that historical understanding needs to move beyond ideological labels.[20] Anchored in the common law, and seen by Coke and those who followed him as equivalent to the Magna Charta's famous "law of the land" clause, the constitutional command that no person "be deprived of life, liberty, or property, without due process of law" was, first and foremost, a guarantee of the right to one's day in court and to at least some part of the proceedings prescribed in common law. It is obvious, but bears noting, that government is not forbidden to deprive people of property, liberty, or life; a court can fine, imprison, and even sentence to death. But it cannot do these things without indictment, trial by jury, confrontation of the accused by witnesses, and the like; though disagreements have long persisted about precisely what the Constitution requires of a trial, all agree that it speaks to the issue. Can a legislature do by statute what a court cannot do without due process? That is how substantive due process cases appeared to the justices who decided them, and to them, the answer seemed obvious. The judges in *Wynehamer* thought that this was precisely what was being attempted: a man was declared a criminal for selling something that he legally owned under the laws of the state, without a showing in court that any wrong or nuisance resulted from his sale, and his property was confiscated by the state. In several of the companion cases, punishment was imposed without a jury trial—the judges' third complaint—and to their mind, this was just a further indication that the legislature had overlooked the protections of due process when it passed the prohibition act.

Due process limitation on attempted exercise of the police power makes its debut in federal constitutional law the following year in the case of *Dred Scott v. Sandford,* and the quick discrediting of that case probably accounts for the slowness of the doctrine's reemergence, despite its active development in state courts and the addition of a Due Process Clause directed against the states in the Fourteenth Amendment. In the first controversy reaching the Supreme Court concerning that amendment, the *Slaughter-House Cases* in 1873, Justice Miller dispatched the due process argument, along with the privileges and immunities claim. The power to establish a slaughterhouse monopoly in New Orleans was within the police power of the state of Louisiana, wrote Miller, quoting Kent and citing *Commonwealth v. Alger,* and there was no reason to think that an amendment everyone knows was designed to protect the freedmen was really meant to "constitute this court a perpetual censor upon all legislation of the States on the civil rights of their own citizens," to "radically change the whole theory of the relations of the State and Federal governments to each other and of both these governments to the people," or "to fetter and degrade the State governments by subjecting them to the control of Congress, in the exercise of powers heretofore universally conceded to them of the most ordinary and fundamental character."[21] Writing for the four dissenters, Justice Field dismissed the monopoly as being established "under the pretence of prescribing a police regulation," cited the *Case of Monopolies* reported by Coke to establish an ancient common-law privilege to practice a lawful trade as "the natural right of every Englishman," and called the "common law of England . . . the basis of the jurisprudence of the United States." With regard to the purpose of the amendment in relation to the freedmen, to Field, the protection of "the equality of right among citizens in the pursuit of the ordinary avocations of life" was precisely the alternative to chattel slavery.[22] In the next major case involving a Fourteenth Amendment due process challenge to state regulation, *Munn v. Illinois* (1877), the majority avoided framing the issue as the police power versus common-law rights by drawing to the former an ancient doctrine of common law that allowed regulation of businesses "affected with a public interest" and thus upholding state regulation of grain elevator rates. To Field's challenge in dissent that this doctrine applied in England specifically to ferries and wharves, not warehouses, and that the police power was defined by the likes of Shaw and Kent to support property rights, not override them, Chief Justice Morrison Waite replied:

A person has no property, no vested interest, in any rule of the common law. That is only one of the forms of municipal law, and is no more sacred than any other. Rights of property which have been created by the common law cannot be taken away without due process; but the law itself, as a rule of conduct, may be changed at the will, or even at the whim, of the legislature, unless prevented by constitutional limitations. Indeed, the great office of statutes is to remedy defects in the common law as they are developed, and to adapt it to the changes of time and circumstances.[23]

To the majority, common law helped frame the interpretation of the Fourteenth Amendment, but it did not lock in place a whole legal regime through the phrase "due process." To Justice Field, the amendment was indeed an adjustment of the American order to guarantee federal judicial protection of individual rights, but for the definition of these rights, he too looked not only to natural but also to common law, in fact assimilating the two in what he thought was their classic form.

Liberty of Contract and the Great (Non-)Dissenter

If the foundational cases concerning the police power at once show the influence of common law in its definition and suggest a tension between common law and its exercise, the subsequent cases bear out the complexity of the relation and the inadequacy of the usual Progressive analysis of the Court's turn-of-the-century jurisprudence. The Progressive argument is, in a nutshell, that a judiciary devoted to the protection of big capital squelched reform by limiting the federal commerce power in the name of the police power of the states and then, in turn, limiting the state police power by "substantive due process." Though this may have been the combined effect of several lines of decision, qualification is needed if one looks at the two most despised decisions of the era: *Lochner v. New York* (1905), which struck down a maximum-hours law for bakers, and *Hammer v. Dagenhart* (1918), which struck down the federal Child Labor Act as exceeding Congress's commerce power by attempting to regulate manufacture. Of the four justices on the Court in both cases, only Holmes votes in accord with the modern way of framing the issues, dissenting in both. Justice Day, author of the Court's opinion in *Hammer,* had joined Justice Harlan's *Lochner* dissent, and Chief Justice White voted with him both times. In the one case, they endorse the state police power against a due process challenge; in the other, they defend it against what they see to be federal interference. Justice McKenna, by contrast, voted with the majority in *Lochner* but joined Holmes's dissent in *Hammer,* perhaps, in the old Federalist spirit, linking secure property rights to federal oversight of a national market. There can be little doubt that had Chief Justice Fuller lived to hear *Hammer,* he would have voted with the majority; in *United States v. E. C. Knight,* he had authored the distinction between commerce and manufacturing on which the *Hammer* opinion was based. Nor is there any doubt that had Justice Harlan endured beyond his third of a century on the Court, the author of *Champion v. Ames* would have voted with the dissenters. But at the very least, it seems problematic to insist that the guiding spirit of the age was precisely the one position on the two leading cases that none of the four justices actually took.[24]

Even a general survey of the "laissez-faire" era in relation to the police power and the common law is beyond the scope of this chapter, but it is worth pausing to note the distinctive position of Justice John Marshall Harlan in relation to these developments. Today, Harlan is known as the "Great Dissenter," principally for his lone opinions in *The Civil Rights Cases* and *Plessy v. Ferguson,* respectively supporting the Civil Rights Act of 1875, which forbade race discrimination in places of public accommodation, and opposing state-mandated segregation. One might add his dissent in *Hurtado v. California,* in which he would have anticipated the twentieth-century "incorporation" of the Bill of Rights through the Fourteenth Amendment and applied the requirement of grand jury indictment in a murder case to the states as an essential element of common-law due process.[25] In the cases concerning the commerce and police powers, Harlan was occasionally a lone dissenter—for example, in *United States v. E. C. Knight Co.,* where he rejected using a distinction between commerce and manufacture to limit Congress's attempt to legislate against combinations (in the old phrase of Coke's) "in restraint of trade"—but he was often joined in dissent, and he wrote several important opinions of the Court. Probably the most notorious in later years is *Adair v. United States,* in which Harlan, writing for a majority of six, struck down a federal law that outlawed railroad contracts in which employees agreed not to join a union as a condition of employment and forbade railroad employers to discriminate against union members in hiring and to prevent others from hiring discharged union employees. Harlan accepted both the Due Process Clause and the Commerce Clause arguments against the act, insisting that in labor relations, "the employer and the employee have equality of right, and any legislation that disturbs that equality is an arbitrary interference with the liberty of contract which no government can legally justify in a free land," and holding that whether an employee joins a union is not a matter of interstate commerce.[26]

On the specific question of free labor contracts, Harlan was clearly, at least in his last years on the Court, within that Court's jurisprudential majority, but generally, the drift of his opinions favored the police power. One example is *Mugler v. Kansas,* sustaining that state's statutes prohibiting the manufacture and sale of intoxicating liquors against a Fourteenth Amendment due process challenge. Here, Harlan wrote for a unanimous or near-unanimous Court (Field alone dissented in one of the companion cases), describing the police power in familiar terms, citing Taney and Shaw, and, in a paraphrase of Field's opinion in *Barbier v. Connolly,* finding that the Fourteenth Amendment was not designed to undermine the police power but "forbade the arbitrary deprivation of life or liberty, and the arbitrary spoilation of property, and secured equal protection to all under like circumstances," something already established in the jurisprudence of many states with their own due process protections. Like Marshall in *McCulloch v. Maryland,* and with a quotation from *Marbury v. Madison,* Harlan qualified his strong statement of government power and judicial deference to account for legislative or lawyerly pretense: "If . . . a statute purporting to have been enacted to protect the public health, the public morals, or the public safety, has no real or substantial relation to those objects, or is a palpable invasion of rights secured by the fundamental law, it is the duty of the courts to so adjudge, and thereby give effect to the Constitution."[27] For all its notoriety, *Lochner v. New York* can be seen to turn on a judgment applying this established principle, at least once the liberty to contract was recognized as a fundamental right by a unanimous Court in *Allgeyer v. Louisiana.*[28] Harlan's *Lochner* dissent is not a dispute with the Court over jurisprudence, but a debate over whether the New York law was valid as a health regulation, which he thought it was, against a majority convinced that the health rationale was a pretense covering favoritism for the laboring class. In this, of course, it differs from Holmes's solo performance, charging the majority not with bad judgment but with bad faith.

Probably Harlan's most influential decision for a Court majority was *Champion v. Ames,* the most important case sustaining an exercise of the federal commerce power between *Brown v. Maryland* in 1827 and *NLRB v. Jones & Laughlin Steel* in 1937. Here, Harlan sustained Congress's power to forbid interstate commerce in lottery tickets: "If a State, when considering legislation for the suppression of lotteries within its own limits, may properly take into view the evils that inhere in the raising of money in that mode, why may not Congress, invested with the power to regulate commerce among the several States, provide that such commerce shall not be polluted by the carrying of lottery tickets from one State to another?" That Harlan assimilates Congress's commerce power in this regard to the states' police power is further evident in his raising and dismissing a due process objection prompted by the liberties expressed in *Allgeyer:* "But surely it will not be said to be a part of anyone's liberty, as recognized by the supreme law of the land, that he shall be allowed to introduce into commerce among the States an element that will be confessedly injurious to the public morals." To the objection that, under this doctrine, Congress might "arbitrarily exclude" any item it wishes from interstate commerce, Harlan replied that although it was not an issue in the case at hand, "the power of Congress to regulate commerce among the States, although plenary, cannot be deemed

arbitrary, since it is subject to such limitations or restrictions as are prescribed by the Constitution."[29] Used to sustain a host of Progressive legislation such as the Pure Food and Drug Act, the White Slave (Mann) Act, and
acts suppressing interstate commerce in pornography and illegal drugs,
Champion was the first case cited in Holmes's dissent in *Hammer v. Dagenhart*. Edward Levi, reviewing the development of commerce doctrine at
midcentury, suggests that the expansion of the federal commerce power in
the New Deal can be seen as an expansion of the principle of *Champion,*
with the concept of moral evil being allowed to develop over time. Harlan
himself had recognized that this was possible, acknowledging that the lottery, "although in general use and somewhat favored in both national and
state legislation in the early history of the country, has grown into disrepute
and has become offensive to the entire people of the Nation." Nor is it an
accident that *Champion* and the line of cases following from it were cited
when the Court upheld the modern Civil Rights Act of 1964 on commerce
grounds in *Heart of Atlanta Motel v. United States*.[30]

   Champion is not a case that invokes the common law, though it is not
hard to hear its echoes in Harlan's confident denunciation of moral evils and
his support for Congress's keeping the channels of commerce unpolluted.
In his famous dissents in the race cases, the link to the common law is much
less tenuous. In dismissing a Thirteenth Amendment claim, the Court in the
Civil Rights Cases insisted on a distinction between civil rights and social
rights, implying that the 1875 act sought to impose the latter when forbidding race discrimination in inns, conveyances, and theaters. At the same
time, the Court acknowledged Congress's power under the Thirteenth and
certainly the Fourteenth Amendment to legislate, as in 1866, to protect
"those fundamental rights which are the essence of civil liberty, namely the
same right to make and enforce contracts, to sue, be parties, give evidence,
and inherit, purchase, lease, sell and convey property, as is enjoyed by white
citizens." Harlan in dissent does not deny the state-action doctrine, but he
does dismiss the distinction between civil and social rights, citing *Munn v.
Illinois* to show that places and vehicles of public accommodation are, in
the doctrine of common law, matters of "quasi public employment," and he
reads the section 5 power of Congress broadly: judges alone can defend
against offending laws once they are passed, but the explicit grant of power
to Congress allows the federal government to be, as we would say today,
proactive.[31] A decade or so later in *Plessy,* facing an offensive state law of
the sort the 1875 statute meant to prevent, Harlan reiterates his common-
law argument that railroads are public highways; adds, with reference to

Blackstone, the definition of personal liberty as concerning especially loco-motion; and concludes, upon his famous supposition that the Civil War Amendments made the Constitution "color-blind," that "if a white man and a black man choose to occupy the same public conveyance on a public high-way, it is their right to do so, and no government, proceeding alone on grounds of race, can prevent it without infringing the personal liberty of each." The majority, of course, had rested segregation laws on the police power, citing Chief Justice Shaw in the 1849 Boston school case; this power was limited only by the requirement that its exercise be "reasonable," and "in determining the question of reasonableness [the legislature] is at liberty to act with reference to the established usages, customs and traditions of the people, and with a view to the promotion of their comfort, and the preser-vation of the public peace and good order."[32] Harlan rejects any such amor-phous reasonableness test as a claim by judges to second-guess legislative policy and, in the context of this case, as an excuse for not facing the con-sequences of the constitutional endorsement of use of the police power to enforce Jim Crow. The majority's reference to "usages, customs and tradi-tions" may sound like a bow to common law, but I think that Harlan would see his legal fiction of "color-blindness" as better grounded, both as a clear rule (and so more protective of liberty) and in the ancient tradition, for the old law of England did not include distinctions based on race.

The Laissez-Faire Court and Its Demise

Before the old jurisprudence of the police and commerce powers met its denouement, it underwent a subtle but important drift away from its com-mon-law foundation under the influence of the modern scientific frame of mind. In contrast to the subtle mix of perspectives represented on the Court in the first two decades of the twentieth century, in the 1920s and 1930s, both sides became more doctrinaire, and voting blocs hardened: on the one side, in support of laissez-faire; on the other, in support of a pragmatism that eschewed as formalistic the traditional distinctions that had animated com-mon law. The issue increasingly became framed as one involving perma-nence and adaptation in constitutional law, with one side urging natural law and positive text and the other urging pragmatic adjustment. Never is the op-position clearer than in the 1934 case *Home Building & Loan Ass'n v. Blais-dell,* where Chief Justice Hughes for the majority upheld as a valid exercise of the police power a Minnesota statute that suspended mortgage foreclo-sures for several years during the Great Depression against the claim that the act impaired the obligation of the mortgage contract, in violation of the Contract Clause. After reviewing the economic crisis at the time the Constitution was written and the subsequent law of contract and remedy, Hughes wrote:

> It is manifest from this review of our decisions that there has been a growing appreciation of public needs and of the necessity of finding ground for a rational compromise between individual rights and public welfare. The settlement and consequent contraction of the public domain, the pressure of a constantly increasing density of population, the interrelation of the activities of our people and the complexity of our economic interests, have inevitably led to an increased use of the organization of society in order to protect the very bases of individual opportunity. Where, in earlier days, it was thought that only the concerns of individuals or of classes were involved, and that those of the state itself were touched only remotely, it has later been found that the fundamental interests of the state are directly affected; and that the question is no longer merely that of one party to a contract as against another, but of the use of reasonable means to safeguard the economic structure upon which the good of all depends.[33]

Economic, social, and conceptual change now justify reading the Constitution in a way different from how it was written, influencing not only the interpretation of particular texts but also the understanding of what is truly fundamental: not God-given rights, but social organization and "economic structure." To Justice Sutherland in dissent, nothing could be plainer than the conflict between the Minnesota statute and the Contract Clause, unless it is that the Founders experienced economic crisis and wrote the Contract Clause to avert the kind of legislation such crises precipitate, on the conviction that such legislation exacerbates what it means to cure.[34]

Sutherland was not naive about the problem of legal change; on the contrary, a decade before *Blaisdell,* he wrote one of the most important opinions justifying it. In *Village of Euclid v. Ambler Realty,* the Court had before it the question of the constitutionality of local zoning ordinances, challenged on due process grounds, and Sutherland wrote to uphold the ordinance over the dissents (without opinion) of Justices Van Devanter, McReynolds, and Butler, whose voice a decade later he would become. The issue of zoning had been considered in many of the states, with mixed results, and Sutherland reviewed these decisions as well as the particular village ordinance before the Court. The "crux" of modern zoning, he found, is "the creation and maintenance of residential districts, from which business and trade of every sort, including hotels and apartment houses, are excluded"; the legal test is whether such exclusion "bears a rational relation to the health and safety of the community." This he readily showed. The occasion for his meditation on legal change is the question of how one moves jurisprudentially from the common law of nuisance to a detailed, comprehensive plan that, as it were, anticipates nuisance by restricting uses of property, thus inevitably altering its value. Sutherland is worth quoting at length, if only for comparison to Hughes a few years later:

> Regulations, the wisdom, necessity, and validity of which, as applied to existing conditions, are so apparent that they are now uniformly sustained, a century ago, or even half a century ago, probably would have been rejected as arbitrary and oppressive. Such regulations are sustained, under the complex conditions of our day, for reasons analogous to those which justify traffic regulations, which, before the advent of automobiles and rapid transit street railways, would have been condemned as fatally arbitrary and unreasonable. And in this there is no inconsistency, for, while the meaning of constitutional guaranties never varies, the scope of their application must expand or contract to meet the new and different conditions which are constantly coming within the field of their operation. In a changing world it is impossible that it should be otherwise. But although a degree of elasticity is thus imparted, not to the *meaning,* but to the *application* of constitutional principles, statutes and ordinances, which, after giving due weight to the new conditions, are found clearly not to conform to the Constitution, of course, must fall.[35]

For Hughes in *Blaisdell,* the change is conceptual; the meaning of the Constitution and its principles changes, or needs to change to stay relevant to a fundamentally altered world. For Sutherland, the basic structure of private property, common law of nuisance, and police power remains stable over time, even though the changing circumstances occasioned by technological and commercial development require that an emphasis on the police power sometimes overtake an emphasis on common law. Sutherland's position thus remains within the tradition of Waite and even Harlan, acknowledging that common law can be altered and improved; at the same time, the example of traffic, meant literally in relation to zoning, reminds the modern reader that improvements designed to enable us to live as we wish more easily often dictate new patterns to which we must then conform.

Sutherland's theoretical sophistication appears as well in his opinions sustaining challenges to statutes on due process grounds, especially in *Adkins v. Children's Hospital.* Here, Sutherland cites the Nineteenth Amendment and married women's property acts as reasons for abandoning the protective concern for women that allowed the *Lochner* Court to sustain maximum-hours legislation for women even as it forbade such legislation for men. He develops the logic of liberty of contract in the matter of a legally mandated minimum wage, finding the statute vague in the standard it furnished the board responsible for setting the minimum wage, and finding the board arbitrary and inconsistent in the distinctions it mandated among employees. Sutherland cannot be charged with being enamored of a principle of formal contractual equality without regard for the factual inequality of contractual negotiations; on the contrary, he remembers the plight of the businessman, writing, "The feature of this statute which, perhaps more than any other, puts upon it the stamp of invalidity is that it exacts from the employer an arbitrary payment for a purpose and upon a basis having no causal connection with his business, or the contract or the work the employee engages to do." His argument has recently been characterized as having a natural-law basis, and that is probably fair; he takes seriously the equal rights of the contracting parties and the limited nature of any contract of employment.[36] There is nothing in the opinion that assumes the old protective stance of the common law, which was often paternalistic even as it privileged liberty of contract. That Sutherland is stepping into new territory is indicated by the fact that Chief Justice Taft, a staunch defender of property rights, dissents; what is more, he adopts a Holmes-like charge against the majority, quietly suggesting that they are driven by economic views, not constitutional ones. Whether or not the charge was fair when leveled by Holmes at the *Lochner* Court, it surely seems that Sutherland was adept at thinking like a laissez-faire economist, whose scientific rationalism had taken the place of the practical reason of the common-law judge.

But economics can be played in different keys, and Hughes finds a different one, more in accord with the economic thinking behind the New Deal. To sustain the statutes at issue in *West Coast Hotel v. Parrish* and *NLRB v. Jones & Laughlin Steel,* he simply realigns the precedents in common-law fashion without altering the principles, adjusting only the rules. In *West Coast Hotel,* the decision that signaled the storied "switch in time that saved nine" by upholding Washington's state minimum wage act, Hughes explicitly overrules *Adkins*, stating the traditional principle that liberty is qualified by protection of "the health, safety, morals, and welfare of the people"; quoting Taft's *Adkins* dissent; and claiming that *Adkins* was out of line with the other precedents, most of which sustained statutes like the one at issue here, which supported regulations protecting women and children. At the end of his opinion, however, he adds, as in *Blaisdell,* a discussion of the depression and the consequences for society of "the denial of a living wage." This "casts a direct burden for their support upon the community," and "the community is not bound to provide what is in effect a subsidy for unconscionable employers."[37]

In *Jones & Laughlin,* Hughes's modernizing is more explicit. He rejects the government's argument that the regulation of industrial labor can be assimilated into the "stream of commerce" line of cases, insisting instead on a judgment about the "close and intimate effect" of labor unrest on interstate commerce. Federal guarantee of the right to organize labor unions is designed to ensure industrial peace, and courts cannot be "asked to shut our eyes to the plainest facts of our national life and to deal with the question of direct and indirect effects in an intellectual vacuum."[38] If the underlying argument in the decision is that "employees have as clear a right to organize and select their representatives for lawful purposes as [an employer] has to organize its business and select its own officers and agents," Hughes does not work out the implications for liberty of contract, perhaps because it would raise the issue of the closed shop; nor does he explicitly overturn *Adair v. United States,* even though it is impossible to see how that decision can stand after *Jones & Laughlin.* As Sutherland had moved away from the array of common-law privileges and police protections in formulating the free-market logic of *Adkins,* so Hughes adopts what he understands to be new and accepted social propositions—the basic tenets of Progressivism— in the place of the old common law. This is Holmes's redefinition of common law as social experience, now as self-conscious judicial mandate, not analysis of inevitable and unconscious effect. That Hughes proceeds to revolutionize judicial doctrine while claiming to follow the weight of precedent only shows him to be adept at what Holmes considered the art of the common-law judge: making new law interstitially, in the light of changing (and judicially determined) social ideals. After *West Coast Hotel,* the liberty of contract is never used again by the Supreme Court to strike a statute, and by *United States v. Darby Lumber* and *Wickard v. Filburn,* the old jurisprudence that sought to limit the reach of congressional power under

the Commerce Clause in the name of the police power of the states seemed
entirely dead.[39]

The Return of the Old Regime?

By explicating his decision in *NLRB v. Jones & Laughlin Steel Corp.* in traditional terms while adjusting their meaning, Chief Justice Hughes naturally paid verbal homage to the old regime: "Undoubtedly the scope of [the
interstate commerce] power must be considered in the light of our dual system of government and may not be extended so as to embrace effects upon
interstate commerce so indirect and remote that to embrace them, in view
of our complex society, would effectually obliterate the distinction between
what is national and what is local and create a completely centralized government."[40] Though there is no similar nod in Justice Jackson's opinion in
Wickard, the passage is quoted in Chief Justice Rehnquist's opinion in
United States v. Lopez in 1995, the first case since the "constitutional revolution" to strike down an act of Congress for exceeding the reach of the
commerce power, even without infringing on any specific constitutional limitation. At issue in *Lopez* was the constitutionality of the Gun Free School
Zones Act of 1990, which made it a federal crime to possess a firearm in or
around a school. In his dissent in this case and in the 2000 case of *United
States v. Morrison,* in which the Court struck part of the Violence against
Women Act of 1994 as beyond the federal commerce power, Justice Breyer
has no trouble finding some connection between the matter complained of—
guns in schools in *Lopez,* rape and sexual assault in *Morrison*—and economic activity, since both might be seen to cause economic loss by relatively
straightforward cost-benefit analysis, but this is not what Rehnquist has in
mind. Any human activity can be assigned some hypothetical monetary
value in modern economic analysis, which means that any activity would
be subject to regulation if analysis could be developed to show a "substantial effect." Rehnquist claims to be following a "substantial effects" test, and
thus *Jones & Laughlin,* but he is not really interested in measuring effect.
Instead, he sees *Lopez* and *Morrison* as involving statutes that would "con-
vert congressional authority under the Commerce Clause to a general [fed-
eral] police power of the sort retained by the states." He quotes Hughes's
statement in *Jones & Laughlin* that the question of how direct the effect of
an activity on interstate commerce must be to enable congressional action
"is necessarily one of degree," but only to show that line-drawing is difficult.
The Court majority in *Lopez,* whatever their protests, would rather require a

categorical inquiry to determine "whether an intrastate activity is commercial or noncommercial."[41] This is not an attempt to revive the distinction between intrastate production and interstate commerce; Congress can apparently draw that line as it chooses. But it is a revival of making categorical distinctions that develop the enumerated kinds of the Constitution—and reflect the various kinds that permeate the common law—rather than conceding to the homogenization of human activity on which economic analysis depends.

If *Lopez* and *Morrison* indicate the Court's willingness to preserve the states' police power from federal aggrandizement, another line of cases arising under the Takings Clause circumscribes that police power in the name of property rights. As we have seen, the old common-law principle of eminent domain—and the American insistence that takings be compensated and restricted to public uses—was paired with and distinguished from due process protection of property. Now, in placing the emphasis on what constitutes a "taking" rather than on what compensation is just or what use is public, the clause can be conceptualized to do the work once given to due process. Curiously, the founding dictum in this line of cases is from Holmes in a 1922 case, *Pennsylvania Coal Co. v. Mahon:* "The general rule at least is that while property may be regulated to a certain extent, if the regulation goes too far it will be recognized as a taking."[42] This, of course, is no rule at all but a characteristically Holmesian replacement of kind with degree, of rule with formula, and an invitation to judicial policy making. Although Holmes is always quoted in the recent cases, the decisions hardly begin to reach the full extent of the principle, which, if taken literally, would have judges second-guessing every act of legislation, perhaps with a cost-benefit analyst on staff. Instead, the decisions are carefully circumscribed. First, they are restricted to regulation of real property. Second, despite the language of degree, the Court has thus far ordered compensation only for a taking that "denies all economically beneficial or productive use of land." Third, the Court has measured the legitimacy of the regulatory taking against the "restrictions [that] background principles of the State's law of property and nuisance already place upon land ownership." In his opinion in *Lucas v. South Carolina Coastal Council,* the principal case in this line, Justice Scalia eschews the old common-law formulation of the police power as competent to regulate "noxious use," on the grounds that "the distinction between regulation that 'prevents harmful use' and that which 'confers benefits' is difficult to discern on an objective, value-free basis," since "the distinction between 'harm-preventing' and 'benefit-conferring' is often in the eye of the beholder."[43] The common law of nuisance remains or returns as the touchstone of legitimacy in land-use regulation, however, as in Justice Sutherland's opinion upholding zoning itself in *Village of Euclid v. Ambler Realty.*

Even in the field where it has seemed most discredited—as an alternative to the modern regulatory state—the common law has proved remarkably resilient, providing a counterpoint to both laissez-faire and state-directed models of economic development, and has been an anchor of tradition against the engine of economic change. In the field of labor relations, where old common-law privileges of practicing a common occupation and freely contracting for the sale of one's labor no longer have constitutional standing, the individualistic bias of the common law runs deep in the culture, to the despair of generations of labor organizers and to the delight of modern advocates of economic restructuring away from a corporatist and toward a market model. Whether the police power is to be understood as sovereign, or whether it is to be understood as defined by the end implicit in the common-law maxim that one should use one's own so as not to harm another's, remains an active question. The new Takings Clause cases almost all involve modern environmental regulation, which, unlike early-twentieth-century zoning, is not oriented toward regulation in the name of human uses; in its more radical moments, it introduces a concern for the nonhuman that is incompatible with or at least sharply restrictive of the very idea of human ownership of things that are not man-made. Still, if modern or postmodern economies are more purely Lockean—where human creativity or "intellectual property" rather than the ownership of land increasingly becomes the paradigm of property claims—old nature survives in the "virtual" world. The old constitutional law of property rights, federal power over interstate commerce, and reserved police powers in the states struck a balance between tradition and invention, between ordered enjoyment and modern development, even if it allowed itself eventually to be subordinated to a too-rigid version of first laissez-faire and then Progressive economics. Whether the new jurisprudence limiting federal police and state environmentalism will restore a balance of private right and public good remains to be seen.

CHAPTER 9

Common Law, Constitution, and World Order

Persistent Precedents and Old Revolutions

Even as commentators make much of the advent of a "conservative" Supreme Court, now that a majority of the justices have been appointed by Republican presidents, the decisions of the "constitutional revolution" of 1937 seem sure to remain largely intact. Whatever the fate of certain doctrines introduced in the Warren and early Burger eras, the justices have been careful not to undo the critical precedents of 1937 and 1938, and even those—such as the advocates of a jurisprudence of original intention—who challenge modern conceptions of the judicial function typically make their appeal to such postrevolutionaries as Justices Frankfurter and Black. For example, the aborted attempt in *National League of Cities v. Usery* by then-Justice Rehnquist to revive constitutional status for limitations on the federal government assumed the form of modern Bill of Rights adjudication, reading the Tenth Amendment as the Court had come to read the First and Fifth.[1] Likewise, proposals from the professoriat to restore constitutional protection to property rights are equally or indeed principally directed against the states as well as against the nation, and the property they mean to secure is defined in the language of modern economics rather than acknowledged in immemorial inheritance.[2] In short, despite some success for the conservative challenge to the economic and social policies of the New Deal and its successors, the constitutional transformation of the age of Roosevelt has not been reversed: Americans, or at least the intelligentsia, continue to make federal politics the primary focus of their attention, and we continue to assume that federal authority can reach as far as we choose.

If there are no effective voices calling for a reversal of the "constitutional revolution," several precedents from the prerevolutionary Court have persisted in full force with scant modification; indeed, these cases are the only pre-1937 cases regularly anthologized in constitutional law casebooks outside of the leading decisions of Chief Justice John Marshall, cases important for having been overturned, several cases anticipating the "revolution," and a few oddities in the area of civil rights whose particular doctrines still stand but whose overall thrust has been reversed. I have in mind as persistent precedents the cases of *Missouri v. Holland* (1920) and *United States v. Curtiss-Wright Export Corporation* (1936). Both cases have to do with foreign relations—in fact, they constitute the critical precedents behind the modern Court's reluctance to examine matters relating to foreign affairs—and between them, they cover the question of foreign affairs in relation to federalism and to the separation of powers. *Missouri v. Holland,* authored by Holmes, can perhaps be assimilated among cases intimating what was to come. Holmes allowed the federal treaty power to support an act that was otherwise found unconstitutional as a violation of the states' sovereign ownership of migratory birds, including in his rationale that the Tenth Amendment must be read "in the light of our whole experience and not merely in that of what was said a hundred years ago."[3] But *Curtiss-Wright,* penned at the height of the constitutional crisis by Justice Sutherland, the intellectual leader of the bloc that chastised the New Deal, is not so easily explained by modern categories. A brief look at the case will help introduce my final theme.

At issue in *Curtiss-Wright* was the constitutionality of a criminal prosecution of dealers who had sold arms to Bolivia during its war with Paraguay over the Chaco. In 1934, a joint resolution of Congress authorized the president to prohibit by proclamation arms sales to the countries engaged in this conflict upon his finding, after consultation with other American governments, that such a prohibition would contribute to peace. President Roosevelt issued a proclamation the same day, revoking the prohibition eighteen months later by further proclamation. The defendants complained, among other things, that the resolution was an unconstitutional delegation of legislative authority, drawing from several contemporary cases in which statutes had fallen for excessive delegation of authority by Congress. Sutherland's strategy was to emphasize "the differences between the powers of the federal government in respect of foreign or external affairs and those in respect of domestic or internal affairs."[4] Widely noted is his finding that the Constitution gives responsibility for the former chiefly to the president, including his reference to "the very delicate, plenary and exclusive power of the President as the sole organ of the federal government in the field of international relations."[5] Less often mentioned is his view that "the federal power over external affairs [is] in origin and essential character different from that over internal affairs." Whereas the list of enumerated powers in the Constitution for the most part transfers from the "general mass of legislative powers then possessed by the states such portions as it was thought desirable to vest in the federal government," power over external relations never belonged to the states in the first place, having at the time of the Revolution passed directly from the British crown to the U.S. Congress. Nor, Sutherland argues, do the framers of constitutions have much discretion in the matter:

> Rulers come and go; governments end and forms of government change; but sovereignty survives. A political society cannot endure without a supreme will somewhere. Sovereignty is never held in suspense. . . . It results that the investment of the federal government with the powers of external sovereignty did not depend upon the affirmative grants of the Constitution. The powers to declare and wage war, to conclude peace, to make treaties, to maintain diplomatic relations with other sovereignties, if they had never been mentioned in the Constitution, would have vested in the federal government as necessary concomitants of nationality.

After citing a number of cases to illustrate his point, Sutherland reiterates the conclusion just quoted, adding: "This the court recognized, and in each of the cases cited found the warrant for its conclusions not in the provisions of the Constitution, but in the law of nations."[6] Just as Holmes in *Missouri v. Holland* had permitted the treaty power a range not circumscribed by particular constitutional provision, so here, with more specific reference to the law of nations, Sutherland finds the constitutive basis of federal power over foreign affairs in a source besides the written text.

In the half century from the decision in *United States v. Curtiss-Wright* to the end of the Cold War, laws such as the one upheld in that case became a staple of American foreign policy, and foreign affairs themselves came to dominate American politics with unprecedented frequency. Although Sutherland's reference to the law of nations was unlikely to be repeated in cases in the interim, his language of sovereign power was not without attractiveness to those who scorned his views of domestic law. The genius of the New Deal and its accompanying "constitutional revolution" was to establish apparently once and for all the sovereignty of federal power in the United States. It certainly seems to have cemented in constitutional law the sovereignty theorists' view of law as the sovereign's command: even the original intentionalists, with their emphasis on purpose and text, take this for granted, though they stress the role of the sovereign people, not a sovereign government, much less a sovereign court acting in the name of sovereign selves. In the rest of this chapter, I explore an alternative understanding of constitutionalism in relation to external affairs, and I do so for two reasons, one historical, one contemporary. Historically speaking, the sovereignty theorists' account of American constitutionalism is, although now regnant, profoundly at odds with the original understanding, which is at least as indebted to the traditions of common law as to those of modern political theory. And today, with the collapse of almost all the totalitarian powers whose states exaggerated and, in the process, helped discredit modern theories of sovereignty, we might do well, in the construction of a new world order, to look for models or even wisdom in accounts of world order before the totalitarian age.

Kent's *Commentaries* and Common Law

To exemplify what I think is the classical account of these things in American constitutional history, I direct attention to the *Commentaries on American Law* by James Kent. Kent was born in 1763 in New York, was educated at Yale during the Revolution, and returned to read law and then to practice in Poughkeepsie, where he attended as a spectator the New York ratification convention in 1788 and later got involved in Federalist politics. After moving his practice to New York City, his reputation for learning and his Federalist connections got him appointed as the first professor of law at Columbia College, but after a successful first year of lectures (less successful in published form), attendance declined, and he submitted his resignation and returned to practice. Beginning in 1797, he held a series of judicial offices in his native state: recorder of the City of New York, judge of the Supreme Court, chief justice of the Supreme Court, and chancellor (the last two entitling him to a seat on the Council of Revision). In 1823, he was forced into judicial retirement on account of his age by a provision of the democratized state constitution adopted (over his efforts as a delegate) in 1821. He eventually returned to the city from Albany, resumed his professorship at Columbia, and resigned again before long, but this time he published an expanded version of his lectures, to great national acclaim, as *Commentaries on American Law,* whose four volumes appeared successively in 1826, 1827, 1828, and 1830. In 1840, at age seventy-seven, he published its fourth edition, remaining active in literary pursuits until his death in 1847.[7]

Kent's *Commentaries* share basic principles and attitudes with the now better-known jurisprudence of his younger contemporary, Justice Joseph Story: that the study of law is a science, but its treatises are propaedeutic,

not encyclopedic; that its precepts are in harmony with natural law, especially as this is reiterated in more certain form by Christianity; that common law is a developing science, especially in the field of commercial law;
and that the Constitution provides the basic principles of American government. Like Blackstone, Kent intended his work as a general but comprehensive introduction to the law, though American rather than English,
and his literate tone of mature authority is not found wanting beside the
famous style of his English predecessor. In the first volume, second part, he
examines the Constitution, focusing on the basic outlines of American government, with particular attention to the circumstances of its formation and
to the special character of the judicial power and federal jurisdiction; he then
proceeds to discuss "the various sources of the municipal law of the several
states," with lectures on statute law, reports of decisions, "the principal publications of the common law," and the civil law. The remaining three volumes are devoted to the law concerning the rights of persons (including
corporations), personal property, and real property, including ample attention
to commercial practice. It is with regard to the last that Kent's distinctive
contribution is usually recognized, since, generalizing from the developing
commercial law of New York, he made available in readily usable form and
with Blackstonian authority a uniform law for the burgeoning commerce of
a developing continent.

In the discussion of the federal Constitution, as well as in his general
remarks on state law, it becomes clear that for Kent, the fabric of American
jurisprudence is provided by common law. He recognizes, of course, the
partial character of the common law's transplantation to the New World. In
addition, the federal courts had determined that they lacked jurisdiction over
common-law crimes, federal criminal law thus being limited to acts deemed
crime by statute. States that declared the common law adopted in their jurisdictions almost always included some qualifying statement, restricting the
adoption to so much of the common law as was deemed consistent with their
institutions and was applicable in the colonies at the moment of separation.
Still, these boundaries notwithstanding, the adoption of common law in
America was to Kent sufficient to include the larger principles of common-
law reasoning and judicial practice, whatever the quibbling over details.
Federal courts may not judge common-law crimes in the absence of a statute, Kent acknowledges, but once a statute has declared criminal behavior,
particular points of definition and criminal process not explicitly detailed
are to be supplied with reference to common-law proceeding. In civil matters in federal courts, he argues, common law indeed applies. That the judi-

cial power established by the Constitution must be understood to be a common-law judiciary Kent takes almost as a matter of course: "though the common law cannot be the foundation of a jurisdiction, not given by the constitution or laws, that jurisdiction, when given, attaches, and is to be exercised according to the rules of common law"; alternatively,

> Though the judiciary power of the United States cannot take cognizance of offenses at common law, unless they have jurisdiction over the person or the subject matter, given them by the constitution or laws made in pursuance of it; yet, when the jurisdiction is once granted, the common law, under the correction of the constitution and statute law of the United States, would seem a necessary and safe guide, in all cases, civil and criminal, arising under the exercise of that jurisdiction, and not specially provided for by statute. Without such a guide, the courts would be left with a dangerous discretion, and to roam at large in the trackless field of their own imaginations.[8]

What, then, is common law in Kent's telling? True to the spirit of written constitutionalism, Kent begins his discussion of law with statutes and constitutions, then turns to consider common law. It "includes those principles, usages, and rules of action, applicable to the government and security of person and property, which do not rest for their authority upon any express and positive declaration of the will of the legislature." In contrast to Blackstone, who stresses the immemorial character of common-law rules, Kent draws attention to their rationality: "A great proportion of the rules and maxims which constitute the immense code of the common law grew into use by gradual adoption, and received, from time to time, the sanction of the courts of justice, without any legislative act or interference." Kent's guarded optimism at the achievements of modern understanding is suggested by these words, but he anchors his definition with a lengthy quotation from the classical seventeenth-century common lawyer Sir Matthew Hale, whose thoughts deserve the attention of "those bold projectors, who can think of striking off a perfect code of law at a single essay": "the common law of England is 'not the product of the wisdom of some one man, or society of men, in any one age; but of the wisdom, counsel, experience, and observation, of many ages of wise and observing men.'"[9] In the ensuing review over several volumes of state law, the common law figures widely, but always, of course, with attention to constitutional and statutory developments in the several states. His most forceful assertion of the general importance of common law, however, comes in the context of his discussion of federal jurisdiction:

> In this view of the subject, the common law may be cultivated as part of the jurisprudence of the United States. In its improved condition in England, and especially in its improved and varied condition in this country, under the benign influence of an expanded commerce, of enlightened justice, of republican principles, and of sound philosophy, the common law has become a code of matured ethics, and enlarged civil wisdom, admirably adapted to promote and secure the freedom and happiness of social life. It has proved to be a system replete with vigorous and healthy principles, eminently conducive to the growth of civil liberty; and it is in no instance disgraced by such a slavish political maxim as that with which the Institutes of Justinian are introduced. It is the common jurisprudence of the people of the United States, and was brought with them as colonists from England, and established here, *so far* as it was adapted to our institutions and circumstances. It was claimed by the congress of the United Colonies, in 1774, as a branch of those "indubitable rights and liberties to which the respective colonies are entitled." It fills up every interstice, and occupies every wide space which the statute law cannot occupy. Its principles may be compared to the influence of the liberal arts and sciences.[10]

The common law in America, to Kent, does not constitute our government or squelch legislative will, but it binds the positive fragments of American law into a single whole, and it does so not by free invention but by bringing reason and experience to bear in the application of law to each particular case.

Introducing the Law of Nations

If the discussion of what Kent, following Blackstone, calls the municipal law of the states comprises the bulk of his *Commentaries,* the work begins, even before its account of the American Constitution and federal law, with nine lectures devoted to the law of nations. In so doing, Kent departs entirely from Blackstone's example, but he sanctions his approach with a principle that echoes back to the first and final paragraphs of the Declaration of Independence, as it echoes forward to the statement of Justice Sutherland in *Curtiss-Wright.* "When the United States ceased to be a part

of the British empire, and assumed the character of an independent nation,"
Kent starts, "they became subject to that system of rules which reason,
morality, and custom, had established among the civilized nations of
Europe, as their public law." Citing an ordinance of the Revolutionary Congress to this effect, Kent explains in his first footnote the domestic sanction for subjection: "The English judges have frequently declared that the
law of nations was part of the common law of England . . . and it is well
settled that the common law of England, so far as it may be consistent with
the constitutions of this country, and remains unaltered by statute, is an essential part of American jurisprudence."[11] From the outset, then, Kent's discussion of the law of nations (which he also calls "national law" or "public
law") and his account of common law are intertwined. Both are forms of
unwritten law, in the sense that neither descends from a supreme legislative power, and both thus depend for their authority on something besides
a sovereign will. In fact, Kent's treatment of the law of nations parallels—
indeed, in the order of presentation in the *Commentaries* it prepares—his
treatment of common law.

The topics of the lectures are as follows:

    I. Of the foundation and history of the law of nations
    II. Of the rights and duties of nations in a state of peace
    III. Of the declaration, and other early measures of a state of war
    IV. Of the various kinds of property liable to capture
    V. Of the rights of belligerent nations in relation to each other
    VI. Of the general rights and duties of neutral nations
    VII. Of restrictions upon neutral trade
    VIII. Of truces, passports, and treaties of peace
    IX. Of offences against the law of nations

Covering nearly 200 pages, the lectures on the law of nations contain a
wealth of material, no doubt much of it superseded by subsequent conventions, but for the purposes of this chapter, what is most interesting is the attitude Kent takes toward his material and the sources of law to which he
looks. In our time, of course, positive conventions seem to overwhelm custom and reason in international law as much as statutes overwhelm common
law in domestic jurisprudence. Kent could see the beginning of this trend
in his own day, but he does not fall prey to international positivism any more
than he does to legal positivism in domestic matters. "The most useful and
practical part of the law of nations is, no doubt, instituted or positive law,

founded on usage, consent, and agreement," he acknowledges, "but it would be improper to separate this law entirely from natural jurisprudence, and not to consider it as deriving much of its force and dignity, from the same principles of right reason, the same views of the nature and constitution of man, and the same sanction of Divine revelation, as those from which the science of morality is deduced."[12] He proceeds: "The law of nations is a complex system, composed of various ingredients. It consists of general principles of right and justice, equally suitable to the government of individuals in a state of natural equality, and to the relations and conduct of nations; of a collection of usages and customs, the growth of civilization and commerce; and of a code of conventional or positive law."[13]

The continuity of law, from the highest level of generality to the lowest, and from the most certain to the most debatable, is thus assured in Kent's understanding. The "perfect equality, and entire independence of all distinct states, is a fundamental principle of public law," Kent declares at the outset of his second lecture,[14] but the fact that states are sovereign persons does not absolve them from being moral persons, in his treatment. That states are moral persons does not, of course, entail that their rights and obligations are identical to those of individuals: states, unlike individuals (except with the authorization of their state), can make war on one another; individuals, unlike states, live under government; and so forth. Still, all the myriad relations into which states and individuals may enter are governed by law and justice—war being no exception—so that for Kent, there is a great chain of law that governs human actions or, better, a web of law whose threads extend throughout all human affairs.

Kent's assumption of legal continuity, and in particular of continuity between the law of nations and common law, avoids a number of the difficulties typically ascribed to international law in our own day. First, the absence of a sovereign legislator is no obstacle to the existence of binding law to the common lawyer, and indeed, Kent discusses the sources of the law of nations much as, later in the *Commentaries,* he lists the sources of municipal law. Treaties and conventions take the place of statutes, to be sure, but the role of custom and the importance of commentators are the same in both systems: what Coke and Blackstone are to common law, so are Grotius and Vattel to the law of nations. Nor does he have difficulty in the international sphere distinguishing abstract theoretical speculation from commentary that illuminates and orders, but does not create, the law: as Hobbes is not Coke, so "the general freedom of trade, however reasonably and strongly it may be inculcated in the modern school of political economy, is but an imperfect right, and necessarily subject to such regulations and restrictions, as each nation may think proper to prescribe for itself."[15] As precedent serves in municipal disputes to provide evidence of the common law, "we now appeal to more accurate, more authentic, more precise, and more commanding evidence of the rules of public law, by a reference to the decisions of those tribunals, to whom, in every country, the administration of that branch of jurisprudence is specially intrusted."[16] Of course, the distinctive characteristics of the foreign sphere lead to distinctive sources of legal evidence: "in the absence of higher and more authoritative sanctions, the ordinances of foreign states, the opinions of eminent statesmen, and the writings of distinguished jurists, are regarded as of great consideration on questions not settled by conventional law."[17] But even these differences from domestic law ought not to be exaggerated, especially since the American law Kent describes applies to a number of distinct jurisdictions, the several states, that typically look to one another in legal matters, just as Kent recommends to the several nations in matters of public law.

If the porous nature of common law provides a model for thinking about the law of nations, Kent leaves no doubt that the actual courts involved in the decision of cases by common law can also serve to settle matters under the law of nations. Political scientists typically speak of courts as though their business were first and foremost to apply the law, so that each system of law should have its own courts, but this reflects the logic of sovereignty rather than the way of thinking characteristic of the common lawyer. Criminal law is, by general understanding (or, strictly speaking, by common law or the law of nations), closely restricted in its territorial reach—or at least it was until very recently—but in civil cases, the business of courts is first of all to settle disputes, and they must bring to bear on the case before them all law that is applicable, whatever its source. As Alexander Hamilton (among Kent's mentors, by the way) wrote in *The Federalist* Number 82, "The judiciary power of every government looks beyond its own local or municipal laws, and in civil cases lays hold of all subjects of litigation between parties within its jurisdiction, though the causes of dispute are relative to the laws of the most distant part of the globe. Those of Japan, not less than those of New York, may furnish the objects of legal discussion to our courts."[18] Thus for Kent, the law of nations, though universal in its precepts, is determined for American citizens in particular cases in American courts. Of course, which courts try which causes, or which persons come before which courts, is a question of jurisdiction, and like all such questions, it must be settled by applicable law, statutory or unwritten. But this understanding of the relation of

law to judging avoids the paradoxes that plague the modern theorist of international law, who must suppose international courts and a cosmopolitan
class to staff them. Kent's discussion of the law of nations always proceeds,
unapologetically, from a point of view within America, at once taking notice
of decisions of distant courts when these, by their learning and wisdom,
exude authority—as he thinks the admiralty decisions in England typically
do—but remaining bound, in the way one is bound in a common-law environment, by the relevant decisions of American courts, and taking guidance,
where guidance is appropriate, from the foreign policy of the United States.
Hence, in considering the right of a sovereign state to confiscate the debts
and funds of an enemy subject during wartime, Kent seems inclined toward
"the weight of modern authority, and of argument, against this claim," but
he acknowledges the contrary judgment of the Supreme Court in *Brown v.
United States,* accommodating the case to his views as best he can.[19] Likewise, he frankly admits that the extensive treatment he devotes to the rights
of neutrals follows in the spirit of Washington's Farewell Address, "as it is
our true policy to cherish a spirit of peace, and to keep ourselves free from
those political connexions which would tend to draw us into the vortex of
European contests."[20] Obviously, Kent does not expect common-law courts
to render judgments about the justice of actual wars, much less to render
them impartially, although he takes the question of just war seriously; rather,
such judgment belongs to the sovereign authority in a state in its own decisions whether to go to war, form alliances, and the like. Far from undoing
the influence of law, this arrangement confirms it, for the matter of who
addresses what concerns is itself the question of jurisdiction.[21]

A third aspect of the relation of common law to the law of nations appears in Kent's sober confidence in the capacity of law for improvement.
Like the common law, the law of nations is a science, and like the other sciences, its improvement is, to Kent's mind, a matter of public record. He
praises advancements, especially in the treatment of private individuals in
time of war, characteristically attributing them to the progress of commercial
relations. He seems to look forward to the development of universal laws
of trade, like the ancient *jus gentium*—although he never writes as though
he thinks progress is irreversible, much less achievable absent conscious human endeavor. Quite often, improvements involve the increasing referral of
matters of public law to judicial tribunals, again with confidence in the general enlightenment of judges and especially in their solicitude for the liberty and property of the individual bearer of rights. When discussing the
slave trade, as when discussing domestic slavery, Kent makes clear his

judgment of where abstract justice leads, but he scrupulously avoids extending the commands of law to the limits of perfect justice where the consensus of the relevant community is reluctant yet to go.[22] His discussion of such matters lacks both the self-righteous indignation of the moral idealist and the aimless pragmatism of the modern realist. The condition for the reality of law, in both the domestic and the foreign spheres, is at once an acceptance of human imperfection and a confidence in the power of reason, working steadily case by case, to aim at the human good.

Liberal Internationalism Today

Kent's integration of the law of nations of his own day seamlessly into American law might make him appear to be a precursor to modern liberal internationalism, and it would be silly to deny some connection. At the same time, something very different is now afoot—not yet in American courts, but in the burgeoning field of international law—that, except for the anomalous persistence of *United States v. Curtiss-Wright,* might pose a serious challenge to American constitutionalism. The new push of liberal internationalism has two dimensions, closely linked. The first involves the insistence that military force be used in concert with other nations, preferably under the aegis of the United Nations (UN) and preferably with the mission of "peacekeeping." Collective security and humanitarian rescue are the only acceptable justifications for military action, on this understanding, and multilateral joint commands are the only acceptable means. Indeed, even multilateralism is suspect if it is used to circumvent the UN, as, for example, in the North Atlantic Treaty Organization (NATO) action in Kosovo. Writes William Ratliff in the *Harvard International Review,* "Most international law scholars . . . have concluded that NATO's action in 1999 was illegal because it lacked UN authorization," though they thought that the bombing was "necessary to accomplish a positive objective."[23]

The second dimension of contemporary liberal internationalism is its development of a vast array of UN conventions and other initiatives designed to universalize liberal public policy on a variety of issues: protection of the environment, women's rights, the designation of international landmarks, prohibitions on chemical and other weapons, promises of political freedom, provision of Western-style birth control, and much more. It goes without saying that some of these objectives are noble, but others are profoundly misguided. Sometimes the end might be good, and easy to trumpet before world opinion, but the means are perverse. Consider the 1997 Kyoto

Protocol for the reduction of greenhouse gases thought to be responsible for global warming, which imposed on the developed world Draconian standards almost certain to cramp their economies, while giving a free ride to developing economies such as India's or China's, where population alone ensures a greater environmental impact. Sometimes the end is itself perverse. Consider here the efforts of the population-control elites to treat abortion as a human right, in open disregard of many people's religious convictions, not to mention biological fact. Sometimes the ambition is vaunting, as in the recent establishment of an International Criminal Court with a worldwide special prosecutor responsible for punishing all genocide, crimes against humanity, war crimes, and aggression. Sometimes it seems to be mere meddling, as in the 1995 visit of the UN World Heritage Committee to inspect proposed mining operations near Yellowstone National Park. In all these matters, the aim seems to be to build up a body of world opinion and "soft law," which can influence and perhaps eventually even determine legal outcomes in particular societies. Indeed, through creative lawyering and in reference to the Alien Tort Statute of 1789, these bodies of so-called customary international law are starting to find their way into American courts, even when the treaties they are founded on have not been ratified by the U.S. Senate.[24]

With reference to ideals such as environmentalism and human rights, the internationalists are deliberately undermining the choices different societies make in ordering their own affairs, thus diminishing their capacity for self-government or sovereignty. But two things need to be noted. First, the apologists for liberal internationalism, or at least plenty of political scientists, deny that sovereignty is being undermined at all. To them, the real threat to sovereignty is global capitalism, whose most powerful players escape the authority of most states. Since sovereignty must be understood on two dimensions, the argument goes, as both independence from outside control and successful domestic control, the rise of international authority in these matters simply involves a limited sacrifice of the former for the sake of the latter. In other words, the international imposition of liberal policies enhances the domestic sovereignty of regulatory liberalism, allowing its proponents, through the pressure of world opinion and sometimes with the help of international resources, to control elements of their own society that previously would have gone ungoverned. From this perspective, what is lost by the sacrifice of external sovereignty except the capacity to do wrong?[25] The second thing to note is that the United States has often played an important role in the formulation of standards that turn out to be so contrary to our interests or understandings that even mainstream liberals are reluctant to urge their acceptance. Daniel Patrick Moynihan noted this phenomenon as long ago as the 1970s in his critique of contemporaneous developments in the UN, but it seems to repeat itself even once it has been exposed. For example, with the International Criminal Court, as with the Law of the Sea Treaty some twenty years before, Americans found themselves forced at the last minute to withdraw from international conventions they had promoted. More seems to be involved here than ordinary political oscillation, or the repudiation by one administration of its predecessors' more partisan achievements. There seems to be a deep confusion about what American attitudes toward world order ought to be.

This, then, is the crux of the problem: America was founded on universal principles—indeed, on the priority of human (or natural) rights—and we feel drawn to modern reformulations of those rights as if to an expansion of our principles. Moreover, though we have a strong tradition of insisting on not being entangled in our actions on the world stage, we have from the beginning been strong advocates of international law—indeed, as a commercial nation, we have always depended on it as a guarantor of free trade.

The problem is, as Jeremy Rabkin showed in his brilliant but undernoticed book *Why Sovereignty Matters* (published as a policy study by the American Enterprise Institute, but researched as a major theoretical statement), we have come to misunderstand our own principles.[26] Our Declaration of Independence asserts for us a place in world affairs in the name of international law and human rights, but it does so precisely through the establishment of constitutional government, of government based on consent of the governed and accountable for its decisions to those subject to its rules. The great fault of the new internationalism, according to Rabkin, is that neither in the making of these new standards nor in their enforcement do the people of the world have a real say, and there is no subsequent accountability for the damage they might do. The example of European integration is instructive here, for the European Union is modeling liberal plans for world government and, given the influence of European states in international organizations, even driving them. An international bureaucracy, accountable to voters only indirectly, is becoming the locus of power in Europe, and its program develops inexorably, despite bare margins at the polls when voters get a rare chance to voice their opinion. The usual means of constitutional control are lacking—certainly the wide variety of means we Americans are used to—including not only elections but also the separation of powers, judicial independence, and the like.

What can be done to protect national sovereignty, and thus national law, against this trend? First, as Rabkin suggests, we need to restore a sense of constitutional limits on which treaties can be made, and at the very least, we need some principles to guide us in determining which multilateral agreements are sound and which are not. He suggests two criteria: international agreements should be about things that cross borders, and the obligations of signatory nations ought to be reciprocal.[27] Treaties that would establish international regimes concerning signatories' domestic concerns should be avoided, as should those in which the failure of one or more parties to adhere to the established standards neither releases the compliant nor allows them to retaliate against the noncompliant in any way. This would save most of our trade agreements, at least those based on the General Agreement on Tariffs and Trade (GATT) model, in which disputes are sent to arbitration and trade improprieties can be countered; it would counsel against repeating or expanding those provisions of the North American Free Trade Agreement (NAFTA) that purport to make joint trade-panel decisions binding on American courts.

Second, with regard to the question of military intervention, but also more generally, we need to restore a sense of the national interest to our considerations, and to restore this sense in light of universal principles. Surely the recent terrorist attacks on the United States give an urgency and plausibility to this objective that it did not have before: we need to find the intellectual resources to develop the idea of the national interest without having to rely on Machiavellian realism and the assertion of collective selfishness. One possibility is the principle of subsidiarity, much developed in twentieth-century Catholic social thought, which insists that decisions that affect people's lives be made at a level as close to the person as possible, allowing for considerations of the common good. Applied impartially, it would seem to counsel against referring all questions of security to an indifferent UN. In the American political tradition, the idea of federalism is analogous to subsidiarity, though the history of federalism warns of the tendency toward unchecked centralization. Both subsidiarity and federalism have the virtue of focusing attention not only on individual human rights but also on the question of self-government and the character of regimes. They point away from the installation of a permanent police force in the aftermath of military intervention and instead favor promoting a decent, locally based regime.

Third, we need to preserve the centrality of the Constitution in our understanding of how our government works. This means jealously guarding the treaty power in the Senate and the war power in Congress as a whole. Both have been seriously eroded over the course of the past century, and though there may have been pressing necessity or tactical advantage behind executive agreements or commander in chief–initiated military engagements, it is an irony of contemporary international development that ceding power to the executive can lead to its slipping out of national hands altogether, as if the branch most able to exercise our sovereignty is also the branch most apt to let it get away. Besides, the executive can have domestic political incentives to negotiate international arrangements that bind his successors in ways that domestic executive orders do not, since the latter are relatively easy to undo. Probably executive authority to negotiate certain matters relating to trade is now irreversible and even advantageous, but we must beware lest, for the sake of material advantage, we trade away an important protection of self-government. Besides, every authority acquiesced in under one administration becomes a precedent for expanded use under the next, a point that ought to be remembered by partisans on both sides.

Finally, the advocates of national authority need to restore clear thinking about international justice and human rights. For example, when we promote democracy, we should be clear that we are promoting not just elections but also constitutional democracy, where popular consent and the rule of law temper each other. When we are asked to endorse human rights, we should include the rights of property, not just because these promote collective wealth—though it seems well proven that they do—but because they buffer liberty and teach responsibility. Above all, when we promote individual liberty, it ought to be in a way more in accord with the traditional understanding of liberty in America as dependent on and contributory to moral order, not as its mortal enemy, a liberty that knows itself not to be license. The intellectual groundwork for talking this way about human rights is, I think, stronger now than it was twenty years ago, even though the decay of social mores has progressed, catching up, as it were, with earlier bad ideas. In short, we need to keep our institutions, thoughts, and words focused on liberty understood as self-government, and on the self as an individual conscience capable of deliberating and acting responsibly with others in the communities of which it is a part.

Sovereignty without a Master

The doctrine of the law of nations Kent develops as the introductory part of his *Commentaries on American Law* can serve as a blueprint for world order in the post–Cold War world—or for the newer order implied by the war on terrorism—no more than the common law he discusses in detail could adequately replace the mass of regulatory legislation that has developed in the twentieth century. Still, the world he depicts deserves renewed attention in this age that seems to demand simultaneously an enhanced capacity for separate peoples to govern themselves and a universal legal order to mediate a world economy growing ever more interlinked. The perspective of common law—the ability at once to focus attention on a particular matter at hand and to draw for its resolution on a universe of reasons—escapes in Kent's presentation the quandary of the theory of sovereignty—too stern an order at home, too lax an order abroad—without falling into the opposite error of domestic anarchy and world despotism. And he certainly suggests that it is possible to acknowledge that standards of lawfulness transcend the political boundaries of particular states without making one's judges, in the style of contemporary Europe, agents of a supranational will.

Conclusion

Do we have a living Constitution? Chief Justice William Rehnquist began a lecture with that question in 1975, when he was in one of his first terms as an associate justice on the Supreme Court.[1] He noted the strangeness of answering in the negative but then proceeded to criticize the concept as it had been employed. Indeed, the notion of a living Constitution has been anathema to conservative judges for over a generation, as the metaphor has been used to explain or justify judges' creative use of constitutional law to enforce the changing agenda of modern liberalism, without regard to long-established precedent, settled popular understanding, or even the language of the Constitution itself, unless at the highest level of abstraction. Actually, as with the appeal to the original intention of the Framers, the conservatives might be said to have won the battle, for liberals now seem reluctant to invoke the image of a living Constitution, though they have hardly abandoned the effort to elicit judicial creativity in the service of their favorite causes.

Yet to invite a common-law perspective on American constitutional law is indeed to accept the idea that the Constitution, or at any rate our constitutionalism, is like a living thing: that it grows and develops; that it adapts to changing circumstances; that, on the one hand, it does this under the guidance of reason or according to laws that reason can grasp, and that, on the other, its destiny is in some decisive respects unknown to those who inhabit its orbit. The men who wrote and ratified the federal Constitution would have denied none of this, it seems to me, even though, by writing down a fundamental law, they meant to mark fixed principles of the regime for generations to come and to outline settled practices by which the course of development and adjustment might proceed. You have missed my point if you think that, by stressing the common-law context of constitutional law, I endorse the notion that constitutional adjudication should make the text of the Constitution as malleable as common law, particularly common law understood as judge-made law in a pragmatic mode. On the contrary, I have tried to show that constitutional meaning has or ought to have stability over time, and that the very possibility of such elemental constancy ought to be

165

what guides all adaptation. At the same time, something central to the genius of America is missed if the Constitution is thought of as an ascetic instrument that commands only self-denial or a creature whose soul is merely public will.

One problem with the metaphor of the living Constitution, as it has been invoked by its proponents and deplored by its detractors, is that both parties take for granted the concept of a living species in Darwinian evolution: an organism that cannot be understood to have a permanent essence or form; that changes in response to extrinsic influence, not intelligent design; that has no purpose nobler than its own survival or the dominion needed for survival in a hostile world. This is hardly the place to assess or even to raise the contemporary controversy over the sufficiency of Darwinian biology as an account of the nature of things, but fortunately, we do not need a definitive disposal of that debate to recognize a few basic truths: that every form of life has intrinsic principles of development that make possible its adaptation to extrinsic circumstance, that the concept of survival of the fittest as applied to social life in the past century and a half has often yielded policies that almost no one is eager to defend, and that the unique endowment and prospect of every human person is grasped by each person in reflecting on life as he or she experiences it. That there is, and for many people in a free and dynamic society, ought to be, a certain indeterminacy—call it adventure, if you like, or trust in providence, if you prefer—in the way life unfolds does not deny that every life well lived conforms to patterns larger than its own imagination and transmits the good things it receives from those who went before to those who follow, suitably enlarged. That life involves both change and continuity is one of the simplest observations of common sense.

To speak of a living Constitution, then, does not mean that in our fundamental law we need to endorse or replicate the popular sensation, so palpable at this historical moment, of careening uncontrollably into a brave new world of science fiction, whether through entrepreneurial genius in the pressure of a competitive market or through vigilant social control in a climate of fear. Quite the contrary, the idea of a living Constitution invites us to engage in dialogue with the wisdom of ages other than our own and to see the verdicts of the moment in the perspective of a larger whole. The common law is not the answer to every question in American constitutional law, and it need not be the only source of American principles; indeed, part of its genius is that it avoided the metaphysical discussions that are at once necessary in the formation of a person's character and productive of bitter political dispute. For all its encouragement of legal sparring, the ways of common law are profoundly peaceable; still, it acknowledged that in times of war there is a place for law of different sorts. To see the judicial power in the common-law perspective, and to see our constitutionalism as a legacy in part of its spirited liberty, can expand the range of possibilities available to those who would understand that constitutionalism, and it can remind us of what our forefathers well knew: that the things that are unwritten and maybe even incapable of being written might yet prove to be, if not always the most urgent, in the long run, the most important things.

NOTES

Introduction

1. Representative examples, which naturally vary quite a bit, include Ronald Dworkin, *Taking Rights Seriously* (Cambridge: Harvard University Press, 1977), and numerous subsequent works; Laurence Tribe, *Constitutional Choices* (Cambridge: Harvard University Press, 1986); Rogers Smith, *Liberalism and American Constitutional Law* (Cambridge: Harvard University Press, 1986); Sanford Levinson, *Constitutional Faith* (Princeton, N.J.: Princeton University Press, 1989); Bruce Ackerman, *We the People: Foundations* (Cambridge: Harvard University Press, 1993), and *We the People: Transformations* (Cambridge: Harvard University Press, 2000); Akhil Amar, *The Bill of Rights: Creation and Reconstruction* (New Haven, Conn.: Yale University Press, 1998); and Cass Sunstein, *One Case at a Time* (Cambridge: Harvard University Press, 2000).

2. Cf. Dworkin, *Taking Rights Seriously,* with Sunstein, *One Case at a Time.* The title can be found in Archibald Cox, *The Warren Court: Constitutional Decision as an Instrument of Reform* (Cambridge: Harvard University Press, 1968).

3. Antonin Scalia et al., *A Matter of Interpretation: Federal Courts and the Law* (Princeton, N.J.: Princeton University Press, 1997); Robert Bork, *The Tempting of America* (New York: Basic Books, 1990); Raoul Berger, *Government by Judiciary: The Transformation of the Fourteenth Amendment* (Cambridge: Harvard University Press, 1977); Gary McDowell, *Curbing the Courts* (Baton Rouge: Louisiana State University Press, 1988); Christopher Wolfe, *The Rise of Modern Judicial Review: From Constitutional Interpretation American to Judge-Made Law* (New York: Basic Books,1986); Walter Berns, *The First Amendment and the Future of American Democracy* (New York: Basic Books, 1976); Keith E. Whittington, *Constitutional Interpretation: Textual Meaning, Original Intent, and Judicial Review* (Lawrence: University Press of Kansas, 1999); and, from a somewhat different perspective, the books that have issued from the controversy surrounding a symposium in the journal *First Things:* Mitchell S. Muncy, ed., *The End of Democracy? The Celebrated* First Things *Debate with Arguments Pro & Con* (Dallas: Spence, 1997), and *The End of Democracy? II: A Crisis of Legitimacy* (Dallas: Spence, 1999).

4. Scalia et al., *A Matter of Interpretation,* p. 7.

5. See, e.g., Melvin Aron Eisenberg, *The Nature of the Common Law* (Cambridge: Harvard University Press, 1988).

170   *Common-Law Liberty*

6. Oliver Wendell Holmes, Jr., "The Path of the Law," in *Collected Legal Papers* (New York: Harcourt, Brace and Howe, 1920), p. 187.

7. Thomas Hobbes, *Leviathan,* chap. 26; William Blackstone, *Commentaries on the Laws of England* (Oxford: Clarendon Press, 1765–1769; facsimile reprint ed., Chicago: University of Chicago Press, 1979), vol. 1, chap. 1.

8. Alexander Hamilton, James Madison, and John Jay, *The Federalist,* ed. Jacob Cooke (Middleton, Conn.: Wesleyan University Press, 1961), nos. 1, 49.

9. For contrast, see Henry P. Monaghan, "Forward: Constitutional Common Law," 89 *Harvard Law Review* 1–45 (1975); and Guido Calabresi, *A Common Law for an Age of Statutes* (Cambridge: Harvard University Press, 1982).

10. James R. Stoner, Jr., *Common Law and Liberal Theory: Coke, Hobbes, and the Origins of American Constitutionalism* (Lawrence: University Press of Kansas, 1992).

11. See Leo Strauss, "Social Science and Humanism," in his posthumously published collection *The Rebirth of Classical Political Rationalism,* ed. Thomas L. Pangle (Chicago: University of Chicago Press, 1989), p. 7.

12. See, for a leading example, Keith E. Whittington, *Constitutional Construction: Divided Powers and Constitutional Meaning* (Cambridge: Harvard University Press, 1999).

13. Aristotle, *Nicomachean Ethics,* book VI, 1141b15-23, tr. Martin Ostwald (Indianapolis: Bobbs-Merrill Co., 1962), pp. 157–58.

Chapter 1. Common Law and Constitution

1. Thomas C. Grey, "Do We Have an Unwritten Constitution?" 27 *Stanford Law Review* 703–18 (1975), and "Origins of the Unwritten Constitution: Fundamental Law in American Revolutionary Thought," 30 *Stanford Law Review* 843–93 (1978); John Hart Ely, *Democracy and Distrust* (Cambridge: Harvard University Press, 1980). The exception to the rule about the disappearance of interest in the unwritten constitution is a fine article by Suzanna Sherry, "The Founders' Unwritten Constitution," 54 *University of Chicago Law Review* 1127–77 (1987). The "jurisprudence of original intention" was thrust into public debate by a much-publicized speech to the American Bar Association by then–Attorney General Edwin Meese III, published as "The Supreme Court of the United States: Bulwark of a Limited Constitution," 27 *South Texas Law Review* 455–66 (1986). For a more developed account, see Robert Bork, *The Tempting of America: The Political Seduction of the Law* (New York: Free Press, 1990); and Robert P. George and Gerard V. Bradley, "Outer Limits: The Commerce Clause and Judicial Review," in *The Supreme Court and American Constitutionalism,* ed. Bradford P. Wilson and Ken Masugi (Lanham, Md.: Rowman and Littlefield, 1998).

2. See, e.g., Ronald Dworkin, *A Matter of Principle* (Cambridge: Harvard University Press, 1985), chap. 6.

3. *Roe v. Wade,* 410 U.S. 113 (1973). The "shadows" are the "penumbras" announced in the basic "right of privacy" case, *Griswold v. Connecticut,* 381 U.S. 479 (1965), at 484.

4. *Planned Parenthood v. Casey,* 505 U.S. 833 (1992).

5. See especially the important work of Hadley Arkes, *Beyond the Constitution* (Princeton, N.J.: Princeton University Press, 1990), and *The Return of George Sutherland: Restoring a Jurisprudence of Natural Rights* (Princeton, N.J.: Princeton University Press, 1994).

6. See Leo Strauss, "Natural Law," in *International Encyclopedia of the Social Sciences,* ed. David L. Sills (New York: Macmillan, 1968).

7. See Robert Nagel, *Constitutional Cultures: The Mentality and Consequences of Judicial Review* (Berkeley and Los Angeles: University of California Press, 1989).

8. I discuss these matters at greater length in *Common Law and Liberal Theory: Coke, Hobbes, and the Origins of American Constitutionalism* (Lawrence: University Press of Kansas, 1992), esp. chap. 1.

9. Albert Venn Dicey, *Introduction to the Study of the Law of the Constitution* (reprint, Indianapolis: Liberty Press, 1982).

10. See, e.g., Thomas Andrew Green, *Verdict According to Conscience* (Chicago: University of Chicago Press, 1985).

11. George Wilson, ed., *The Reports of Sir Edward Coke* (Dublin: J. Moore, 1793), vol. 8, preface; Sir Edward Coke, *Institutes of the Laws of England,* part II (London, 1642; reprint, New York: Garland Publishing, 1979), p. 47. See also Stoner, *Common Law and Liberal Theory,* p. 21.

12. See Stoner, *Common Law and Liberal Theory,* chaps. 8, 10.

13. Reprinted in Jack P. Greene, ed., *Colonies to Nation, 1763–1789: A Documentary History of the American Revolution* (New York: W. W. Norton, 1975), p. 245.

14. "Codification of the Common Law," in William W. Story, ed., *The Miscellaneous Writings of Joseph Story* (Boston: Little, Brown, 1852), p. 701. On the more general question of the reception of common law in America, see Kermit Hall, *The Magic Mirror: Law in American History* (New York: Oxford University Press, 1989), pp. 12 ff.; and William E. Nelson, *Americanization of the Common Law: The Impact of Legal Change on Massachusetts Society, 1760–1830* (Cambridge: Harvard University Press, 1975).

15. Thomas Jefferson, *Writings* (New York: Library of America, 1984), p. 38.

16. I discuss this matter at greater length in *Common Law and Liberal Theory,* pp. 188–89.

17. Nelson, *Americanization of the Common Law;* see also Shannon Stimson, *The American Revolution in the Law: Anglo-American Jurisprudence before John Marshall* (Princeton, N.J.: Princeton University Press, 1990).

18. *The Federalist,* ed. Jacob Cooke (Middletown, Conn.: Wesleyan University Press, 1961), nos. 9, 51, and nos. 14, 88.

19. In Max Farrand, *The Framing of the Constitution of the United States* (New Haven, Conn.: Yale University Press, 1913), appendix II, p. 226.

20. See the rules for interpretation of statutes in William Blackstone, *Commentaries on the Laws of England* (1765; reprint, Chicago: University of Chicago Press, 1979), 1:87–91.

21. *The Federalist,* pp. 529, 526, 528.

22. Farrand, *Framing of the Constitution,* appendix II, p. 226; appendix III, pp. 232, 229.

23. *The Federalist,* no. 82, p. 553.

24. Ibid., no. 83, p. 562.

25. See Herbert J. Storing, "The Constitution and the Bill of Rights," in *Essays on the Constitution of the United States,* ed. M. Judd Harmon (Port Washington, N.Y.: Kennikat Press, 1978).

26. Joseph Story, *A Discourse Pronounced upon the Inauguration of the Author as Dane Professor of Law in Harvard University* . . . (Boston: Hilliard, Gray, Little, and Wilkins, 1829); reprinted in Joseph Story, *Miscellaneous Writings, Literary, Critical, Juridical, and Political* (Boston: James Munroe and Co., 1835), pp. 440–76. Page numbers in the following notes refer to the original imprint.

27. Ibid., pp. 41, 4–5.

28. Quoted in James McClellan, *Joseph Story and the American Constitution* (Norman: University of Oklahoma Press, 1971), p. 61.

29. Story, *Discourse,* pp. 6, 7, 9–10.

30. Coke, *Institutes of the Laws of England,* 1: 97b.

31. Story, *Discourse,* pp. 8–9, 52–53.

32. Ibid., pp. 20–21, 34–35.

33. Ibid., p. 55.

34. *Swift v. Tyson,* 16 Peters (41 U.S.) 1 (1842).

35. Ibid., at 18–19.

36. For a fine discussion of *Swift v. Tyson* and of its constitutional implications, see William T. Braithwaite, "The Common Law and Judicial Power: An Introduction to Swift-Erie and the Problem of Transcendental versus Positive Law," in *Law and Philosophy: The Practice of Theory, Essays in Honor of George Anastaplo,* ed. John A. Murley, Robert L. Stone, and William T. Braithwaite (Athens: Ohio University Press, 1992), 2:774–818.

37. *Erie R. Co. v. Tompkins,* 304 U.S. 64 (1938).

38. See Edward H. Levi, *An Introduction to Legal Reasoning* (Chicago: University of Chicago Press, 1949), esp. pp. 27 ff.

39. Oliver Wendell Holmes, Jr., *The Common Law* (Cambridge: Harvard University Press, 1963), p. 32.

40. Oliver Wendell Holmes, Jr., *Collected Legal Papers* (New York: Harcourt, Brace and Howe, 1920), p. 269.

41. Ibid., pp. 186–87.

42. See, e.g., Melvin Aron Eisenberg, *The Nature of the Common Law* (Cambridge: Harvard University Press, 1988); from the dean of the school of law and economics, a self-conscious Holmesian and now an influential federal judge, see Richard A. Posner, *Economic Analysis of Law,* 4th ed. (Boston: Little, Brown, 1992).

43. See Stoner, *Common Law and Liberal Theory*, pp. 53 ff.

44. See Morton J. Horwitz, *The Transformation of American Law, 1780–1860* (Cambridge: Harvard University Press, 1977).

45. Story, *Discourse,* pp. 20–21. As a young man, Thomas Jefferson wrote an essay in which he attempted to expose this proposition as a seventeenth-century error or fraud, and in his later years, he digs it out again and stands by his youthful opinion. See Jefferson, *Writings,* pp. 1321–29, 1494–95.

46. Cf. *Roe v. Wade* with *Skinner v. Oklahoma,* 316 U.S. 535 (1942), *Meyer v. Nebraska,* 262 U.S. 390 (1923), and *Pierce v. Society of Sisters,* 268 U.S. 510 (1925).

Chapter 2. Fighting Words

1. H.B. 1331, Regular Session, 1990. Bill on file at the House Docket Office of House Legislative Services, Baton Rouge, Louisiana.

2. *Chaplinsky v. New Hampshire,* 315 U.S. 568 (1942), at 571–72.

3. *R.A.V. v. St. Paul,* 505 U.S. 377 (1992).

4. *Abrams v. United States,* 250 U.S. 616 (1919), at 630.

5. Paul Rahe, *Republics Ancient and Modern: Classical Republicanism and the American Revolution* (Chapel Hill: University of North Carolina Press, 1992), p. 35. The account of the history of political thought that follows is much indebted to Rahe's remarkable book.

6. That man is political because he is rational is clear from *Politics,* book I, 1253a; that he would not need the city if he were perfectly rational, that is, a god, is announced in the same passage. (See also Aristotle, *Nicomachean Ethics,* book X, 1177b.) At least half this sentiment is echoed in Publius's famous statement, "If men were angels, no government would be necessary" (Jacob E. Cooke, ed., *The Federalist* [Middletown, Conn.: Wesleyan University Press, 1961], no. 51, p. 349).

7. Aristotle, *Nicomachean Ethics,* book III, 1112b.

8. See chapter 3.

9. See Rahe, *Republics Ancient and Modern,* book II; Harvey C. Mansfield, Jr., "The Religious Issue and the Origin of Modern Constitutionalism," in *How Does the Constitution Protect Religious Freedom?* ed. Robert A. Goldwin and Art Kaufman (Washington, D.C.: American Enterprise Institute, 1987); and Walter Berns, *The First Amendment and the Future of American Democracy* (New York: Basic Books, 1976), chap. 1.

10. Consider Hobbes, Locke, and Blackstone, respectively.

11. See Harvey C. Mansfield, Jr., "Responsibility versus Self-Expression," in *Old*

Rights and New, ed. Robert A. Licht (Washington, D.C.: American Enterprise Institute, 1993).

12. E.g., *Cantwell v. Connecticut,* 310 U.S. 296 (1940), and *West Virginia v. Barnette,* 319 U.S. 624 (1943).

13. Berns, *The First Amendment,* p. 83; Rahe, *Republics Ancient and Modern,* p. 706.

14. *Abrams v. United States,* 250 U.S. 616, at 630.

15. Ibid.

16. Leonard Levy, *Emergence of a Free Press* (New York: Oxford University Press, 1985).

17. Berns, *The First Amendment,* esp. chaps. 2–5.

18. See Harvey C. Mansfield, Jr., *Statesmanship and Party Government* (Chicago: University of Chicago Press, 1965); Alexis de Tocqueville, *Democracy in America* (New York: Harper and Row, 1966), vol. 1, part 2, chap. 2, pp. 174 ff.

19. See Madison's April 4, 1800, letter to Jefferson, where, looking forward to a Republican victory in the federal elections that year, he writes, "Such a demonstration of the rectitude & efficacy of popular sentiment, will be the more precious, as the late defection of France has left America the only Theatre on which true liberty can have a fair trial" (Gaillard Hunt, ed., *The Writings of James Madison* [New York: G. P. Putnam's Sons, 1906], 4: 408).

20. *The Federalist,* no. 10, pp. 57, 59.

21. *United States v. Hudson and Goodwin,* 7 Cranch (11 U.S.) 32 (1812). Cf. Levy's discussion of Justice Story's suppression of his dissent in *Emergence of a Free Press,* p. 279.

22. See James Morton Smith, *Freedom's Fetters: The Alien and Sedition Laws and American Civil Liberties* (Ithaca, N.Y.: Cornell University Press, 1956), p. 421.

23. See my *Common Law and Liberal Theory: Coke, Hobbes, and the Origins of American Constitutionalism* (Lawrence: University Press of Kansas, 1992), chap. 10.

24. William Blackstone, *Commentaries on the Laws of England* (1765; reprint, Chicago: University of Chicago Press, 1979), 4:150–51.

25. Edward Coke, *Reports,* ed. George Wilson (Dublin: Moore, 1793), 3:125.

26. Blackstone, *Commentaries,* 4: 151–53.

27. These appear sequentially in *The Writings of James Madison,* 6:326–31, 332–40, 341–406.

28. Berns, *The First Amendment,* chap. 2.

29. *Writings of James Madison,* 6:375–76, 373, 381, 380.

30. Ibid., pp. 386–89.

31. This phrase was apparently taken from a 1775 pamphlet by Virginian Arthur Lee, where it was used to somewhat different effect: "The right of *property* is the guardian of every other right, and to deprive a people of this, is in fact to deprive them of their liberty" (emphasis added). Quoted in James W. Ely, Jr., *The Guardian*

of Every Other Right: A Constitutional History of Property Rights (New York: Oxford University Press, 1992), p. 26.

32. *Writings of James Madison,* 6:393–97.

33. Ibid., pp. 386, 402.

34. Ibid., p. 393.

35. Julius Goebel, Jr., ed., *The Law Practice of Alexander Hamilton* (New York: Columbia University Press, 1964), 1:775 ff., esp. p. 789.

36. Ibid., pp. 809–10; cf. *Writings of James Madison,* 6:335.

37. Goebel, *Law Practice of Alexander Hamilton,* 1:811.

38. Ibid., pp. 829–30.

39. Ibid., pp. 813, 818, 820.

40. See ibid., pp. 844–48.

41. James Kent, *Commentaries on American Law,* 4th ed. (New York: James Kent, 1840), 2:23.

42. Tocqueville, *Democracy in America,* vol. 1, part 2, chap. 3.

43. See, e.g., Jackson's dissent in *Beauharnais v. Illinois,* 343 U.S. 250 (1952).

44. *Gitlow v. New York,* 268 U.S. 652 (1925), at 673. See the discussion in Berns, *The First Amendment,* pp. 155 ff.

45. *Chaplinsky v. New Hampshire,* 315 U.S. 568, at 573.

46. *New York Times v. Sullivan,* 376 U.S. 254 (1964), at 280–82. The Supreme Court defines "actual malice" to mean publication with knowledge that the published statement is false or reckless disregard for whether it is true or false.

47. Ibid., at 270 ff. This case has recently been characterized as "motivated by an implicit purpose of stretching the principle of free speech, beyond what in its own context would seem reasonable, in order to stimulate a more aggressive press and a more active self-government" (Lee C. Bollinger, "The End of *New York Times v. Sullivan:* Reflections on *Masson v. New Yorker Magazine,*" 1991 *Supreme Court Review* 40).

48. *Cohen v. California,* 403 U.S. 15 (1971), at 23, 25.

49. For a similar periodization, see Mark A. Graber, *Transforming Free Speech: The Ambiguous Legacy of Civil Libertarianism* (Berkeley and Los Angeles: University of California Press, 1991).

50. *R.A.V. v. St. Paul,* 505 U.S. 377 (1992), at 392.

51. Cass Sunstein, *Democracy and the Problem of Free Speech* (New York: Free Press, 1993).

Chapter 3. Religious Liberty and Common Law

1. Alexis de Tocqueville, *Democracy in America,* trans. George Lawrence (New York: Harper and Row, 1966), vol. 1, part 2, chap. 8, p. 267.

2. *Employment Division, Department of Human Resources of Oregon v. Smith,* 494 U.S. 872 (1990).

3. *Sherbert v. Verner,* 374 U.S. 398 (1963). See *Smith v. Employment Division, Department of Human Resources, and ADAPT,* 301 Or. 209 (1986).

4. The refusal to work Saturdays was at issue in *Sherbert;* the refusal to build weapons had cost the petitioner his job in *Thomas v. Review Board of the Indiana Employment Security Division,* 450 U.S. 707 (1981).

5. *Employment Division, Department of Human Resources of Oregon v. Smith,* 485 U.S. 660 (1988), at 673–74.

6. See *City of Boerne v. Flores,* 521 U.S. 507 (1997).

7. Justice O'Connor objected strenuously to the abandonment of the "compelling interest test" in *Smith,* but she joined the majority in the judgment, finding the state's interest in its drug laws compelling against the free-exercise claim. Justice Blackmun, joined by Justices Brennan and Marshall, joined Justice O'Connor on the question of the "test" but dissented from the result. In general, a compelling-interest test is a device by which the Court allows a statute to stand only if it can be persuaded that the statute serves an extremely serious purpose that government is allowed or required to pursue.

8. *Smith,* 494 U.S. 872, at 884.

9. Ibid., at 881.

10. Ibid., at 888, 890.

11. Ibid., at 878–79.

12. The citation for *Gobitis* is 310 U.S. 586 (1940); it was overturned three years later by *West Virginia Board of Education v. Barnette,* 319 U.S. 624 (1943), as Justice O'Connor points out in her concurrence in *Smith* (494 U.S. 872, at 902). In fairness to Justice Scalia, one should note that *Barnette* struck down the compulsory flag salute on free-speech grounds, while Frankfurter's opinion in *Gobitis* had upheld it against a claim of religious liberty.

13. See Antonin Scalia, "The Rule of Law as a Law of Rules," 56 *University of Chicago Law Review* 1175 (1989). For a scholarly critique of balancing tests and the formulaic style of opinion writing they spawned, especially during the Burger years, see Robert Nagel, *Constitutional Cultures: The Mentality and Consequences of Judicial Review* (Berkeley: University of California Press, 1989), esp. chap. 7.

14. In *Everson,* 330 U.S. 1 (1947), Frankfurter joined the dissenting opinions of Justices Jackson and Rutledge. The released-time cases are *Illinois ex rel McCollum v. Board of Education,* 333 U.S. 203 (1948), and *Zorach v. Clauson,* 343 U.S. 306 (1952). The Sunday-closing cases begin with *McGowan v. Maryland,* 366 U.S. 420 (1961). For an influential discussion of the jurisprudence of the Religion Clauses sympathetic to Frankfurter's perspective, see Philip B. Kurland, "Of Church and State and the Supreme Court," 29 *University of Chicago Law Review* 1 (1961); also Mark Tushnet, "'Of Church and State and the Supreme Court': Kurland Revisited," 1989 *Supreme Court Review* 373.

15. Quoted from *Lee v. Weisman,* 505 U.S. 577 (1992), at 584. The citation for *Lemon* is 403 U.S. 602 (1971).

16. *Marsh v. Chambers,* 463 U.S. 783 (1983); *Allegheny County v. ACLU,* 492 U.S. 573 (1989), at 655. The various calls for reconsideration of the *Lemon* test are cited by Justice Scalia in his *Weisman* dissent, 505 U.S. 577 (1992), at 643. Justice Thomas gathers four votes for a lenient no-establishment test in *Mitchell v. Helms,* 530 U.S. 793 (2000).

17. *Allegheny,* 492 U.S. 573, at 670.

18. *Lee v. Weisman,* 505 U.S. 577, at 632, 645, 641.

19. Ibid., at 638.

20. Walter Berns, *The First Amendment and the Future of American Democracy* (New York: Basic Books, 1976), pp. 1–2.

21. Ibid., p. 32.

22. Ibid., p. 48.

23. Ibid., p. 13. See also Michael J. Malbin, *Religion and Politics: The Intentions of the Authors of the First Amendment* (Washington, D.C.: American Enterprise Institute, 1978), whose reading of the congressional debates over the First Amendment harmonizes with Berns's.

24. Berns, *The First Amendment,* p. 60.

25. See Michael McConnell, "Accommodation of Religion," 1985 *Supreme Court Review* 1.

26. Michael McConnell, "The Origins and Historical Understanding of the Free Exercise of Religion," 103 *Harvard Law Review* 1410 (1990). His more recent article is "Free Exercise Revisionism and the *Smith* Decision," 57 *University of Chicago Law Review* 1109 (1990).

27. "Memorial and Remonstrance," appended to *Everson v. Board of Education,* 330 U.S. 1 (1947), at 64. See McConnell, "Origins of Free Exercise," pp. 1430–55.

28. Cf. Justice Souter's concurring opinion in *Lee v. Weisman.* For a defense of taking the Virginians' experience as determinative of the clause's meaning, see Douglas Laycock, "'Nonpreferential' Aid to Religion: A False Claim About Original Intent," 27 *William and Mary Law Review* 875 (1986).

29. Thomas Curry, *The First Freedoms: Church and State in America to the Passage of the First Amendment* (New York: Oxford University Press, 1986). Other works that document the accommodation of religion in the states at the time of the Founding include Robert Cord, *Separation of Church and State: Historical Fact and Current Fiction* (New York: Lambeth Press, 1982); and Gerard V. Bradley, *Church-State Relationships in America* (Westport, Conn.: Greenwood Press, 1987).

30. McConnell, "Origins of Free Exercise," p. 1425.

31. Ibid., p. 1516.

32. See Charles A. Lofgren, "The Original Understanding of Original Intent?" 5 *Constitutional Commentary* 77 (1988).

33. See, e.g., Berns, *The First Amendment,* pp. 234–35.

34. McConnell, "Accommodation of Religion," p. 6.

35. Tocqueville, *Democracy in America,* vol. 2, part 2, chap. 15, p. 546.

36. McConnell, " Origins of Free Exercise," p. 1515.

37. Alexander Hamilton, James Madison, and John Jay, *The Federalist Papers* (New York: Mentor, 1961); cf. pp. 324–25, with p. 79. See also Berns, *The First Amendment,* pp. 27–30, and especially Thomas Lindsay, "James Madison on Religion and Politics: Rhetoric and Reality," 85 *American Political Science Review* 1321 (1991).

38. For McConnell's remark on ecumenism, see "Origins of Free Exercise," p. 1516. On the way religious liberty under the Constitution appears from one perspective of faith, see John Courtney Murray, *We Hold These Truths: Catholic Reflections on the American Proposition* (Kansas City, Mo.: Sheed and Ward, 1960), esp. chap. 2.

39. This, it should be noted, seems to be the conclusion of Gerard Bradley's reading in historical context of the words of the Establishment Clause. See his *Church-State Relationships in America,* esp. chap. 7. More generally, see Ellis Sandoz, *A Government of Laws: Political Theory, Religion, and the American Founding* (Baton Rouge: Louisiana State University Press, 1990).

40. See McConnell, "Origins of Free Exercise," pp. 1444–45 and n. 186.

41. See, e.g., Edward Levi, *An Introduction to Legal Reasoning* (Chicago: University of Chicago Press, 1949).

42. Cf. *Smith,* 494 U.S. at 881–82, with McConnell, "Free Exercise Revisionism," pp. 1121–22.

43. McConnell, "Free Exercise Revisionism," pp. 1127–28.

44. Ibid., p. 1112.

45. See William Blackstone, *Commentaries on the Laws of England* (reprint, Chicago: University of Chicago Press, 1979), 1:86–88.

46. See McConnell, "Origins of Free Exercise," esp. pp. 1455 ff., and "Free Exercise Revisionism," pp. 1128 ff.; also Bradley, *Church-State Relationships in American Law.*

47. Cf. John Stuart Mill, *On Liberty* (Indianapolis: Hackett Publishing Co., 1979), p. 1.

48. See, generally, Curry, *The First Freedoms;* Murray, *We Hold These Truths;* Bradley, *Church-State Relationships in America;* and, with particular reference to the importance of common law, Sandoz, *A Government of Laws.*

49. See Blackstone, *Commentaries,* vol. 4, chap. 4.

50. McConnell, "Origins of Free Exercise," p. 1433.

51. John Locke, *A Letter Concerning Toleration,* ed. Mario Montuori (The Hague: Martinus Nijhoff, 1963), pp. 89–93.

52. On the relation of ancient common law and ecclesiastical law, see R. H. Helmholz, *Canon Law and the Law of England* (London: Hambledon Press, 1987), esp. chap. 1.

53. Of modern interest here is a series of American cases that involved the courts in settling disputes over church property, usually in the wake of a schism. The basic

federal case, decided as a matter of general common law rather than constitutional law, is *Watson v. Jones,* 13 Wallace 679 (1872). Its principle—that in civil disputes that ultimately involve matters of religious doctrine, the civil courts must defer to authoritative solution by the tribunals of the relevant church—is now considered a matter of federal constitutional law under the Religion Clause of the First Amendment. See *Jones v. Wolf,* 443 U.S. 595 (1979); *Presbyterian Church v. Hull Church,* 393 U.S. 440 (1969); *Kreshik v. St. Nicholas Cathedral,* 363 U.S. 190 (1960); *Kedroff v. St. Nicholas Cathedral,* 344 U.S. 94 (1952).

54. William Sampson (reporter), *The Catholic Question in America* (New York: Edward Gillespy, 1813), p. 9.

55. McConnell features this case in "Origins of Free Exercise," pp. 1410–12, 1504–6, but considers only the constitutional argument. It should also be noted that the precedent established by the case was never universally accepted, and the question of clerical privilege from legal testimony remains a matter of uncertainty in American law today. See Michael Clay Smith, "The Pastor on the Witness Stand: Toward a Religious Privilege in the Courts," 29 *The Catholic Lawyer* 1 (1984).

56. Sampson, *The Catholic Question in America,* pp. 107–8.

57. Ibid., p. 103.

58. *Ashwander v. T.V.A.,* 297 U.S. 288 (1936), at 346.

59. Quoted in Sampson, *The Catholic Question in America,* pp. 109–10.

60. On the distinctiveness of modern judicial review, see, e.g., Nagel, *Constitutional Cultures;* Robert Clinton, *Marbury v. Madison and Judicial Review* (Lawrence: University Press of Kansas, 1989); Christopher Wolfe, *The Rise of Modern Judicial Review* (New York: Basic Books, 1986); and, for an attempt to reconcile the common-law character of certain modern decisions with the constitutional pegs from which they hang, see Henry P. Monaghan, "Foreword: Constitutional Common Law," 89 *Harvard Law Review* 1 (1975).

61. *Wisconsin v. Yoder,* 406 U.S. 205, where the Court relied on testimony from a scholarly expert on the Amish religion. The dissenters in *Smith* relied on published texts on peyotism and, like the Oregon Supreme Court, on a 1964 California case, *People v. Woody,* 61 Cal. 2d 716.

62. *Thomas v. Review Board of the Indiana Employment Security Division,* 450 U.S. 707 (1981).

63. See note 53. Actually, the most recent of the property cases, *Jones v. Wolf,* somewhat complicates the matter; see Justice Powell's dissent in that case, 443 U.S. at 610.

Chapter 4. Common Law and Constitutionalism in the Abortion Case

1. *Roe v. Wade,* 410 U.S. 113 (1973).

2. *Planned Parenthood of Southeastern Pennsylvania v. Casey,* 505 U.S. 833 (1992).

3. More precisely, although the reporting scheme was upheld in principle, the part

pertaining to spousal notification was overturned, and the Court left open the possibility that the scheme, though "facially" valid, would prove unconstitutional in practice.

4. *Casey,* 505 U.S. 833, at 846.

5. *Eisenstadt v. Baird,* 405 U.S. 438 (1972), at 453; quoted in *Casey,* 505 U.S. 833, at 896.

6. *Casey,* 505 U.S. 833, at 871, 851.

7. Ibid., at 852. The "undue burden" language appeared in opinions by Justices O'Connor and Kennedy in previous abortion cases, although with varying meaning, as the Joint Opinion itself acknowledges, at 874–78. The appearance of the phrase "unduly burdensome" in Chief Justice Burger's concurrence in *Doe v. Bolton,* 410 U.S. 179 (1973), the companion case to *Roe* in which the Court struck down in its entirety Georgia's modernized abortion statute, suggests a possible origin of the standard.

8. *Casey,* 505 U.S. 833, at 852.

9. Ibid., at 853 (emphasis added).

10. Ibid., at 856.

11. Ibid., at 863.

12. One wonders, for instance, whether this might not explain the drift toward dissent in abortion cases by Chief Justice Burger, who wrote in his concurrence in *Doe v. Bolton* (410 U.S. 179, at 208), "I do not read the Court's holdings today [in *Doe* and *Roe*] as having the sweeping consequences attributed to them by the dissenting Justices; . . . Plainly the Court today rejects any claim that the Constitution requires abortions on demand."

13. Alexander Bickel, *The Least Dangerous Branch: The Supreme Court at the Bar of Politics* (Indianapolis: Bobbs-Merrill, 1962).

14. *Casey,* 505 U.S. 833, at 866–67.

15. Ibid., at 958 (opinion of Chief Justice Rehnquist).

16. *Cooper v. Aaron,* 358 U.S. 1 (1958); *Casey,* 505 U.S. 833, at 868.

17. *Casey,* 505 U.S. 833, at 867.

18. *Akron,* 462 U.S. 416 (1983), and *Thornburgh,* 476 U.S. 747 (1986); cf. *Casey,* 505 U.S. 833, at 882, and Justice Scalia's catalogue of overrulings, at 994.

19. *Roe v. Wade,* 410 U.S., at 153, 164. Cf. *Casey,* 505 U.S. 833, at 884: "Whatever constitutional status the doctor-patient relation may have as a general matter, in the present context it is derivative of the woman's position. The doctor-patient relation does not underlie or override the two more general rights under which the abortion right is justified: the right to make family decisions and the right to physical autonomy."

20. *Casey,* 505 U.S. 833, at 901.

21. Ibid., at 896–98.

22. See *Roe v. Wade,* 410 U.S. 113, at 165, 132 ff.

23. See *Brief of the American Academy of Medical Ethics . . .* , filed by Professor

Joseph W. Dellapenna of Villanova University; also John Keown, *Abortions, Doctors, and the Law: Some Aspects of the Legal Regulation of Abortion in England from 1803 to 1982* (Cambridge: Cambridge University Press, 1988), esp. chap. 1. The much-publicized *Brief of 250 American Historians,* by Professor Sylvia A. Law of New York University, does not address *Roe*'s findings concerning the common law but simply picks up the tale with an interpretation of the causes behind the nineteenth-century antiabortion statutes.

24. *Bowers v. Hardwick,* 478 U.S. 186 (1986).

25. Ibid., at 199.

26. Ibid., cf. 206 with 190.

27. *Michael H. v. Gerald D.,* 491 U.S. 110 (1989), at 124, 122; quoting *Snyder v. Massachusetts,* 291 U.S. 97 (1934), at 105.

28. *Michael H. v. Gerald D.,* 491 U.S. 110, at 127–28, n. 6. Significantly, Justices O'Connor and Kennedy, who, with Chief Justice Rehnquist, joined the bulk of the opinion, expressly refused to consent to this note. It merits reiteration here that the assimilation of statutes to common-law tradition is itself such a tradition, since statutes were often held simply to declare common law, not to change it. For the limit a widespread custom places on use of the Due Process Clause to abridge that custom, see Justice Scalia's dissent in *Lee v. Weisman,* 505 U.S. 577 (1992), at 643.

29. *Poe v. Ullman,* 367 U.S. 497 (1961), at 542; quoted in *Casey,* 505 U.S. 833, at 849–50.

30. *Meyer v. Nebraska,* 262 U.S. 390 (1923), and *Pierce v. Society of Sisters,* 268 U.S. 510 (1925), are generally taken to be the first cases in which a noneconomic due process liberty was affirmed by the Supreme Court.

31. See the sources cited in note 23; more generally, see John T. Noonan, ed., *The Morality of Abortion: Legal and Historical Perspectives* (Cambridge: Harvard University Press, 1970).

Chapter 5. The Common Law of the Family and the Constitutional Law of the Self

1. Alexander Hamilton, James Madison, and John Jay, *The Federalist,* ed. Jacob Cooke (Middletown, Conn.: Wesleyan University Press, 1961), no. 15, p. 93.

2. William Blackstone, *Commentaries on the Laws of England* (1765; reprint, Chicago: University of Chicago Press, 1979), vol. 1, chaps. 14–17.

3. See Stephen Parker, *Informal Marriage, Cohabitation and the Law 1750–1989* (New York: St. Martin's Press, 1990).

4. Blackstone, *Commentaries,* 1:430.

5. Ibid., pp. 432–33. With characteristic irony, Blackstone adds, "Yet the lower rank of people, who were always fond of the old common law, still claim and exert their antient privilege."

6. Ibid., p. 411.

7. James Kent, *Commentaries on American Law,* 4th ed. (New York: James Kent, 1840), vol. 2, part 4, lectures 26–32.

8. Ibid., p. 187. The ambiguity concerns whether the praise is meant for only the continental system or for the English as well; I would suppose he means the latter.

9. See Alexis de Tocqueville, *Democracy in America* (New York: Harper and Row, 1966), vol. 2, part 3, chaps. 8–12.

10. See, e.g., Blackstone, *Commentaries,* 1:442–43; Kent, *Commentaries* 2:208–9. This distinctive trait of common law was declared as early as the Statute of Merton in 1235.

11. See *Women in American Law,* vol. 1, *From Colonial Times to the New Deal,* ed. Marlene Stein Wortman (New York: Holmes and Meier, 1985), vol. 2, *The Struggle toward Equality from the New Deal to the Present,* by Judith A. Baer (New York: Holmes and Meier, 1991); also Marcia Mobilia Boumil and Stephen C. Hicks, *Women and the Law* (Littleton, Colo.: Fred B. Rothman, 1992); Kermit L. Hall, ed., *Women, the Law, and the Constitution: Major Historical Interpretations* (New York: Garland Publishing, 1987); Susan Gluck Mezey, *In Pursuit of Equality: Women, Public Policy, and the Federal Courts* (New York: St. Martin's Press, 1992). See Milton C. Regan, Jr., *Family Law and the Pursuit of Intimacy* (New York: New York University Press, 1993), for a postmodern perspective. Interesting as historical documents along the way are *A Survey of the Legal Status of Women in the Forty-eight States* (Washington, D.C.: National League of Women Voters, 1930), and, from the eve of the revolution, Leo Kanowitz, *Women and the Law: The Unfinished Revolution* (Albuquerque: University of New Mexico Press, 1969). Recall the account of the development of common law over a similar period in chapter 1.

12. See Marylynn Shannon, *Women and the Law of Property in Early America* (Chapel Hill: University of North Carolina Press, 1986), who argues that developments in American common law toward the independence and equality of wives had begun already in the aftermath of the Revolution.

13. *Bradwell v. State,* 16 Wallace (83 U.S.) 130 (1873), at 141.

14. *Muller v. Oregon,* 208 U.S. 412 (1908).

15. See *Adkins v. Children's Hospital of the District of Columbia,* 261 U.S. 525 (1923).

16. On the New Deal as designed to replace the regime of common law, see Cass Sunstein, "Constitutionalism after the New Deal," 101 *Harvard Law Review* 421–510 (1987).

17. *Poe v. Ullman,* 367 U.S. 497 (1961), at 552.

18. Ibid., at 542, a passage quoted approvingly in the joint opinion of Justices O'Connor, Kennedy, and Souter in *Planned Parenthood v. Casey,* 505 U.S. 833 (1992).

19. *Griswold v. Connecticut,* 381 U.S. 479 (1965), at 484.

20. *Eisenstadt v. Baird,* 405 U.S. 438 (1972), at 453. For an incisive critique of this sort of reasoning in equal protection cases, see Robert Nagel, *Constitutional Cul-*

tures: The Mentality and Consequences of Judicial Review (Berkeley and Los Angeles: University of California Press, 1989).

21. *Roe v. Wade,* 410 U.S. 113 (1973); *Casey,* 505 U.S. 833, at 851, 897.

22. *Hoyt v. Florida,* 368 U.S. 57 (1961); *Reed v. Reed,* 404 U.S. 71 (1971).

23. *Craig v. Boren,* 429 U.S. 190 (1976). The other cases alluded to are *Taylor v. Louisiana,* 419 U.S. 422 (1975), and *Frontiero v. Richardson,* 411 U.S. 677 (1973).

24. *Frontiero v. Richardson,* 411 U.S. 677 (1973), at 687.

25. *United States v. Virginia,* 518 U.S. 515 (1996).

26. Quoted in ibid., at 528.

27. Ibid., at 530.

28. Ibid., at 566. For his developed dismissal of the common law as a basis for constitutional jurisprudence, premised on his understanding of common law in Holmesian terms as judge-made law, see Antonin Scalia, *A Matter of Interpretation: Federal Courts and the Law* (Princeton, N.J.: Princeton University Press, 1997).

Chapter 6. Peremptory Challenge

1. *Batson v. Kentucky,* 476 U.S. 79 (1986).

2. *Swain v. Alabama,* 380 U.S. 202 (1965).

3. *Batson,* 476 U.S. 79, at 102 ff.

4. Ibid., at 127.

5. *Holland v. Illinois,* 493 U.S. 474 (1990).

6. *Powers v. Ohio,* 499 U.S. 400 (1991); *Edmonson v. Leesville Concrete Co., Inc.,* 500 U.S. 614 (1991).

7. *Georgia v. McCollum,* 505 U.S. 42 (1992).

8. *J.E.B. v. Alabama ex rel T.B.,* 511 U.S. 127 (1994).

9. *McCollum,* 505 U.S. 42, at 60–62. The citation for *Strauder* is 100 U.S. 303 (1880).

10. See William Blackstone, *Commentaries on the Laws of England* (reprint, Chicago: University of Chicago Press, 1979), 3:349 ff., 4:342 ff.; J. H. Baker, *An Introduction to English Legal History,* 2nd ed. (London: Butterworths, 1979), esp. chap. 5; Thomas Andrew Green, *Verdict According to Conscience* (Chicago: University of Chicago Press, 1985); James P. Levine, *Juries and Politics* (Pacific Grove, Calif.: Brooks/Cole, 1992), chap. 2.

11. William Nelson, *Americanization of the Common Law* (Cambridge: Harvard University Press, 1975), chaps. 1–4; Shannon Stimson, *The American Revolution in the Law: Anglo-American Jurisprudence before John Marshall* (Princeton, N.J.: Princeton University Press, 1990).

12. See Jack Greene, ed., *Colonies to Nation, 1763–1789: A Documentary History of the American Revolution* (New York: Norton, 1975), pp. 64, 158, 245, 256, 299.

13. Ibid., pp. 333, 343.

14. *Duncan v. Louisiana,* 391 U.S. 145 (1968); *Williams v. Florida,* 399 U.S. 78 (1970); *Apodaca v. Oregon,* 406 U.S. 404 (1972); *Ballew v. Georgia,* 435 U.S. 223 (1978); *Burch v. Louisiana,* 441 U.S. 130 (1979).

15. Blackstone, *Commentaries,* 4:346–47.

16. *United States v. Marchant,* 12 Wheaton (25 U.S.) 480 (1827); the quotation is at 482. See also the account of the history of the peremptory challenge in *Swain v. Alabama,* 380 U.S. 202, at 201 ff.

17. *United States v. Shackleford,* 18 Howard (59 U.S.) 588 (1856).

18. *Lewis v. United States,* 146 U.S. 370 (1892); the quotation is at 376.

19. *Stilson v. United States,* 250 U.S. 583 (1919), at 586.

20. Ibid., at 587.

21. *Patton v. United States,* 281 U.S. 276 (1930).

22. Ibid., at 290. At issue in this part of the case is whether the issue of complete waiver must be raised in order to allow the defendant to accept a verdict by an eleven-man jury when, as happened in the actual case, a juror took ill before deliberations. Justice Sutherland ruled that it must: waiving a unanimous verdict by a twelve-man jury meant waiving the right to a jury.

23. Ibid., at 307. Sutherland also notes that American practice in colonial times often differed from the English rule, allowing waiver of trial by jury.

24. Blackstone, *Commentaries,* 1:123.

25. *Smith v. Gould,* 2 Ld. Raym. 1274–75 (92 Eng. Rep. 338) (1708). Cf. the report in 2 Salkeld. 666–67 (91 Eng. Rep. 567).

26. Quoted in Kermit Hall, *The Magic Mirror: Law in American History* (New York: Oxford University Press, 1989), p. 130.

27. *Strauder v. West Virginia,* 100 U.S. 303 (1880); cf. *Civil Rights Cases,* 109 U.S. 3 (1883); *Plessy v. Ferguson,* 163 U.S. 537 (1896).

28. *Strauder,* 100 U.S. 303, at 308–10.

29. *Virginia v. Rives,* 100 U.S. 313 (1880); *Ex parte Virginia,* 100 U.S. 339 (1880).

30. *Strauder,* 100 U.S. 303, at 309.

31. *Ex parte Virginia,* 100 U.S. 339, at 361.

32. *Norris v. Alabama,* 294 U.S. 587 (1935); see the cases cited in Justice Goldberg's dissent in *Swain,* 380 U.S. 202, at 228–29, and in Justice Scalia's dissent in *Powers,* 499 U.S. 400, at 418.

33. *Swain,* 380 U.S. 202, at 220–21, 221–22, 219.

34. *Batson,* 476 U.S. 79; the quotation is at 101.

35. Ibid., at 88, 99.

36. Ibid., at 137–38.

37. Ibid., at 96. The new case was *Powers v. Ohio,* 499 U.S. 400 (1991).

38. *Powers,* 499 U.S. 400, at 407, quoting Alexis de Tocqueville, *Democracy in America* (New York: Schocken, 1961), 1:337.

39. *Edmonson,* 500 U.S. 614, at 624–25, 630–31.

40. *McCollum,* 505 U.S. 42, at 70.

41. *Swain,* 380 U.S. 202, at 222, quoting *Hayes v. Missouri,* 120 U.S. 68 (1887), at 70; see also Justice Marshall's concurrence in *Batson,* 476 U.S. 79, at 107.

42. *J.E.B. v. Alabama ex rel T.B.,* 511 U.S. 127 (1994); *Taylor v. Louisiana,* 419 U.S. 522 (1975).

Chapter 7. The Judicial Science of Politics

1. Cf. *Nixon v. United States,* 506 U.S. 224 (1993), with *Bush v. Gore,* 531 U.S. 98 (2000). See Robert Nagel, "Political Law, Legalistic Politics: A Recent History of the Political Question Doctrine," 56 *University of Chicago Law Review* 643–69 (1989).

2. *Missouri v. Jenkins,* 495 U.S. 33 (1990). The case returned to the Supreme Court as *Missouri v. Jenkins,* 515 U.S. 70 (1995). Without reversing their earlier action, the Court moved to limit the district court's new remedial order.

3. *Brown v. Board of Education (Brown I),* 347 U.S. 483 (1954).

4. *Brown v. Board of Education (Brown II),* 349 U.S. 294 (1955), at 300, 299, 301.

5. *Cooper v. Aaron,* 358 U.S. 1 (1958).

6. *Griffin v. Prince Edward County School Board,* 377 U.S. 218 (1964).

7. *Green v. New Kent County School Board,* 391 U.S. 430 (1968), at 435, 436.

8. *Swann v. Charlotte-Mecklenburg Board of Education,* 402 U.S. 1 (1971).

9. *Keyes v. School District,* 413 U.S. 189 (1973).

10. *Milliken v. Bradley* [II], 433 U.S. 267 (1977), at 280–81.

11. The bar to interdistrict remedies in cases without interdistrict violation was announced in *Milliken v. Bradley* [I], 418 U.S. 717 (1974). Recently, the Court has been faced with the issue of when a school system has sufficiently desegregated so that judicial supervision can be lifted. See *Board of Education of Oklahoma City v. Dowell,* 498 U.S. 237 (1990), and *Missouri v. Jenkins,* 515 U.S. 70 (1995).

12. *Jenkins,* 495 U.S. 33, at 60. The case and the plan are described in Justice White's opinion of the Court (at 37–45) and in Justice Kennedy's concurrence (at 59–60).

13. Ibid., at 41.

14. *Griffin,* 377 U.S. 218, at 233.

15. *Jenkins,* 495 U.S. 33, at 55–57.

16. Ibid., at 67–68.

17. Ibid., at 71–75.

18. Ibid., at 70–71, 68. The quotation from *Milliken II* originates in 433 U.S. 267 at 291.

19. *Rutan v. Republican Party of Illinois,* 497 U.S. 62 (1990). The individual cases are described at 65–68. There was apparently no question in the case about whether the Governor's way of proceeding, by establishing a freeze and then granting patronage exceptions, was authorized by State law.

20. *Elrod v. Burns,* 427 U.S. 347 (1976); *Branti v. Finkel,* 445 U.S. 507 (1980).

Justice Stevens, who had just joined the Court, did not participate in *Elrod*. His lower court opinion, from which he quotes generously in his concurrence in *Rutan*, can be found in *Illinois State Employees Union v. Lewis*, 473 F.2d 561 (1972).

21. *Elrod*, 427 U.S. 347, at 367–68 (Justice Brennan's plurality opinion) and 374–75 (Justice Stewart's concurrence); *Branti*, 445 U.S. 507, at 518.

22. *United Public Workers v. Mitchell*, 330 U.S. 75 (1947); see also *CSC v. Letter Carriers*, 413 U.S. 548 (1973).

23. To compound the irony further, on the same day the Court's decision in *Rutan* was announced, an attempt in Congress to repeal the Hatch Act failed by a close vote.

24. *Shelton v. Tucker*, 364 U.S. 479 (1960); *Elfbrandt v. Russell*, 384 U.S. 11 (1966); *Keyishian v. Board of Regents*, 385 U.S. 589 (1967).

25. *Perry v. Sindermann*, 408 U.S. 593 (1972), at 597; quoted in *Elrod*, 427 U.S. 347, at 359, and *Branti*, 445 U.S. 507, at 514–15.

26. Justice Powell's dissent in *Elrod* was joined by Chief Justice Burger and Justice Rehnquist. In *Branti*, with the same Court, Powell was joined again by Rehnquist and in part by Justice Stewart, who had concurred in *Elrod* on narrower grounds; Burger, who had also written separately in dissent in *Elrod*, as if to emphasize the point, joined the majority in *Branti*, without separate explanation.

27. *Rutan*, 497 U.S. 62, at 74–75. Political scientists Larry Sabato and Frank Sorauf, as well as a *Congressional Quarterly Guide*, are cited to show that parties have survived the decline in patronage.

28. Ibid., at 91.

29. Ibid., at 92–94.

30. See Robert Nagel, *Constitutional Cultures: The Mentality and Consequences of Judicial Review* (Berkeley and Los Angeles: University of California Press, 1989), esp. chaps. 6, 7.

31. *Rutan*, 497 U.S. 62, at 95–96. In a pair of footnotes, Justice Scalia responds to Justice Stevens's open challenge to his approach. To the objection that *Brown v. Board of Education* shows the inadequacy of reliance on tradition, Scalia responds that tradition has authority only in the absence of clear textual commands, and the Fourteenth Amendment itself, read together with the Thirteenth, "leaves no room for doubt that laws treating people differently because of their race are invalid." As for the tradition overlooking this and upholding segregation, it was never "open . . . and unchallenged," as Justice Harlan's *Plessy* dissent proves. To Stevens's claim that the right-privilege distinction has been abandoned by the Court, making anachronistic Scalia's distinction between government as lawmaker and government as employer, he responds that his colleague has reversed the order of theory and holding in constitutional cases: "The order of precedence is that a constitutional theory must be wrong if its application contradicts a clear constitutional tradition; not that a clear constitutional tradition must be wrong if it does not conform to current constitutional theory." On the question of the place of tradition in constitutional interpretation according to Scalia, see his opinions in *Michael H. v. Gerald D.*, 491

U.S. 110 (1989), and *Burnham v. Superior Court of California, County of Marin,* 495 U.S. 604 (1990).

32. *Rutan,* 497 U.S. 62, at 102.

33. Ibid., at 103–4, 109.

34. Ibid., at 113.

35. Cass Sunstein, "Constitutionalism after the New Deal," 101 *Harvard Law Review* 421–510 (1987); see esp. pp. 422–25.

36. Cf. *Rutan,* 497 U.S. 62, at 114, where Justice Scalia calls it precisely that.

37. In speaking of ad hoc prudence, I have in mind a common criticism made of the Burger Court, aimed especially at the chief justice and perhaps also at Justice Powell. Whatever the validity of the charge in those cases, which I am not ready to admit, it is not easily extended to the likes of Justice Scalia, whose theoretical abilities, as opposed to inclinations, no one ought to doubt.

38. As, for instance, the Republicans discovered in the matter of the presidential primary, a creature of the Democrats that at once solved the modern Republicans' problem of finding a popular candidate and created the modern Democrats' quandary of struggling to identify an electable one.

Chapter 8. Commerce, Property, and Police

1. One of the most complete formulations is Justice Field's in *Barbier v. Connolly,* 113 U.S. 27 (1884), but there are many others. See William J. Novak, *The People's Welfare: Law and Regulation in Nineteenth-Century America* (Chapel Hill: University of North Carolina Press, 1996), esp. pp. 13–17. Novak suggests the continental origin of the term *police,* which is not found (to my knowledge) in Coke or the earlier common lawyers. The concurrence of federal and state commerce powers was established in *Cooley v. Board of Wardens,* discussed later.

2. See Michael Les Benedict, "Laissez-Faire and Liberty: A Re-evaluation of the Meaning and Origins of Laissez-Faire Constitutionalism," 3 *Law and History Review* 293–331 (1985); and especially Howard Gillman, *The Constitution Besieged: The Rise and Demise of* Lochner *Era Police Powers Jurisprudence* (Durham, N.C.: Duke University Press, 1993).

3. See, e.g., Robert G. McCloskey, *The American Supreme Court* (Chicago: University of Chicago Press, 1960).

4. For an interesting discussion, see William H. Rehnquist, "The Changing Role of the Supreme Court," 14 *Florida State University Law Review* 1 (1986).

5. *Swift v. Tyson,* 16 Peters (41 U.S.) 1 (1842).

6. I discuss the political theory of property at greater length in "Property, the Common Law, and John Locke," in *Natural Law and Contemporary Public Policy,* ed. David F. Forte (Washington, D.C.: Georgetown University Press, 1998), pp. 193–218.

7. William Blackstone, *Commentaries on the Laws of England* (reprint, Chicago: University of Chicago Press, 1979), vol. 4, chap. 13.

8. Ibid., pp. 162, 167.

9. Ibid., vol. 3, chap. 13.

10. Thomas Cooley, *A Treatise on Constitutional Limitations* (Boston: Little, Brown, 1868), chap. 16, p. 572.

11. *Commonwealth v. Alger,* 7 Cush. (61 Mass.) 53 (1851), at 95–96.

12. Ibid., at 84–85. Cooley does not quote the phrase that all property is derived from government.

13. *Prigg v. Pennsylvania,* 16 Peters (41 U.S.) 539 (1842).

14. *Roberts v. City of Boston,* 5 Cush. (59 Mass.) 53 (1849).

15. *Gibbons v. Ogden,* 9 Wheaton (22 U.S.) 1 (1824), at 203; *Brown v. Maryland,* 12 Wheaton 419 (1827).

16. *Charles River Bridge v. Warren Bridge,* 11 Peters (36 U.S.) 420 (1837), at 547–48.

17. *The License Cases,* 5 Howard (46 U.S.) 504 (1847), at 583.

18. *Cooley v. Board of Wardens,* 12 Howard (53 U.S.) 299 (1851).

19. *Wynehamer v. People,* 13 N.Y. 378 (1856).

20. See James W. Ely, Jr., "The Oxymoron Reconsidered: Myth and Reality in the Origins of Substantive Due Process," *Constitutional Commentary* 16 (1999): 315–45.

21. *Slaughter-House Cases,* 16 Wallace (83 U.S.) 36 (1873), at 62, 78.

22. Ibid., at 104, 109.

23. *Munn v. Illinois,* 94 U.S. 113 (1877), at 134.

24. *Lochner v. New York,* 198 U.S. 45 (1905); *Hammer v. Dagenhart,* 247 U.S. 251 (1918); *United States v. E. C. Knight,* 156 U.S. 1 (1895); *Champion v. Ames,* 188 U.S. 321 (1903).

25. *The Civil Rights Cases,* 109 U.S. 3 (1883); *Plessy v. Ferguson,* 163 U.S. 357 (1896); *Hurtado v. California,* 110 U.S. 516 (1884).

26. *Adair v. United States,* 208 U.S. 161 (1908), at 175.

27. *Mugler v. Kansas,* 123 U.S. 623 (1887), at 663, 661.

28. *Allgeyer v. Louisiana,* 165 U.S. 578 (1897).

29. *Champion v. Ames,* 188 U.S. 321 (1903), at 356, 357, 362–63.

30. Ibid., at 358; Edward Levi, *An Introduction to Legal Reasoning* (Chicago: University of Chicago Press, 1949); *Heart of Atlanta Motel v. United States,* 379 U.S. 241 (1964).

31. *The Civil Rights Cases,* 109 U.S. 3 (1883).

32. *Plessy v. Ferguson,* 163 U.S. 357 (1896), at 557, 550.

33. *Home Building & Loan Ass'n v. Blaisdell,* 290 U.S. 398 (1934), at 442.

34. Ibid., at 467, quoting Charles Warren.

35. *Village of Euclid v. Ambler Realty Co.,* 272 U.S. 365 (1926), at 390, 391, 387 (emphasis in original).

36. *Adkins v. Children's Hospital,* 261 U.S. 525 (1923), at 588. See Hadley Arkes, *The Return of George Sutherland* (Princeton, N.J.: Princeton University Press, 1994).

37. *West Coast Hotel v. Parrish,* 300 U.S. 379 (1937), at 399.
38. *NLRB v. Jones & Laughlin Steel Corp.,* 301 U.S. 1 (1937), at 41.
39. *United States v. Darby Lumber,* 312 U.S. 100 (1941); *Wickard v. Filburn,* 317 U.S. 111 (1942).
40. *NLRB v. Jones & Laughlin,* 301 U.S. 1, at 37.
41. *United States v. Lopez,* 514 U.S. 549 (1995), at 566; *United States v. Morrison,* 529 U.S. 598 (2000). The quickly overturned case of *National League of Cities v. Usery,* 426 U.S. 833 (1976), attempted to limit the commerce power by finding in the Tenth Amendment a positive right of the states to structure their own governments; the new cases restore the older concept of limiting what counts as commerce, treating the police power of the states as reserved, if extensive. On the recent commerce cases as inspired principally by a concern for keeping the federal courts free of the routine enforcement of criminal law, see Ann Althouse, "Inside the Federalism Cases: Concern about the Federal Courts," *Annals of the American Academy of Political and Social Science* 574 (2001): 132–44.
42. *Pennsylvania Coal Co. v. Mahon,* 260 U.S. 393 (1922), at 415.
43. *Lucas v. South Carolina Coastal Council,* 505 U.S. 1003 (1987), at 1015, 1029, 1026, 1024.

Chapter 9. Common Law, Constitution, and World Order

1. See *National League of Cities v. Usery,* 426 U.S. 833 (1976), overruled in *Garcia v. Metropolitan Transit District,* 469 U.S. 428 (1985).
2. Richard Epstein, *Takings* (Chicago: University of Chicago Press, 1986).
3. *Missouri v. Holland,* 252 U.S. 416 (1920), at 433.
4. *United States v. Curtiss-Wright Export Corporation,* 299 U.S. 304 (1936), at 315.
5. Ibid., at 320.
6. Ibid., at 316–19.
7. See John Theodore Horton, *James Kent: A Study in Conservatism, 1763–1847* (New York: D. Appleton-Century, 1939), which is, to my knowledge, the only book-length biography of Kent ever published. But see also the collection of his letters and memoranda edited by his grandson, William Kent, *Memoirs and Letters of James Kent, LL.D.* (Boston: Little, Brown, 1898).
8. James Kent, *Commentaries on American Law,* 4th ed. (New York: James Kent, 1840), 1:343n., 341. See generally lectures 16 and 21.
9. Ibid., pp. 471–72.
10. Ibid., pp. 342–43. The "slavish maxim" Kent has in mind is *Quod principi placuit legis habet vigorem:* "What pleases the prince has the force of law."
11. Ibid., p. 1.
12. Ibid., p. 2.
13. Ibid., p. 3.

14. Ibid., p. 21.

15. Ibid., p. 32.

16. Ibid., p.18.

17. Ibid.

18. Alexander Hamilton, James Madison, and John Jay, *The Federalist,* ed. Jacob E. Cooke (Middletown, Conn.: Wesleyan University Press, 1961), p. 555.

19. Kent, *Commentaries,* 1:64 ff. The citation for *Brown v. United States* is 8 Cranch (12 U.S.) 110 (1814).

20. Ibid., p. 115.

21. Kent's felicitous combination of a respect for the law of nations and a stern sense of national sovereignty also appears in his discussion of piracy, which is suggestive in relation to the threat of international terrorism today. He writes, "Pirates have been regarded by all civilized nations as the enemies of the human race, and the most atrocious violators of the universal law of society. . . . Every nation has a right to attack and exterminate them without any declaration of war; for though pirates may form a loose and temporary association among themselves, and re-establish in some degree those laws of justice which they have violated with the rest of the world, yet they are not considered as a national body, or entitled to the laws of war as one of the community of nations" (ibid., p. 183). He proceeds, however, to explain that the Barbary states are now recognized as national bodies, so the pirates they sponsor are treated as their privateers; and he notes cases in which jurisdiction over pirates was disputed.

22. Compare Kent, *Commentaries,* 1:191 ff. with 2:247 ff.

23. William E. Ratliff, "'Madeleine's War' and the Costs of Intervention: The Kosovo Precedent," *Harvard International Review* 22, no. 4 (winter 2001): 70.

24. The Kyoto Protocol, the International Criminal Court, and the UN World Heritage Committee's visit to Montana are discussed in Jeremy Rabkin, *Why Sovereignty Matters* (Washington, D.C.: AEI Press, 1998), to which much of what follows is indebted. Like much modern common law, the "customs" here at issue are judge-made, or at least administrator-made.

25. See, e.g., Stephen Krasner, "Globalization and Sovereignty," in *States and Sovereignty in the Global Economy,* ed. David Smith, Dorothy J. Solinger, and Steven C. Topik (London: Routledge, 1999), pp. 34–52; or Samuel Barkin, "Resilience of the State: The Evolution and Sustainability of Sovereignty," *Harvard International Review* 22, no. 4 (winter 2001): 42–46.

26. Rabkin, *Why Sovereignty Matters,* esp. chap. 4.

27. Ibid., chap. 6, pp. 69–70.

Conclusion

1. William H. Rehnquist, "The Notion of a Living Constitution," 54 *Texas Law Review* 693 (1976).

BIBLIOGRAPHIC ESSAY

Rather than to catalog the books that have passed across my desk over the years that I composed this study or to reiterate the particular sources cited in the notes, I have appended a brief essay about recent books on constitutional law and common law, and how I would situate this book among them.

Common-Law Liberty was conceived as a sort of sequel to my study of the common-law roots of the American Constitution, *Common Law and Liberal Theory: Coke, Hobbes, and the Origins of American Constitutionalism* (Lawrence: University Press of Kansas, 1992), and so naturally I would refer the reader who is interested in the historical and theoretical background to the current study there. Since the earlier work was published, of course, much has been written on the topic. Two books deserve particular mention here: Robert Lowry Clinton, *God and Man in the Law: The Foundations of Anglo-American Constitutionalism* (Lawrence: University Press of Kansas,1997) and Paul O. Carrese, *The Cloaking of Power: Montesquieu, Blackstone, and the Rise of Judicial Activism* (Chicago: University of Chicago Press, 2003).

I set out to write for the shelf of books about judicial review and its exercise by the United States Supreme Court. As I indicated in the first pages of my introduction, this literature has frequently fallen into two camps. Dominant over the past generation have been the authors who propose theories of judicial review and, more precisely, theories that defend judicial initiative in promoting egalitarian and civil-libertarian reform against the charge that it is undemocratic. Alexander Bickel, *The Least Dangerous Branch: The Supreme Court at the Bar of Politics* (Indianapolis: Bobbs-Merrill Co., 1962), is still the best in the genre, and one of the most moderate. More recent influential works include Ronald Dworkin, *Taking Rights Seriously* (Cambridge: Harvard University Press, 1977) and his subsequent works; John Hart Ely, *Democracy and Distrust: A Theory of Judicial Review* (Cambridge: Harvard University Press, 1980); the many books by Cass R. Sunstein, especially *One Case at a Time: Judicial Minimalism on the Supreme Court* (Cambridge: Harvard University Press, 1999); and Terri Peretti, *In Defense of a Political Court* (Princeton, N.J.: Princeton University Press, 1999).

The opposing tradition has stressed a jurisprudence of original intention or of textualism. For the former, see Walter Berns, *The First Amendment and the Future of American Democracy* (New York: Basic Books, 1976) and other works; Raoul

Berger, *Government by Judiciary: The Transformation of the Fourteenth Amendment* (Cambridge: Harvard University Press, 1977); and Robert H. Bork, *The Tempting of America: The Political Seduction of the Law* (New York: Free Press, 1990). Textualism is advanced (and in accompanying essays critiqued) in Antonin Scalia, *A Matter of Interpretation: Federal Courts and the Law* (Princeton, N.J.: Princeton University Press, 1997). See generally, Keith E. Whittington, *Constitutional Interpretation: Textual Meaning, Original Intent, and Judicial Review* (Lawrence: University Press of Kansas, 1999).

Lest the reader think that principled argument for judicial initiative is entirely a liberal project, or that the conservative voice in constitutional law is only a call for restraint, consult Richard Epstein, *Simple Rules for a Complex World* (Cambridge: Harvard University Press, 1995); Hadley Arkes, most recently *Natural Rights and the Right to Choose* (New York: Cambridge University Press, 2002); and Michael Greve, *Real Federalism: Why It Matters, How It Could Happen* (Washington, D.C.: AEI Press, 1999).

Many of the most interesting books on judicial review in recent years, however, fit into none of these schemes. On the left, Sanford Levinson, *Constitutional Faith* (Princeton, N.J.: Princeton University Press, 1989), provides a revealing look at the civil religion of liberal constitutionalism. From a conservative or rather skeptical perspective, the books of Robert F. Nagel are insightful, especially *Constitutional Culture: The Mentality and Consequences of Judicial Review* (Berkeley and Los Angeles: University of California Press, 1989) and *The Implosion of American Federalism* (New York: Oxford University Press, 2001). Keith E. Whittington, *Constitutional Construction: Divided Powers and Constitutional Meaning* (Cambridge: Harvard University Press, 1999), puts on the table the question of authoritative constitutional interpretation outside the courts. Mark Tushnet's interesting thought-experiment, *Taking the Constitution Away from the Courts* (Princeton, N.J.: Princeton University Press, 1999), calls a few bluffs, if not his own, while Jeremy Waldron, *The Dignity of Legislation* (Cambridge: Cambridge University Press, 1999), develops an alternative to Dworkin in the language of philosophical jurisprudence. I have restricted myself here to books by single authors, but many important questions concerning judicial review and its consequences are vetted in the edited collections that grew out of a controversial symposium published in the journal *First Things:* Mitchell S. Muncy, ed., *The End of Democracy? The Judicial Usurpation of Politics* (Dallas: Spence Publishing Co., 1997) and *The End of Democracy? II: A Crisis of Legitimacy* (Dallas: Spence Publishing Co., 1999). And I would not want to neglect Harvey C. Mansfield, Jr., *America's Constitutional Soul* (Baltimore: Johns Hopkins University Press, 1991).

Constitutional and legal history have burgeoned in recent years, not least in the work of political scientists, as the old Progressive paradigm that dominated constitutional studies for most of the twentieth century has begun to unravel. Robert McCloskey, *The American Supreme Court* (Chicago: University of Chicago Press,

1960), remains a classic touchstone. Other useful overviews include Rogers M. Smith, *Liberalism and American Constitutional Law* (Cambridge: Harvard University Press, 1985); William Lasser, *The Limits of Judicial Power: The Supreme Court in American Politics* (Chapel Hill: University of North Carolina Press, 1988); and especially Christopher Wolfe, *The Rise of Modern Judicial Review: From Constitutional Interpretation to Judge-Made Law* (New York: Basic Books, 1986). Some insightful recent studies that properly pay special attention to state law in the era when it remained primary if not supreme include Howard Gillman, *The Constitution Besieged: The Rise and Demise of* Lochner *Era Police Powers Jurisprudence* (Durham, N.C.: Duke University Press, 1993); William J. Novak, *The People's Welfare: Law and Regulation in Nineteenth-Century America* (Chapel Hill: University of North Carolina Press, 1996); and John J. Dinan, *Keeping the People's Liberties: Legislators, Citizens, and Judges as Guardians of Rights* (Lawrence: University Press of Kansas, 1998). Perhaps here mention should be made of the books of several law professors whose constitutional histories specifically address the question of whether the Civil War and the amendments that followed from it effected a constitutional transformation: Bruce Ackerman, *We the People: Vol. 1 (Foundations)* (Cambridge: Harvard University Press, 1991) and *Vol. 2 (Transformations)* (Cambridge: Harvard University Press, 1998); and Akhil Reed Amar, *The Bill of Rights: Creation and Reconstruction* (New Haven, Conn.: Yale University Press, 1998).

On the common law, for an account of the contemporary orthodoxy that common law is judge-made law, see Melvin Aron Eisenberg, *The Nature of the Common Law* (Cambridge: Harvard University Press, 1988), but consult as well the works of Sunstein and especially Epstein, cited above. Still the best introduction to common-law reasoning, because it is ironic rather than dogmatic, and because it situates common-law reasoning in relation to statutory and constitutional interpretation, is Edward H. Levi, *An Introduction to Legal Reasoning* (Chicago: University of Chicago Press, 1949). But one really learns the way of reasoning of common law by reading cases, lots of them, and one sees best how common-law reasoning develops by reading the nineteenth-century cases, before judges felt free to describe their function as law-making. The most valuable overview I have found to substantive law—constitutional and general, federal and state—in America is Kermit L. Hall, *The Magic Mirror: Law in American History* (New York: Oxford University Press, 1989).

Finally, there is no substitute for engaging the books from which—alongside the cases themselves—American lawyers once learned the law, common and constitutional. William Blackstone's four-part *Commentaries* were critical, and two of the American editions are of particular interest for the editor's notes adjusting Blackstone's account of English law to the American context: that edited by Virginia lawyer and jurist St. George Tucker (Philadelphia : W.Y. Birch and A. Small, 1803) and that edited by prominent Michigan judge and legal author Thomas M. Cooley (2nd ed., Chicago: Callaghan, 1872). Joseph Story's *Commentaries on the Consti-*

tution of the United States (Boston: Hilliard, Gray, 1833) has been recognized for years as a constitutional law classic by a Supreme Court justice and law professor who wrote on numerous other topics as well. To my mind, the classic synthesis of American common law and constitutional law is to be found in James Kent, *Commentaries on American Law*, 4 vols. (4th ed., New York: James Kent, 1840). When in the aftermath of the Civil War Cooley was editing Blackstone to bring him up to date, Kent's *Commentaries* appeared in an edition with critical notes by Oliver Wendell Holmes, Jr. (12th ed., Boston: Little, Brown, 1873). Indeed, in Holmes's notes one finds the germs of change.

INDEX

Jefferson, Thomas
alleged libel against, 40–41
on Committee of Revisors and
common law, 14
"constitutions" in his Declaration draft,
15
contrasted to the Jeffersonians on
freedom of the press, 35
preference for Coke over Blackstone,
37
religion and state, 55
Jeffersonians. *See* Republican party
(Jeffersonian)
Jehovah's Witnesses, 34
Jenkins, Missouri v. [495 U.S. 33 (1990);
515 U.S. 70 (1995)], 108, 110–15,
121
Johnson, William, 36
*Jones & Laughlin Steel, National Labor
Relations Board v.* [301 U.S. 1
(1937)], 138, 143–45
Judge-made law, xii, 3, 10, 86, 144,
165
Judges
according to Holmes and in the early
republic, 28
as agents of supranational will, 164
as policy makers, 122–23
their common-law character, 11–12,
18–19
Judicial activism, 2, 3, 7, 76
Judicial power, 5, 18, 80, 152–53
Judicial restraint, 2, 51, 87
Judicial review, 54, 122
Judiciary Act of 1789, 19–20, 26
Jurisprudence, 22
Jury
and Bill of Rights, 20
as democratic element in common law,
81
as distinctive mark of common law, 12
and due process, 134
its early history, 93–98
in English libel law, 37, 41
peremptory challenges, 91–106
and race, 91–93, 98–106

under the Sedition Act, 36
women and, 89
Jus gentium, 158
Justinian's *Institutes,* 154

Kansas, Mugler v. [123 U.S. 623 (1887)],
137–38
Kansas City, Missouri, School District,
110–15
Kennedy, Anthony
in *Casey* Joint Opinion, 66–77
on custom, 58
opinion in *Missouri v. Jenkins,* 112–14,
123
opinions in religion cases, 49–50
in *Powers v. Ohio* and *Edmonson v.
Leesville Concrete Co.,* 104–05
joins Scalia in *Rutan* dissent, 118
Kent, James
adopts Hamilton's argument on libel,
42
biography, 151
on family law, 82–83
jurisprudence and view of common
law, 151–54
on law of nations, 154–59, 163–64
quoted in *Slaughter-House Cases,* 134
recommends St. German, 127
writer of national legal *Comentaries,*
20
Kentucky Resolutions, 36, 40
Kenyon, Lord, 62
King's Bench, 11, 13
Kohlmann, Anthony, 61–62
Kosovo, 159
Kurtzman, Lemon v. [403 U.S. 602
(1971)], 49
Kyoto Protocol, 159–60

Labor, 127, 137, 143–44, 147
Laissez-faire, 85, 136–45
Lateran Council of 1215, 94
Law
its definition as command of the
sovereign, 107
See also Common law

210 *Common-Law Liberty*

Seventh Amendment, 21, 95

Sex discrimination, 105, 143

Sexual revolution, 86–87

Shackleford, United States v. [18 Howard (59 U.S.) 588 (1856)], 97

Shaw, Lemuel, 129, 131, 137, 140

Sherbert v. Verner [374 U.S. 398 (1963), 47

Sindermann, Perry v. [408 U.S. 593 (1972)], 116–17, 119

Sixth Amendment, 92, 95, 98, 103–04

Slaughter-House Cases [16 Wallace (83 U.S.) 36 (1873)], 84–86, 134–35

Slavery

Kent on, 158–59

unknown to English law, 82, 98–99, 130–31

Smith, Employment Division, Department of Human Resources of Oregon v. [494 U.S. 872 (1990)], 47–51

Smith v. Gould [92 Eng. Rep. 338 (1708)], 99

Social Security, 86

Society of Sisters, Pierce v. [268 U.S. 510 (1925)], 48

Somerset v. Stewart (Somerset's Case) [98 Eng. Rep. 499 (1772)], 99, 130

Souter, David, 66–77

South Carolina Coastal Council, Lucas v. [505 U.S. 1003 (1992)], 146–47

Sovereignty

defined as police power, 132

and internationalism, 160–64

in Madison's *Report*, 40

and moral personhood, in Kent, 156

no concern in *Rutan* for states', 122

of Parliament, 13

political scientists deny internationalism undermines, 160

power of taxation an attribute of, 113

its quandary, 164

Sutherland on, 150–51

Spinoza, Baruch, 51

Stamp Act Congress, 94

State-action doctrine, 139

State of nature, 79

State ratifying conventions, 20

States

and common law, 14–15, 26, 79

development of law in, 20

differ on peremptory challenges in early republic, 97

need to consider their law to interpret Religion Clauses, 58

relation to federal government like international law, 157

rights, Field on, 101

Stereotypes, 104

Stevens, John Paul, 66–67, 115, 117–18

St. German, Christopher, 127

Stilson v. United States [250 U.S. 583 (1919)], 97, 103

Story, Joseph

on common law and Constitution, 21–25

on common law in America, 14

compared to Kent, 151–52

dissent in *Charles River Bridge*, 132

on jury, 96–97

opinion in *Prigg v. Pennsylvania*, 130

opinion in *Swift v. Tyson*, 25–26

writer of national legal treatises, 20

Strauder v. West Virginia [100 U.S. 303 (1880)], 93, 99–101

Strict scrutiny test, 117, 119

Subsidiarity, 162

Sullivan, New York Times v. [376 U.S. 254 (1964)], 44

Sunstein, Cass, 45, 121–23

Supremacy Clause, 19, 71, 80, 112

Supreme Court of the United States, *passim*

Supreme Judicial Court of Massachusetts, where Holmes sat, 11

Sutherland, George, 147

on jury, 98

on legal change, 141–44

opinion in *Curtiss-Wright*, 149–50, 154

reasoning contrasted to Powell's, 103

Unwritten constitution, 9, 78
Unwritten law, 167
  Aristotle on, vii
  and the family, 90
  at the Founding, 79
  and the Ninth Amendment, 21
  police power as, 131
  power of judicial review itself as, 19
  Story on common law, 22
  and written constitutions, 15
Usery, National League of Cities v. [426 U.S. 833 (1976)], 148

Vattel, Emerich de, 156
Venire, 91, 101–03
Verner, Sherbert v. [374 U.S. 398 (1963), 47
Vicinage, 95
Village of Euclid v. Ambler Realty [272 U.S. 365 (1926)], 141–42, 147
Virginia, 14, 100
Virginia, Ex parte [100 U.S. 339 (1880)], 100
Virginia, United States v. [518 U.S. 515 (1996)], 89–90
Virginia Military Academy (VMI), 89–90
Virginia Plan
  and the (failed) negative on state laws, 19
  common law thinking alters it, 17
Virginia Resolutions, 36, 38–40
Virginia Resolves of 1769, 94
Virginia Statute on Religious Freedom, 53
Virginia v. Rives [100 U.S. 313 (1880)], 100
Virtue, 52

Waite, Morrison, 135, 142
War, 156, 158, 167

Warren Bridge, Charles River Bridge v. [11 Peters (36 U.S.) 420 (1837)], 132
Warren Court, 1–2, 95, 148
Washington, George, 41, 52, 158
Welfare state, 86
Weisman, Lee v. [505 U.S. 577 (1992)], 50–51, 57
West Coast Hotel v. Parrish [300 U.S. 379 (1937)], 70, 143–44
West Virginia, Strauder v. [100 U.S. 303 (1880)], 93, 99–101
Whiggism, 16
White, Byron, 50
  concurrence in *Batson v. Kentucky,* 102
  opinion in *Bowers v. Hardwick,* 74
  opinion in *Missouri v. Jenkins,* 111–12, 114
  opinion in *Planned Parenthood v. Casey,* 66, 68
  opinion in *Swain v. Alabama,* 101–03, 105
White, Edward, 136
White flight, 110
Wickard v. Filburn [317 U.S. 111 (1942)], 144–45
Wilson, James, 37
Women
  and coverture, 81–83
  equal rights for, 84–86, 89–90, 159
Written constitution, 79, 150
Wynehamer v. People [13 N.Y. 378 (1856)], 133–34
Wythe, George, 14

Yellowstone National Park, 160
Yoder, Wisconsin v. [406 U.S. 205 (1972)], 48, 52, 64

Zenger, Peter, 94
Zoning, 141–42, 147